BLOCKCHAIN
BITCOIN
AND THE
DIGITAL ECONOMY

BLOCKCHAIN
BITCOIN
AND THE
DIGITAL ECONOMY

Len Mei, Ph.D.

MERCURY LEARNING AND INFORMATION
Dulles, Virginia
Boston, Massachusetts
New Delhi

Publisher: David Pallai
MERCURY LEARNING AND INFORMATION
22841 Quicksilver Drive
Dulles, VA 20166
info@merclearning.com
www.merclearning.com
1-800-232-0223

L. Mei. *Blockchain, Bitcoin, and the Digital Economy.*
ISBN: 978-1-68392-835-5

Library of Congress Control Number: 2022936048

222324321   Printed on acid-free paper in the United States of America.

CONTENTS

PREFACE

Bitcoin, the first *cryptocurrency*, is arguably the most explosive asset in human history. Since its inception in 2009, Bitcoin's market capitalization has grown from zero to over $560 billion by January of 2022.[1] This increase was almost unthinkable just a few years ago. Since Bitcoin first appeared, many other cryptocurrencies have sprung to life. There are thousands of different cryptocurrencies currently and that number increases almost daily.[2] Cryptocurrencies have a combined market capitalization of approximately $2 trillion.

Many people believe that the cryptocurrency market is nothing more than a bubble. Indeed, the value of cryptocurrencies has endured violent ups-and-downs. However, such explosive growth is more than just speculation. The underlying technology of any cryptocurrency, the *blockchain*, shows enormous potential to usher in all kinds of change. Regardless of the future value of cryptocurrencies, the blockchain technology is here to stay.

We are at the beginning of a digital revolution, propelling the world into an era of a digital economy. In the U.S., the overall economy grows at an average rate of 2% a year, while the digital economy is growing at 10%. Today, the digital economy in the U.S. is roughly 10% of the total economy. But by 2030, that number is forecasted to be 22% of the total economy. Blockchain, together with the other nascent technologies, such as artificial intelligence (AI), big data, the Internet of Things (IoT), and many others are the driving forces of this coming digital revolution, also known as the 4th Industrial Revolution.

Blockchain technology is derived from cryptography, a branch of computer science. What makes blockchain technology unique from traditional cryptography is that it was combined with the technology of the Internet. It transformed the Internet from a platform of information, data transfer, and storage into a platform of asset transfer and storage. Suddenly, the Internet and online world finds itself capable of performing many financial functions with the security and speed unmatched by the world's traditional financial systems.

For example, the Bank of England released a report on how to use the blockchain technology to strengthen its real-time settlement system; Swift proposed a block-linked roadmap; IMF released the first digital currency report. Gartner estimates that blockchain could produce \$176 billion in business value by 2025.[3]

The birth of blockchain technology in the first decade of the 21st century obviously was not an accident. A number of factors drove the innovation, but blockchain mainly relied on the maturity of Internet technology itself, the advance in computer science capabilities, the spread of cheap computing power, and high speed, high bandwidth communication technology, as well as things such as the globalization of e-commerce and trade.

Blockchain technology is still at the nascent stage. It is evolving and changing. Thousands of startups and large companies are experimenting with it for the development of new applications. Blockchain's application to cryptocurrencies has caught the attention of the news media. However, in time, its other applications may have a much more profound impact.

Blockchain is revolutionary because, for the first time, we can transfer objects with a monetary value over the Internet and store them in the database securely and quickly.

Before the invention of Bitcoin in 2009, nobody could figure out a way to make a digital currency work. Since the replication of data on the network is easy, such data cannot represent an asset. This is the double-spending problem. This changed when a person called Satoshi Nakamoto invented Bitcoin using blockchain technology in 2009. If blockchain can create and transact digital currency, it can also create and transact any and all digital assets.

Blockchain-based smart contracts and distributed apps open up a wide frontier for transaction applications. Blockchain can create an immutable digital identity, which provides a chain of custody and proof of the ownership of assets, furnishing all the elements necessary to conduct financial activities online.

However, blockchain is not the only technology that is altering many aspects of the financial, business, and trade systems today. It is the combination of artificial intelligence, blockchain, big data, communication, Internet technology, computing power, and many others to cause a drastic shift in the best and most efficient ways to do things.

With the development of blockchain, there is also a newly evolved technology called *fintech*, short for financial technology. Fintech promises to revolutionize the financial industry just like automation revolutionized manufacturing. These new technologies can add trillions of dollars to the global economy. The implications are staggering.

This book discusses basic concepts and fundamentals of blockchain technology, the issues in development and potential applications, and its use in cryptocurrency. We will also discuss fintech, its status and applications, and some aspects of the digital economy. This subject is vast and quickly changing, so it is impossible to cover the subject entirely in one book. This book serves as a comprehensive introduction and background to anyone who is interested in blockchain technology and cryptocurrency. This survey provides ample opportunity to do further research on any of the topics covered. Many references are cited to make further exploration easier.

Len Mei, Ph. D.
April 2022

1. *https://www.investing.com/crypto/*

2. *https://www.statista.com/statistics/863917/number-crypto-coins-tokens/*

3. "Predicts 2018: top predictions in blockchain business", *https://www.gartner.com/doc/3827065/predicts--top-predictions-blockchain*

CHAPTER 1

WHAT IS BLOCKCHAIN?

Blockchain is the technology that gave birth to Bitcoin, Ethereum, Dogecoin, and every other cryptocurrency in existence, helping to ignite a revolution in the digital economy. Blockchain is a technology to transact, distribute, and store digital information on the Internet. It does so by linking blocks of data and distributing them across a network.

1.1 INTRODUCTION

The data in blockchain is secure and immutable. The first application of blockchain was to create a digital currency – Bitcoin. However, blockchain is now being applied in other ways, such as for product traceability and copyright protection, as well as financial transactions, entertainment, publishing, energy, healthcare, and other industries.[1] It can be used across the entire value chain, benefiting businesses and consumers alike.

Blockchain is an encrypted database technology. It enables immutable data to be accessible by parties involved in a transaction securely, thus it is an ideal universal irrefutable depository for all transactions. Such a capability allows blockchain to transform the way that individuals, organizations, businesses, and entire industries collaborate and interact with one another. With its capability of guaranteeing data security, blockchain technology will be a foundation for many industries in the future.

One of the difficulties in using the blockchain today is the difficulty in developing apps. Such an effort requires extensive blockchain knowledge and ingenuity. However, this is about to change. The blockchain enabled network for service, or Blockchain Service Network (BSN), is embedding blockchain technology into Internet protocols, which will allow anyone to develop and implement blockchain-enabled apps, such as those for remittances, cross-border settlements, and travel. In BSN, blockchain implementation is standardized. Such a network removes the difficult blockchain development work from the users and provides turn-key blockchain solutions to users.

A standardized blockchain platform allows for plug-and-play applications. Even small-to-medium-sized enterprises (SME) or an individual can afford to access the critical tools to participate in the digital economy. Developers can use a single private key to deploy and manage decentralized applications (Dapps) on multiple frameworks, and to realize interconnectivity and mutual communication between Dapps. These Dapps retain the unique features of a smart contract and consensus mechanism.

BSN will greatly reduce the cost of development of blockchain-enabled applications and accelerate the adoption of blockchain technology. It is envisioned that BSN can facilitate increased global trade and bilateral economic activity through more efficient cross-border trade, investment, and international collaboration. According to market research firm Grand View Research in California, the global blockchain market size was valued at $5.92 billion in 2021 and will grow 86% annually to 2030.[2]

A typical blockchain application involves several basic components: participants, assets, access control, and transactions. Its value chain ranges from hardware manufacturing, software platforms, and cybersecurity to application services, investments, media, and human resources.

Since blockchain resides on the Internet and its objective is to move "valuable assets," whether it is money or contracts, it is also known as the Internet of Value (IoV).[3]

The difference between the Internet as we know it today and the IoV is the asset value of the contents. The Internet today can move duplicated copies of data around. These data are for information only. The data in blockchain applications are either original or a verified copy of an asset that is as good as the original. When blockchain technologies spread more widely, many, many more applications will be developed.

A significant number of these applications will be targeted for financial uses. These applications are known as *fintech*, short for "financial technology."

Many blockchain applications are revolutionary and create paradigm shifts. Blockchain technology can automate financial industries, just as robots automate manufacturing. Banks, stock exchanges, insurance companies, supply chain managers, and land registration companies are experimenting with blockchain technology. Other potential blockchain applications include medical records management, vote tracking, identity management and protection, long-term record storage, chain-of-custody for insurance policies, and the management of legal documents, such as those for real estate ownership.

When blockchain is used in conjunction with other technologies, such as the IoT (Internet of Things), it allows companies to track virtually every kind of digital record and transaction, which requires privacy and confidentiality. This is because all kinds of data collected by the IoT can be constructed as a blockchain.

Other names for blockchain are Mutual Distributed Ledger (MDL), or Distributed Ledger Technology (DLT). A *ledger* is a chronological record of transactions. The word "Mutual" denotes the shared nature of the distributed ledger. It is a special type of the more generalized distributed ledger.

In addition to being a distributed ledger, blockchain is also a distributed database. It enables multiple parties to share and update data in a safe and secure way, even if they do not trust each other. Blockchain allows for the secure transfer and storage of assets online. Blockchain can be used in a wide variety of applications to perform transactions or exchange value safely and securely.

Blockchain's fundamental construction mechanisms make this technology unique: It is distributed in a P2P network, decentralized, and encrypted. The signed, encrypted, validated new transactions are bundled together into a "block." The new block links to the previous verified block in the blockchain cryptographically. As such, the blocks are forming a permanent and immutable chain of records. It is as if each new page of the ledger, when filled, is bound to the previous page of the ledger. The balance at the beginning of a new page must match that of the end of the previous page. In this way, the balances on each page form a chain with the balances of previous pages. Multiple copies of the identical ledger stored in different locations will receive a duplicated new page so that all the ledger books are instantly updated and identical to each other. In doing so, any altered copy will be different from the original so that the alteration can be easily identified.

Identical copies of the blockchain are replicated across all nodes in the network. In the construction of Bitcoin's blockchain, a new block is generated and attached to the blockchain every 10 minutes, and all copies of the blockchain automatically update themselves. During this short interval, different versions of the blockchain may appear in different nodes. This phenomenon is called *forking*. When a new block emerges by consensus, it is attached to all the blockchain copies to make all of them identical. Forks dissipate quickly and automatically.

The nodes communicate over a network and collaboratively construct the blockchain without relying on a central authority. Faults can appear when individual nodes crash, the communication between nodes fail, or there is a malicious attack. However, because there are many more nodes, the record remains safe. Such safe record keeping is achieved by a *consensus protocol*. That is, the identical copies kept by majority nodes are considered as the authentic copy.

The number of nodes is so vast that it is impossible to alter the transaction replicated in the majority of the nodes to form a consensus. In addition, all data are vertically integrated along the chain in the blockchain. Any attempt to alter the data inevitably creates a discrepancy among the data in the sequential blocks and different copies of the blockchain. Regular updates prevent any attempt to alter the data, making it immutable.

Blockchain is accessible to anyone on the Internet. Therefore, it can be regarded as a public Internet ledger. All copies of the blockchain are more than just secure sequential distributed databases. Because they can be trusted, they offer the ability to simplify and automate transactions and make it easier and cheaper to conduct financial activities.

Blockchain resides on the Internet. In many ways, the blockchain network is similar to the Internet and really is something of a subset of the Internet. On the Internet, Web servers or HTTP servers manage Web applications. In the same way, in the blockchain network, the *consensus servers* manage distributed applications. The application sends a transaction to the platform, which handles communication and consensus. When the community agrees on the order of transactions, it then changes the state, which is recorded in the distributed database.

Bitcoin was the first application of blockchain technology. It is also fair to say that blockchain was invented to create Bitcoin. P2P (peer to peer) distribution and decentralization are built into the Bitcoin blockchain and some of the first blockchain applications. As Bitcoin started to proliferate, interest in blockchain technology grew. Since the idea of Bitcoin was initially developed, countless industries, from financial services to health care, have begun contemplating how to leverage the technology for themselves.

Blockchain's distributed nature, validation and encryption methods, and trust mechanisms are evolving to meet the needs of developers.

As applications have evolved, the basic mechanism of constructing blockchain has also changed. Some of its derivatives are far from the idealistic distributed, decentralized blockchain originally invented for Bitcoin. However, this does not diminish the importance of blockchain technology. This evolution contributed to creating fintech, which would not be salient without the blockchain technology.

1.2 DISTRIBUTED COMPUTING

Modern computing infrastructure is becoming more distributed for many reasons. First, the price of CPUs/GPUs and storage media (memories and disk drives) has decreased. These provide computing power and data storage on a broad scale. They are not only cheaper than before, but also more powerful, thanks to the progress made in semiconductor technology.

In 1971, the first commercial integrated circuit (IC) made by Intel – the Intel 4004 – had 2,300 transistors. In 2021, the most advanced IC had 54 billion transistors (an example is the NVIDIA GA100). Today, a single smartphone has more computing power than NASA did in 1969, when the United States first put a man on the moon.[4]

The ever-increasing communication speed and bandwidth make remote services possible. Powerful applications residing in the cloud provide supercomputing power at the fingertip. Therefore, data processing is no longer confined in one location. This is known as *distributed computing*.

Widespread computing and communications generate high volumes of data. Cheap storage also encourages data safeguarding by replication; when one of the storage devices fails, valuable data are not lost. Almost all the online applications access data remotely and process these data either locally or remotely. In this way, distributed computing co-exists with a distributed database.[5]

When multiple computers are processing the same dataset, they may generate different outputs. For example, searching the same keywords using Google on different days may give different results. In some applications, this may not be acceptable. To avoid conflict, distributed systems need a consensus mechanism. A consensus mechanism is a fundamental necessity in the distributed systems as it guarantees the consistency of the outcome of a process. *Consensus* is a mechanism of reaching a collective agreement on some value, and it makes it possible for a distributed system to act as a single entity. A distributed computing system without consensus is like a city without traffic lights.

In the world of blockchain-based distributed computing, there are two types of consensus mechanisms: hashing power (computer power) and economic power. Before 2016, economic power was the only type of consensus. However, as the power of Bitcoin miners became more concentrated, hashing power became stronger. In 2022, roughly 10% of the Bitcoin miners controlled 90% of the Bitcoin mining.[6]

1.3 CENTRALIZATION VS. DECENTRALIZATION

Another characteristic of blockchain is the concept of decentralization. Distribution applies to the location of data: A *distributed database* resides in many computer nodes, whereas a non-distributed database resides in one location. A *centralized database* has an owner or central authority overseeing the database, while a decentralized database does not.

Blockchain for Bitcoin is decentralized, which has led many to believe that blockchain in general is decentralized. However, it is not true: A blockchain can also be centralized.

The word "decentralization" does not have a clear definition in the context of blockchain technology. As the technology evolves, the blockchain technology also evolves.

Vitalik Buterin, the founder of Ethereum – another popular cryptocurrency – defined centralization through architectural, political, and logical concepts.[7] *Architectural centralization* refers to the database distribution nature of the ledger; an architectural decentralized database is the same as a distributed database. *Political centralization* refers to the ownership or presence of a central authority. *Logical centralization* refers to the state and the behavior of the blockchain. Buterin considered blockchain politically and architecturally decentralized, but logically centralized. This is true for certain types of blockchain.

When a blockchain is not truly public and has an owner, it is called the *permissioned blockchain*.[8] The permissioned blockchain is politically centralized because its owner controls it. To access a permissioned blockchain, transactions, validation, and other privileges require permission from the owner/administrator, who retains control over how the blockchain operates.[9] Since there are many privileges that have different levels of centralization, this makes the exact boundary between decentralization and centralization blurry at best.

The permissioned blockchain is also called the private blockchain, or consortium blockchain. This is because the creator of a permissioned blockchain has a specific object in mind for its application. There are many permissioned blockchain platforms, such as Hyperledger Fabric, Tendermint, Symbiont Assembly, R3 Corda, Iroha, Kadena, Chain, Quorum, and MultiChain.

To differentiate the centralized nature of the permissioned blockchain, the originally developed Bitcoin-like decentralized P2P blockchain is now called the permissionless blockchain, or the public blockchain. The difference between the permissionless (or public) blockchain and permissioned (or private) blockchain is akin to that of the Internet and an intranet. While the Internet belongs to the public, intranets are internal and private and belong to individual particular organizations. It can also be compared to a public park and private garden. Anyone can visit a public park, but one needs permission to visit a private space. In a permissionless blockchain – such as Bitcoin's blockchain – anyone can be a user or run a node, invoke transactions, and participate in the consensus process. In the permissioned blockchain, the participation is by invitation only.

Most of the Bitcoin nodes receive data from other nodes, checking its validity, and passing it on further without doing the mining work. Nodes accept the block only if all transactions in it are valid and not already spent. There are over 15,000 reachable full nodes at any given time. However, the actual number of computers running the full nodes in the Bitcoin network can be much larger.[10] (The United States alone has 12.1% of all the full nodes in the Bitcoin network, followed by Germany at 9.64%, and France at 3.2%.) These full nodes constitute the Bitcoin community, and within the Bitcoin community, a small group of full nodes operate as miners. The hashing power resides in the miners, but the economic power resides in the Bitcoin community.

A permissioned blockchain can be distributed, but is not necessarily decentralized. Even a centralized permission blockchain still offers benefits over a traditional centralized database, although, the claim is sometimes rebuked by critics. Some of the benefits are as follows:

- Each participant retains full control over assets;
- The data are encrypted and cannot be altered easily, and are therefore considered safe;
- Alterations are traceable;
- Control of the database is distributed across entities;
- The loss of any one server does not compromise the network.

There are different degrees of the centralization or decentralization. For example, in the Bitcoin or Ethereum platform, miners can create coins and anybody can be a miner. This is distinguishably decentralized vs. a national digital currency, which can only be created by the government. The decentralization is relative: for example, Bitcoin is more decentralized than Ethereum.

The Bitcoin platform can create up to 21 million Bitcoin as coded in the software. Nobody can change the protocol unless there is a consensus in the Bitcoin community. This is the designed decentralization. The maximum number of ETH (the Ethereum currency) that can be created is around 100 million, which has also been codified. However, Ethereum Foundation holds the power to change the protocol, including the capacity for its coins. In this aspect, Ethereum is less decentralized than Bitcoin.

Nevertheless, Ethereum allows anyone to develop an application on its platform. There are multiple clients written by independent parties, but the Ethereum Foundation has control only over its own client. Furthermore, if the Ethereum Foundation forces a change in its own client, and some people do not agree, they can split off as a hard fork. This is what happened in the Ethereum and Ethereum Classic split. From this point of view, Ethereum is still considered decentralized.

Figure 1.1 shows the degree of centralization for three criteria: authority, power, and control. There is no such thing as a 100% decentralized system or centralized system. Each system has its own degree of centralization for authority, power, and control – independently represented by lines AB, AC, and AD. Point E indicates the degree of centralization of authority. Likewise, Point F is for power and point G is for control. When the point is closer to the apex, the degree of centralization is higher. Therefore, we can use a triangle formed by the vertexes of three lines connecting three points along the axis of power, control, and authorization (triangle EFG) to represent the degree of decentralization.

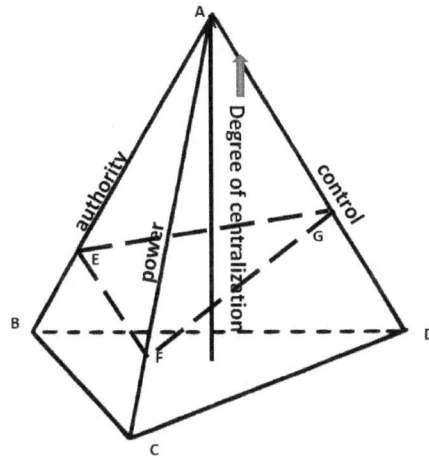

FIGURE 1.1 Degree of centralization.

Permissioned blockchain development was very important because most fintech applications are this type. Some decentralized properties for the permissionless blockchain do not apply to the permissioned blockchain. Permissioned blockchains do have owners, who act as centralized authorities to the blockchain. These two branches of blockchain are evolving in very different directions as they have a different philosophies and applications.

Both types of blockchain guarantee the validity of transactions by recording them in a connected distributed system with a secure validation mechanism. Most blockchain applications reside in a network of computers connected to the Internet. Some blockchain applications reside in a cloud environment. Each computer node – a client – performs validation and relays the transaction to the next node. These computer nodes store a copy of the blockchain they validate.

The blockchain can be as long as the history of transactions of a particular asset it represents. In the case of Bitcoin, it creates a block every 10 minutes and grows 6 blocks per hour, 144 blocks per day or 52,560 blocks per year. It contains all the transaction history of Bitcoin. In addition, it exists in all the nodes in the Bitcoin blockchain network, so it is impossible to alter the data and make them consistent throughout the chain during the 10-minute interval. The 10-minute period is a result of the Proof of Work (PoW) algorithm, which takes miners 10 minutes to construct a block with hash lower than the target value.

A permissionless blockchain network is a subset of the Internet. Every node is equal and joins the network voluntarily, which is a form of mass collaboration. The incentive for participating in the network as a miner is the chance of winning Bitcoin. In addition, the incentive for participating in the network as a full node is to have the most private and secure way to use Bitcoin.

Blockchain technology creates a channel for the peer-to-peer transaction and may change the way we make all types of transactions. The technology provides a distributed transaction ledger that connects each transaction to its previous transactions, protecting them all with encryption. The blockchain tracks and verifies digital assets so they cannot be hacked or copied without permission. It operates without the need for intermediaries. The high level of security is why blockchain is used for cryptocurrency, but it can also be used for other assets, anything from votes in an election to stocks, tax payments, and property deeds.

What is revolutionary about the blockchain is that it decentralizes ownership and control of assets, and by doing this, it remodels fundamental structures in our society. It also replaces the traditional trust wholly or partially by cryptographic technology. By doing so, it removes one of the biggest barriers to transact valuables. From this point of view, it is the most important invention since paper money. It will stimulate the transactions or economic activities between unknown parties – globally – which was previously impossible without the third party as trust element. Blockchain technology has the potential to allow untapped economic activities that are currently impeded by a lack of trust.

The global economy is based on the power and trust we place in intermediaries like banks, governments, utilities, and large technology companies such as Facebook and Google, because we have no alternative. They add no value to transactions beyond the trust, yet they wield tremendous power over us all, make money from the transactions, and slow the transactions down in the process. If transactions and assets remain secure without these intermediaries, then we do not need them; we can retain our own property and stop paying them to insert themselves into various processes.

Interestingly, blockchain will take power and wealth away from even relatively new corporate intermediaries like Uber and Facebook. Imagine that if drivers and passengers can contract themselves securely without risking their identities or financial information, then the intermediary – here Uber – is extraneous.

However, the permissionless blockchain has its weakness. Because there is no central authority, any change requires majority consensus. Sometimes, the consensus fails because of different interests that different groups in the blockchain community represent. This was apparent in the 2017 disparity in fixing Bitcoin's scaling issues, where miners were pitted against users. It ended up with a split of the Bitcoin blockchain.[11]

There are many potential applications of the blockchain technology. Since it is a transaction-based system, the most obvious applications are in the financial sector. For example, international remittances, which amount to over $400 billion in transactions per year, are one of the primary targets of blockchain. It not only cuts out the intermediary to handle the transaction, thus lowering the cost, but it is fast and secure. Cryptocurrency can transact across national borders instantly. This greatly promotes e-commerce on a global scale.

Blockchain is secure because it is encrypted, and its network does not have the vulnerability of a single system that computer hackers can exploit. Most of the service industries, such as banking, real estate, and insurance, will be transformed beyond recognition by blockchain technology.

Banks will need to add value rather than simply guard money and move it around, because, with blockchain, buyers and sellers will be able to verify the presence of funds and exchange them on their own.

Utility companies will also change as individuals switch to highly efficient renewable sources and store extra power; they can then sell their reserve power locally, effectively creating multiple mini-grids — unless utility companies include consumers as partners.

Even governments might eventually have a less involved role in its governance and a more streamlined bureaucracy with the help of blockchain. While societies would still probably opt for group decision-making and policymaking processes, with blockchain the execution of programs and distribution of benefits could be managed efficiently without as much corruption.

When technologies such as self-driving cars come onto the scene, blockchain technology will help prevent malicious attacks on the autonomous driving and help to ensure safety.

1.4   PERMISSIONED VS. PERMISSIONLESS

We have briefly discussed the permissioned vs. permissionless blockchain. In a blockchain such as Bitcoin and Ethereum, any user can join the network and start mining. One does not need anyone's permission to join the blockchain. In addition, one does not have to prove his/her identity to anyone – as long as one can commit the processing power to be part of the network and extend the blockchain. The permissionless blockchain is like a public park that anyone can walk in. Since the network is open to all, the only way to make the transactions secure is that the participating nodes do the block verification by performing PoW/PoS/dBFT type of work. It is just like you need to buy a ticket to go to a public zoo.

As more large corporations embrace blockchain technology, they are creating applications that are very specific and only involve certain parties. For example, if a bank develops a blockchain application to serve its clients, naturally, it will only allow its clients to use such application. In this type of permissioned blockchain, the central authority establishes the trust. To open an account at a bank or apply for a credit card, the necessary ID and financial information of the applicant already serve as a kind of "trust."

There are two aspects of the permission: one is the right to access, the other is the right to validate transactions. In the permissioned blockchain, only a restricted group of users (who have access by invitation) has the rights to validate the block transactions. The right to validate transactions is more restrictive than the right to access. In the real world, there are also different levels of privilege: a bank's client has the right to see his account balance and to write a check, but he does not have the right to change the account maintenance fee or to see other clients' balances.

Similarly, in a blockchain belonging to a bank, the right of validation is restricted to the bank's network nodes, and the right of access is restricted to the bank's clients. Therefore, the permissioned blockchain is like a private club where only admitted members can enter. In addition, there are different levels of members that have different privileges and rights.

The permissioned blockchain has an owner who approves the participation membership. The owner builds the blockchain to serve his purpose. When banks and financial institutions build blockchain applications, they use the permissioned blockchain to do so. A national digital currency also uses the permissioned blockchain because the digital currency has an owner – the central bank.

The permissionless blockchain needs to provide coins as the incentive to validate the blocks and build the blockchain, which requires resources. However, in the permissioned blockchain, the token does not serve this purpose anymore. Unless transactions require tokens, the blockchain does not need tokens. Some permissioned blockchains are token-less blockchains where the owner controls the validators and block-creators – they do this for different reasons other than receiving tokens (for example, someone whose job is to operate a blockchain application as a part of their business operation).

As a result, the validation work can be very different in these two types of blockchains. In the permissionless blockchain, PoW or PoS (Proof of Stake) mining is necessary to achieve consensus. The Bitcoin blockchain uses hashing power to build trust, and Ethereum currently is using PoW but is moving to a consensus mechanism using PoS.

Permissioned blockchains already operate based on the trust of the institution that owns it; therefore, their blockchains do not require PoW to validate transactions. The institution (e.g., bank) provides the trust. The most important attribute of their blockchain application is security and efficiency. They can use a simplified version of PoS or dBFT or use very different kinds of consensus algorithms like RAFT, Paxos, or PBFT.

Even without the PoW or PoS consensus mechanism, the permissioned blockchain still has the following advantages:

- Privacy – only members have rights to view the transactions;
- Scalability – by not using the resource-intensive PoW, a permissioned blockchain can be easily scaled up; and
- Access Control – a permissioned blockchain can restrict access to the data within the ledger as the owner (bank) desires.

SETL, a London-based company, has created a permission-based blockchain settlement and payment system that can move cash and assets in real-time to settle market transactions.[12] It maintains a distributed ledger of ownership and transaction records, simplifying the process of matching, settlement, custody, registration, and transaction reporting. The platform enables investors and distributors to easily subscribe and redeem fund units via a direct connection with the asset management company, thereby removing the need for the transfer agent, which in turn reduces transaction costs. The platform increases transparency, optimizes operational workflow, and enables the development of new value-added services.

In summary, the permissioned blockchain is a closed, private blockchain with an owner. It has a certain degree of centralization. In a way, permissioned and permissionless blockchains can be thought of in terms of a comparison of the Internet and an intranet. The Internet is a robust high-capacity global network for transmitting information within an organization. This enables many enterprises to make use of virtual private networks (VPNs), which use the Internet as a backbone but encrypt the organization's traffic over these public pipes. VPNs allow enterprises to enjoy the Internet's economy of scale while ensuring that their data is not visible to outside observers. One can imagine a comparable process playing out between the permissionless/public blockchain and permissioned/private blockchain.

1.5   BITCOIN

As mentioned earlier, the concept of blockchain evolves from cryptography, a computer science discipline that focuses on encryption technology to ensure the security of data stored or transferred digitally. It has become more important since the volume of data generated and stored by humans has grown exponentially.

In 2008, a computer scientist named Satoshi Nakamoto wrote a paper to propose the use of cryptography to create a digital currency called Bitcoin.[13] In his original publication, he envisioned a purely peer-to-peer version of electronic cash that allows sending online payments safely and directly from one party to another over the Internet without going through a financial institution.

In building the Bitcoin platform, he included several elements, including a digital signature, network timestamp, and hashing into a chain of blocks of data. Such a chain forms a record that is unchangeable without redoing the PoW. The basic concept of the blockchain technology was born. As long as a majority of owners in the nodes do not collaborate to attack the network, the data are safe.

The network itself requires minimal structure. Any computer on the Internet can be a node if it is running the Bitcoin software downloaded from Bitcoin's platform. Nodes broadcast messages on a best effort basis – they are free to leave and rejoin the network at will. The functionality of the Bitcoin blockchain does not depend on a particular node, and this flexible structure makes the Bitcoin network easy to grow.

The blockchain encryption uses public and private "keys." The public key is the user's address on the blockchain. It is a destination that people can send Bitcoin to across the network. It is also where a transaction record is kept. The public and private key pair represent the ownership of the Bitcoin. The asset tied to the public key belongs to the owner of the public key. The private key is a password that gives its owner access to his digital assets. Consider the following analogy: a public key is like a post office box number and private key is like the key to open the box. The box itself can store valuable objects.

Another analogy is as follows: if the blockchain is a ledger book, the public key is the page number plus the line number where a transaction is recorded. By providing such information, one can immediately identify a transaction.

The pair of public and private keys is one entity, because the public key is generated from the private key by elliptic curve multiplication.[14] The creation of a public key from a private key is a one-way process. It is impossible to recreate the private key from the public key. Protecting the private key is essential to protect the digital assets associated with the private key. Therefore, safeguarding the private key is critical to the possession of the Bitcoin stored in the corresponding public key. Many forms of "wallets" can safeguard the private keys. Figure 1.2 shows Bitcoin public and private keys in printed form.[15]

Even without considering all the current and possible applications of blockchain technology, the technology itself is a breakthrough in computer science. It is built upon more than 20 years of research in cryptographic currencies and 40 years of development efforts in cryptography by thousands of researchers around the world. Satoshi Nakamoto put the pieces together in a useful form. He incorporated all the essential elements into one place: the Bitcoin software.

Bitcoin is a solution to a long-standing issue with digital cash: the double-spend problem – a digital file cannot have any value as an asset because anyone can copy or duplicate it with minimal effort. Satoshi Nakamoto proposed a solution to the double spending problem in his original paper published in 2008.

He constructed the Bitcoin platform that hashes the transaction into an ongoing chain of hash-based Proof-of-Work, forming a record that cannot be changed without redoing the Proof-of-Work.

The ownership of Bitcoin is nothing more than the receipt or record of the transaction, which contains payer, payee, transaction time, and the amount.

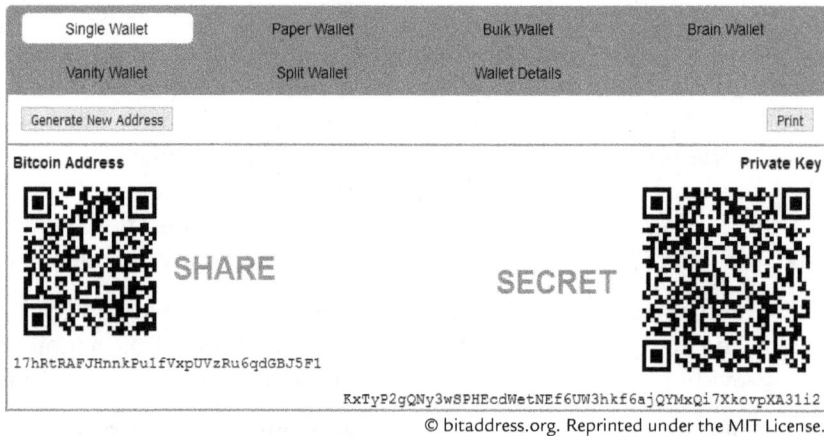

FIGURE 1.2 A printed Bitcoin Public Key and Private Key.

The payer and payee are represented by their respective public addresses. The transaction is recorded in the payee's public address in the blockchain. You prove your ownership by showing your public key with a private key. Only the person who has the private key can spend the Bitcoin stored in the public key address.

After you spend the Bitcoin stored in a particular address, this address becomes invalid, because the Bitcoin in this address has passed to another address. You cannot use the same address again. This prevents double spending. The transaction is broadcasted to the Bitcoin network, much like you send a message in Twitter. A group of nodes called "miners" catch transactions floating in the network. They verify if the address is valid before accepting the transaction. If the address has been used as a payer in the previous transaction, the transaction is rejected.

When there are enough transactions to fill the block, the block is complete. The miner who completes a block first wins the race. Other miners stop constructing their unfinished blocks. There is only one winner per block. All other unverified blocks dissipate. Bitcoin nodes doubly verify the validity of all the transactions in the winner's block before the block becomes official and is attached to the blockchain. There is little chance that the Bitcoin in an address can be spent twice. The transactions included in the block are eliminated from the pools of transactions in circulation in the Bitcoin network. The construction of the next block then starts. This process repeats every 10 minutes.

In the first quarter of 2021, the price of Bitcoin reached almost $60,000 and the market cap of Bitcoin grew to well over $600 billion, as shown in

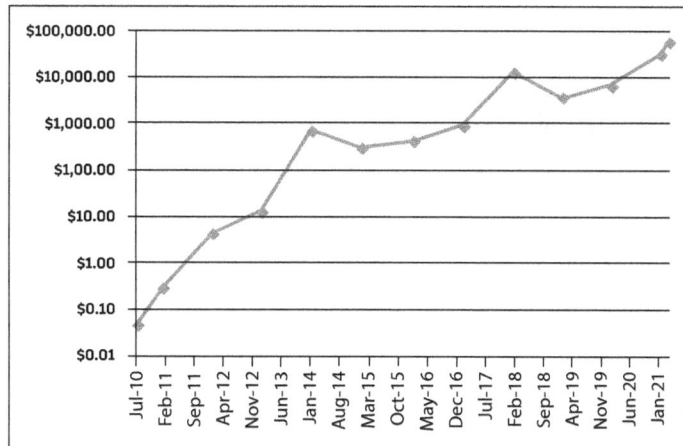

FIGURE 1.3 Year-by-year Bitcoin price.

Figure 1.3.[16] If we include Bitcoin Cash, which is a fork of the Bitcoin, the combined market capitalization is greater. This is the proof that the concept of Bitcoin proposed by Satoshi Nakamoto has enormous popularity.

Today, more businesses accept Bitcoin as payment. In Japan, over 260,000 stores accept Bitcoin as legal tender. In the U.S., large, brand name companies also accept Bitcoin as payments, such as Whole Foods, Expedia, Home Depot, CVS, Subway, and Microsoft.

The main Bitcoin merchants processing solutions for vendors to accept Bitcoin are BitPay and Coinbase in the U.S. and Coinify in Europe. Mobile payment functionality for quick point-of-sale Bitcoin purchases will further stimulate a greater adoption of Bitcoin.

In Chapter 2, we discuss Bitcoin and how it works in much more detail.

1.6 PROLIFERATION OF BLOCKCHAIN TECHNOLOGY

Blockchain technology has not only created many cryptocurrencies, but is also the foundation of fintech. Hundreds of applications are flourishing, and many of them will have a significant impact in the near future.

With such explosive potential applications, blockchain technology is in a pivotal phase. The activity is not limited to the startups, as a number of large companies, including financial, technological, and logistic companies, are embracing blockchain technology.

Today, cryptocurrency seems to dominate blockchain applications, however, digital currency is not the only application of blockchain. Hundreds of transactional applications are in development using blockchain technology. Some people consider it the biggest invention since the invention of the Internet itself.

The nascent blockchain industry is developing a new generation of transactional applications that establish trust, accountability, and transparency at their core while streamlining business processes and legal constraints. It is akin to an operating system for marketplaces, data-sharing networks, micro-currencies, and decentralized digital communities. It has the potential to reduce the cost and complexity of real-world transactions, and therefore greatly improves the efficiency of economy.

There is no lack of effort to introduce blockchain into financial applications. For example, Linux Foundation hosts an open source, collaborative software development platform, known as Hyperledger, in conjunction with the leaders in finance, banking, and the IoT, supply chains, manufacturing, and technology to develop the applications in their respective fields.[17] This approach ensures the transparency, longevity, interoperability, and support required to bring blockchain technologies to mainstream commercial adoption.

R3, the largest blockchain consortium, raised $107 million from global financial institutions like SBI Group, Bank of America Merrill Lynch, HSBC, Intel, ING, Banco Bradesco, Itaü Unibanco, Barclays, UBS, and Wells Fargo to develop commercial applications for the MDL technology.[18]

Once again, the Internet has spawned the greatest value generating, revolutionary technological breakthrough since the invention of e-commerce (e.g., Amazon) and online advertisement through a search engine (Google). There is no reason to doubt that blockchain will not be able to give birth to giant companies on a par with Amazon and Google. In fact, there is every reason to believe that blockchain technology will make an even bigger impact on the world than search engines and e-commerce. Not since the invention of the Web itself has a technology promised broader and more fundamental revolution than blockchain.

1.7 INITIAL COIN OFFERING (ICO)

Blockchain technology is creating a completely new financial market called the Initial Coin Offering (ICO). ICO is a process whereby the cryptocurrency companies sell their newly launched crypto coins. ICO bypasses the regulated capital-raising process required by venture capitalists or banks. In an ICO campaign, the early backers of the project buy a percentage of the newly issued cryptocurrency. The proceeds are to fund the company. The ICO process is also known as *crowd sales*. Ethereum, a company that developed a blockchain protocol, which can transact smart contracts in a distributed network, is a great success story of the ICO.

Much like the traditional angel funding, the startup company with a vision to create a business generates a project plan. The project plan includes a business plan with a whitepaper. The plan describes the project mission and vision, detail plan, execution strategy, technological approach, target market, potential applications, goals, risks, and its differentiation from other similar projects, funding needed for execution, number of new coins the founders keep for themselves, and the ICO campaign period.

The aim of the startup is to attract and convince enthusiasts and supporters to buy some of the distributed crypto coins. These coins are tokens. If the money raised does not meet the minimum required fund at the end of ICO campaign period, the ICO event fails. The startup returns the money to the subscribers of the ICO. Otherwise, the new coin is born, and the money raised goes to fund the startup.

Early investors in the operation are usually motivated to buy the crypto coins in the hope that the plan becomes successful, and the coins will increase value.

In the ICO model, the return on investment does not come from the shares of the company that they invest, but from the blockchain-based token. For example, an Ethereum token was worth of $1.00 on January 2016, it became $349.06 on June 10, 2017. It was a successful investment in a very short period.

The token represents an ownership of the blockchain network of the proposed project, not the company. This is a radically new way of investment. The ownership is the direct asset rather than the company holding the asset. Eventually, if the project becomes valuable, the token value will increase. Of course, if the project fails, the coin will become worthless.

Today, the blockchain technology is still in the incubation stage. Many projects may fail. However, when the appropriate application appears, its growth will be explosive. In the process, it can create many millionaires. However, like any investment, investors need to do due diligence to understand the underlying technology to know whether it has any potential. Today, because the financial authorities do not yet regulate the ICO process, its risk is high.

Many blockchain companies that have done ICOs have found success, raising tens of millions of dollars at a significant valuation. In fact, blockchain startup companies have raised more capital from ICOs than traditional early-stage and venture capital funding.

Instead of building a new blockchain from scratch, one can also build projects on the existing, open blockchain platforms. Over the past year, an increasing number of blockchain projects have utilized the Ethereum protocol to distribute unique tokens in a decentralized and transparent manner. The tokens released by independent Blockchain projects and companies are compatible with the Ethereum network and its native token.

1.8 BLOCKCHAIN PLATFORMS

Bitcoin is the first blockchain platform, but by no means the only one. In the last decade, many blockchain platforms have been developed. Each one has its own characteristics and uniqueness. They all target certain applications. The technology has applications in many sectors, such as capital markets and trade, finance, healthcare, energy, and government (taxation).

For instance, the technology could potentially be applied to capital markets to eliminate the need for reconciling various ledgers by providing a shared and synchronized blockchain among participants. In this section, we discuss some of the most important ones.

Many startups are developing products and services in this space: for example, Chain Core is a blockchain platform for issuing and transferring financial assets on a permissioned blockchain infrastructure.[19] Corda is a distributed ledger platform with a pluggable consensus.[20] Credits is a development framework for building permissioned distributed ledgers.[21] Ethereum is a decentralized platform that runs smart contracts on a custom-built blockchain.[22] HydraChain is an Ethereum extension for creating permissioned distributed ledgers for private and consortium chains.[23] Hyperledger Fabric supports the use of one or more networks, each managing different assets, agreements, and transactions between different nodes.[24] Hyperledger Iroha is a simple and modularized distributed ledger system with an emphasis on mobile application development. Hyperledger Sawtooth Lake is a modular blockchain suite in which transaction business logic is decoupled from the consensus layer. The list goes on and on.

Moody's published a report that identified over 120 on-going projects among the issuers that it rates.[25] In the report, Moody evaluated the platforms in development by their efficiency in terms of speed, cost, security, and reliability, as well as the auditability of the processes. The longer-term viability of these platforms depends on whether their positives by leveraging blockchain technology will outweigh their negatives, and their market acceptance. Not all of them will be successful, but many of them will be.

For blockchain technology to make an impact on the existing establishment, there are many challenges. Among the challenges are the compatibility of blockchain technology with the existing systems, the need for the development of industry standards, and questions about regulatory compliance. It is essential that new blockchain-based systems can upgrade the existing systems without causing an interruption in service.

Many of the blockchain platforms in development are trying to address these challenges. Instead of blockchain technology toppling the existing establishment, it likely will greatly improve the security, efficiency, and cost of the existing systems.

REFERENCES

1. "What is a blockchain", Nick Williamson, *https://www.finyear.com/What-is-a-Blockchain_a34985.html*

2. *https://www.grandviewresearch.com/industry-analysis/blockchain-technology-market*

3. "The Internet of Value – Exchange", *https://www2.deloitte.com/content/dam/Deloitte/uk/Documents/Innovation/deloitte-uk-Internet-of-value-exchange.pdf*

4. *http://www.northeastern.edu/levelblog/2016/04/21/smartphones-supercomputer-in-your-pocket/*

5. "Distributed Computing: Fundamentals, Simulations and Advanced Topics", H. Attiya et al., Wiley, second edition, 2004.

6. *https://fortune.com/2021/10/26/bitcoin-mining-capacity-ownership-concentration-top-investors-nber-study/*

7. "The meaning of decentralization", Vitalik Buterin, Medium, *https://medium.com/@VitalikButerin/the-meaning-of-decentralization-a0c92b76a274*

8. "Consensus-as-a-service: a brief report on the emergence of Permissioned, distributed ledger systems", Tim Swanson, Great Wall of Numbers, *http://www.ofnumbers.com/2015/04/06/consensus-as-a-service-a-brief-report-on-the-emergence-of-Permissioned-distributed-ledger-systems/*

9. "What has been the reaction to Permissioned distributed ledgers?", *http://www.ofnumbers.com/2015/04/26/what-has-been-the-reaction-to-Permissioned-distributed-ledgers/*

10. *https://bitnodes.io/*

11. *https://en.wikipedia.org/wiki/Bitcoin_scalability_problem*

12. *https://setl.io/*

13. "Bitcoin: A Peer to Peer Electronic Cash System": Satoshi Nakamoto white paper *https://bitcoin.org/bitcoin.pdf*

14. *https://medium.com/blockthought/how-does-Bitcoin-validate-transactions-a-primer-21e007f3a9d3*

15. Generated from bitaddress.org

16. *https://bitinfocharts.com/*

17. *https://www.hyperledger.org/community*

18. *https://www.r3.com/*

19. *https://www.blockchain-council.org/blockchain/chain-core-technology-works/*

20. *https://www.corda.net*

21. *https://credits.com*

22. *https://ethereum.org/en/*

23. *https://hydrachain.org*

24. *https://www.hyperledger.org*

25. *https://bravenewcoin.com/insights/moodys-new-report-identifies-25-top-blockchain-use-cases-from-a-list-of-120*

CHAPTER 2

BITCOIN

Bitcoin, the first application of blockchain, was the motivation for the development of the technology. Many of the other digital currencies and applications are variations of that initial Bitcoin application. By understanding the inner workings of the Bitcoin blockchain, it is easier to understand other applications of blockchain technology, including applications other than crypto.

The objective of the Bitcoin platform is to address the root problem of a fiat currency: the extensive trust network that is required to make it work. Bitcoin replaces the trust with the use of cryptographic proof and decentralized networks.

Wei Dai at Microsoft published the earliest proposal for an "anonymous, distributed electronic cash system" in November 1998. Dai called it "b-money."[1] In his proposal, Dai first described the Proof-of-Work concept using the Hashcash algorithm, although he did not use the term "Proof-of-Work." Dai's proposal advanced three key concepts, which eventually became the cornerstone of Bitcoin:

- Transaction: Funds are exchanged through broadcasting and digital signatures.
- Verification: The transaction is verified by authentication with cryptographic hashes and updated to the collective ledger.
- Reward: Whoever does the work is rewarded for their effort.

Dai did not put his idea into practical use, however, and it remained simply an academic curiosity. Ten years later, Nakamoto took the b-money concept further when he created Bitcoin. He first published the software on the Bitcoin Core website in January 2009.[2] The Bitcoin nodes use the Core software to create the Bitcoin network. Over the course of the following 13 years, Bitcoin Core has served as the main branch of Bitcoin development.

After the disappearance of Nakamoto in April 2011, Bitcoin developers continued to support the Bitcoin Core website and make changes to the Bitcoin protocol.[3] By March of 2022, it was in version 22.0. To keep the promise of decentralization, Bitcoin Core does not take a position in the implementation of any modification to the Bitcoin software – it is up to the Bitcoin community to decide.[4]

The first block on the Bitcoin blockchain – known as block 0 or the Genesis Block – was mined on January 3, 2009, according to the timestamp in the block header (See Figure 2.1).[5] Nakamoto made the Bitcoin software available online to the public on January 8, 2009. The second user, Hal Finney, a Cal Tech-educated computer scientist, mined Bitcoin a few days later. Finney also contributed to the Proof-of-Work concept used in the Bitcoin platform through the publication of his paper on the topic in 2007, two years before the appearance of Bitcoin.[6] Because Bitcoin's platform is distributed and decentralized, Bitcoin Core created, but does not own, the system. As a reference client of Bitcoin, Bitcoin Core cannot enforce the changes to the Bitcoin software. Rather, the Bitcoin community must reach a consensus on critical decisions. Such a consensus creates difficulty at times because of the conflicts of interest from different parties involved in the Bitcoin community. It is the inherent shortcoming of the leaderless state of Bitcoin platform.

2.1 BITCOIN MINING

Bitcoin is a digital file that records transactions like a ledger, and the Bitcoin blockchain bears many similarities to a paper ledger, where each page can record many transactions. Likewise, in a blockchain, each block can record many Bitcoin transactions. Each page in the ledger is bonded to the next page. The balance at the end of each page carries to the next page, thus forming a link between pages. In the same manner, each block of Bitcoin is bonded to the previous block by a hash to form a chain.

Each node in the Bitcoin network keeps an updated copy of the Bitcoin blockchain that contains a complete transaction history of Bitcoin. New transactions are broadcast to the network. A special type of node in the Bitcoin

```
00000000  01 00 00 00 00 00 00 00  00 00 00 00 00 00 00 00   ................
00000010  00 00 00 00 00 00 00 00  00 00 00 00 00 00 00 00   ................
00000020  00 00 00 00 3B A3 ED FD  7A 7B 12 B2 7A C7 2C 3E   ....;£íý z{.²zÇ,>
00000030  67 76 8F 61 7F C8 1B C3  88 8A 51 32 3A 9F B8 AA   gv.a.È.Ã^ŠQ2:Ÿ¸ª
00000040  4B 1E 5E 4A 29 AB 5F 49  FF FF 00 1D 1D AC 2B 7C   K.^J)«_Iÿÿ...¬+|
00000050  01 01 00 00 00 01 00 00  00 00 00 00 00 00 00 00   ................
00000060  00 00 00 00 00 00 00 00  00 00 00 00 00 00 00 00   ................
00000070  00 00 00 00 00 00 FF FF  FF FF 4D 04 FF FF 00 1D   ......ÿÿÿÿM.ÿÿ..
00000080  01 04 45 54 68 65 20 54  69 6D 65 73 20 30 33 2F   ..EThe Times 03/
00000090  4A 61 6E 2F 32 30 30 39  20 43 68 61 6E 63 65 6C   Jan/2009 Chancel
000000A0  6C 6F 72 20 6F 6E 20 62  72 69 6E 6B 20 6F 66 20   lor on brink of
000000B0  73 65 63 6F 6E 64 20 62  61 69 6C 6F 75 74 20 66   second bailout f
000000C0  6F 72 20 62 61 6E 6B 73  FF FF FF FF 01 00 F2 05   or banksÿÿÿÿ..ò.
000000D0  2A 01 00 00 00 43 41 04  67 8A FD B0 FE 55 48 27   *....CA.gŠý°þUH'
000000E0  19 67 F1 A6 71 30 B7 10  5C D6 A8 28 E0 39 09 A6   .gñ¦q0·.\Ö¨(à9.¦
000000F0  79 62 E0 EA 1F 61 DE B6  49 F6 BC 3F 4C EF 38 C4   ybàê.aÞ¶Iö¼?Lï8Ä
00000100  F3 55 04 E5 1E C1 12 DE  5C 38 4D F7 BA 0B 8D 57   óU.å.Á.Þ\8M÷º..W
00000110  8A 4C 70 2B 6B F1 1D 5F  AC 00 00 00 00            ŠLp+kñ._¬....
```

FIGURE 2.1 The Bitcoin Genesis block.

network, called *miners*, collect, validate, and record new transactions to form new blocks. This process of forming a new block is better known as Bitcoin mining. The transaction history is transparent and the Bitcoin blockchain contains a complete history of the Bitcoin transactions since its creation. Therefore, it makes the verification possible.

One of the differences between Bitcoin's ledger and a traditional paper ledger is that each node in the Bitcoin network maintains a copy of the most updated Bitcoin ledger, while the person who handles the transactions maintains the paper ledger.

In the Bitcoin platform, there are many anonymous users, and trust does not exist. The Bitcoin platform uses special mathematical functions to produce a secret code to replace and improve upon the trust. Such mathematical functions guarantee the value of Bitcoin in a way trust simply cannot.

Bitcoin's blockchain consists of blocks containing a sequence of digitally signed transactions since the genesis block was mined. Each Bitcoin in existence was created by the Bitcoin platform, which pays the miners in Bitcoin as a reward for creating the blocks. A miner's job is essentially validating the transactions to create a new block per a set of rules provided by the Bitcoin platform. It is like the accountant who maintains the paper ledger by validating and recording the transactions to receive payment for his service.

Besides receiving Bitcoin by creating blocks, miners also receive transaction fees in Bitcoin. As the Bitcoin platform grows more mature, the former reward diminishes, while the latter reward becomes more important. It has certain impact to the transactions. We will discuss this in more detail later.

Just like a check can be transferred by the payer to the payee when endorsed by the payer, Bitcoin can also be transferred from one person to another. More like money than a check, the same Bitcoin can transfer hands many times. The person who receives the Bitcoin can endorse the same Bitcoin and pay it to another person. Since all the transaction history of this particular Bitcoin is recorded in the blockchain, one can examine all the previous transactions to verify the chain of ownership, most importantly, to make sure that such a Bitcoin has not been spent twice by the same owner.

2.2   HOW DOES BITCOIN WORK?

The Bitcoin network is a peer-to-peer (P2P) network – there is no central authority in charge of creating currency or verifying transactions, all the work is performed in the network with distributed computing power. All the computers connected to the Bitcoin network are called "nodes."

There are three types of nodes in the Bitcoin network: miners, complete nodes, and partial nodes. Miners perform the work of transaction verification, encryption, and building the blocks. Nodes have the responsibility of validating the blocks built by the miners. *Complete nodes* carry a complete copy of the blockchain, while *partial nodes* carry only part of the blockchain. Miners are rewarded for their work of building blocks with newly created Bitcoin, while other nodes are strictly volunteers. Currently, there are over 15,000 complete nodes in the Bitcoin network. Anyone can join the Bitcoin network as a node by downloading and executing Bitcoin software.

The Bitcoin software encrypts each transaction – the sender and the receiver are identified only by a string of numbers – their public keys – which are public information. Buyers and sellers remain anonymous, but everyone can see that a coin has moved from address A to B, and the address is for one-time-use only, thus preventing any double spending.

The central idea of Bitcoin is that it can be used as a currency. We can best understand the concept of Bitcoin transactions by studying the representation of the transaction scheme in Nakamoto's original paper, shown in Figure 2.2.[7]

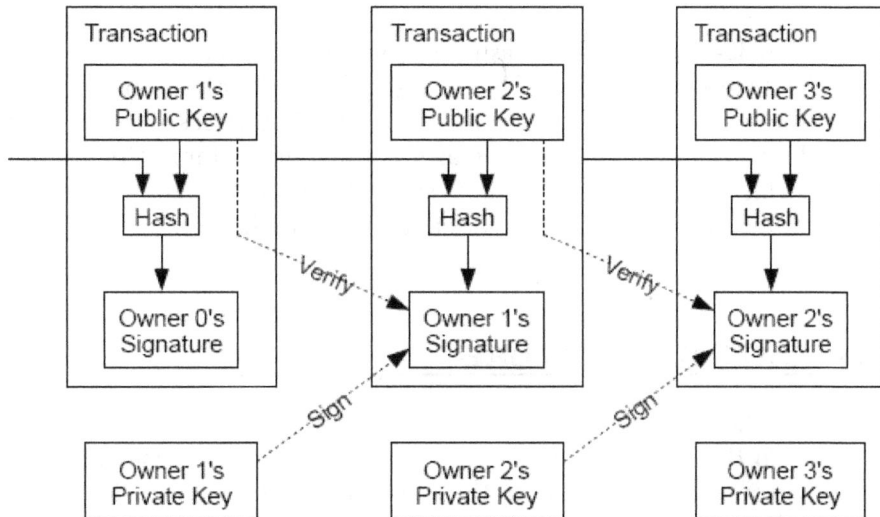

FIGURE 2.2 Illustration of Bitcoin transaction in the original publication.

A transaction involves three elements: a record of the previous transaction, payer's private key, and payee's public key. The private key is payer's evidence of ownership of Bitcoin. Since a Bitcoin transaction record does not exist outside of the blockchain, to receive a Bitcoin, one must create a new address in the Bitcoin network or the public key. The public key can be created by an online wallet. Once these three elements are in place, the transaction is broadcast to the Bitcoin network, much like a message is sent from a Twitter account to many others.

Miners collect these transactions and validate them. The first step of validation is to verify payer's public key. If the public key has been used in a previous transaction, that means such Bitcoin has been spent already, and it cannot be spent again. Such a transaction is invalid and discarded. This solves the so-called double spending issue. It guarantees that no Bitcoin can be used in two different transactions. The second step in the validation is to verify payer's digital signature. From Figure 2.3, we can see that the signature is the hash of previous transaction and payee's public key fused with payer's private key. The validation is done by making sure that the public key forms a pair with the private key. Only the one whose private key matches the public key is the true owner of the Bitcoin.

Each transaction is converted into an alphanumerical string. This action is called *hashing*. In the Bitcoin platform, the hashes are done by an algorithm called SHA-256, which is a version of the Secure Hash Algorithm. It generates 32-byte or 256-bit hash code, and the possible combinations of such hash code are in the order of 1 x , roughly the order of number of all the atoms in the universe, which is infinite for practical purposes. Therefore, the hash can be considered collision-free as it is functionally impossible to find two input strings with the same hash. As such, the hash of a data string is unique. More discussion of hashes is included later in this chapter.

2.3   DIGITAL SIGNATURE

Digital signing is a process that fuses the transaction data (amount and date) with the identity of the owner (private key) mathematically. It produces an output that contains both the transaction data and the identity of the owner. Others can verify the signature but not alter it. This process is like signing a document where the ink of the signature fuses into the paper document – your signature on the document can be verified but not altered.

In Bitcoin, a transaction must be signed by the owner of the Bitcoin – the signature is a unique string of numbers generated by a signing algorithm using the owner's private key. A digital signature is a hash value from the transaction data encrypted with the private key (Figure 2.3). The signing algorithm performs three functions:

- Authentication, that the message was created by a known sender (For example, in the real world, the signer of a document must produce his ID and sign in front of a notary public.)
- Non-repudiation, that the sender cannot deny having sent the message (In the real world, the signer cannot deny his signature either.)
- Ensuring integrity, that the message was not altered in transit (In the real world, every page of the document must be initialed by the signer.)

The generation of a signature combines the private key with the transaction data. When a hash function and asymmetric cryptography (public-private keys) are combined, digital signatures are created.

Since the transaction data comes from the Internet as a message, it is possible that it could be intercepted and modified by malicious actors during the transmission to steal the asset. Software libraries such as OpenSSL and libsecp256k1 are used to secure communications against malicious attacks. (OpenSSL was the original library used in Bitcoin and libsecp256k1 is the new software library used for the same purpose; it is 2 to 5 times faster than the original.)

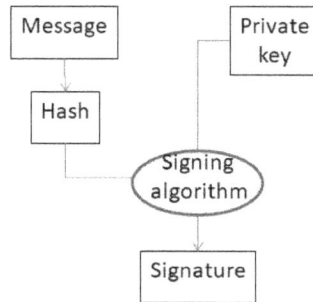

FIGURE 2.3 Digital signature flow.

The Bitcoin signature verification algorithm works in the following way: It takes the payer's public key, message, and signature as inputs (the verification does not need the private key of the signer). Since the signature already contains the private key, the verification algorithm has all the information about the payer and transaction.

The verification algorithm first decrypts the message using the sender's public key to produce a digest, then the verification algorithm calculates another digest from the signature. Since the private key is embedded in the signature, the two digests will match only when the public key used for the verification corresponds to the private key in the signature. If they match, the signature is valid. otherwise, the sender does not have the proper private key to use the Bitcoin.

When the transaction is completed, the Bitcoin has a new owner, represented by the new public key. The new owner can then use this Bitcoin in a new transaction, repeating the process described above.

The public key is the Bitcoin address, and its blockchain contains all the history of Bitcoin transactions. By verifying the public key, the Bitcoin platform ensures that such a public key has never been used as a payer before. This prevents double spending.

There are many digital signature algorithms. The most popular ones are RSA (Rivest, Shamir, Adleman) and DSS (Digital Signature Standard). Bitcoin's platform uses an algorithm called ECDSA, or Elliptic Curve Digital Signature Algorithm. Bitcoin's platform chose ECDSA because it produces signatures and public keys much smaller than RSA or DSS at similar security levels. The RSA signature and public key are 128 bytes each as compared to 48 bytes-long signatures and 25 bytes-long public keys produced by ECDSA. Even so, the signature is a large portion of the transaction data size.

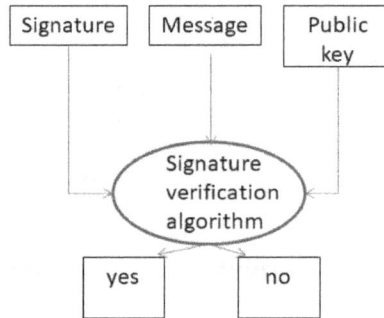

FIGURE 2.4 Digital signature verification flow.

One problem with the signature is that it consumes precious block space, which leaves less space for transaction data. Currently, each block can contain only up to 3,000 transactions. This limits the transaction rate of the Bitcoin platform to 3,000 transactions every 10 minutes, because it takes 10 minutes to mine each block. This is a far from sufficient ratio when Bitcoin becomes popular worldwide. For example, the current credit card transactions worldwide are about 750,000 per 10 minutes, or 250 times greater than Bitcoin. Without any improvement, this would set the maximum Bitcoin transaction volume to be no more than 0.4% of the current credit card transaction market. The lack of efficiency in generating signatures has also had an impact on Bitcoin mining.

One of the proposals to reduce the transaction data size, and therefore increase the transaction rate of the Bitcoin platform, is to separate the signature from the transaction data. This proposal is called Segregated Witness, or SegWit for short, which we will discuss SegWit in more detail later in the book.

2.4 MULTISIG

In the real world, there is sometimes a need for two or more people to agree in order to spend funds. In Bitcoin transactions, this can also be done. The signature scheme used is called multisig, short for multisignature. You can do this by creating a multisig wallet, and the transaction is sent to a multisig address.

The multisig scheme is made possible by the use of P2SH (Pay-to-Script-Hash), which is a mini programming language that was activated on April 1, 2012.[8] The script consists of two parts: opcodes (operational codes) and data. In this case, the data also define who needs to sign to spend the Bitcoin at this address in addition to the other transaction data, such as signature and public key. At the same time, it also locks the output. The funds sent to the P2SH address with script specifying the private keys to unlock the funds will require these private keys to sign in order to spend it.

A multisig scheme can also be used for a single signer to enhance the security. For example, the Bitcoin can be deposited in an address which requires two keys, one kept by the user, and one kept by the exchange. Both keys need to be present to spend the funds. The multisig structure is gaining popularity exponentially, thanks to the wider adaption of the multisig wallet.[9]

2.5   BITCOIN WALLETS

When you buy Bitcoins, you need to first create a private key and public key pair. The Bitcoins you buy will be deposited in your new public key, which is the address in the Bitcoin blockchain that your transaction is recorded. The private key is the password which allows you to spend the Bitcoins. It is long and random and is impossible to remember by heart. If you lose the private key, you lose the Bitcoins. Therefore, it is important to safeguard the private key.

Keys are small data files. They are among millions of files on your disk drives. It is not easy to keep it safe, especially if you have many keys. If you lose it, you are out of luck. Believe or not, it happens quite often.

For example, if the hard drive where you keep your private key crashes, you lose your Bitcoins. The most notable case is when a U.K. man accidentally threw out his hard drive – he lost $280 million of Bitcoins (in 2022 dollars).[10] Online wallets are not always safe either. In 2019, Gerald Cotton – the owner of QuadrigaCX, the largest Bitcoin exchange in Canada – died unexpectedly. He was the only one in control of his company's wallets, and as a result, the firm lost $190 million worth of crypto, all belonging to its customers.[11]

You can find out a list of "dormant" Bitcoin addresses, which have no movement for at least three years.[12] The address 1FeexV6bAHb8ybZjqQMjJrcCrHGW9sb6uF holds the most Bitcoins – 79,958 Bitcoins, valued at $3 billion as of March 2022.[13]

Blockchain data firm Chainalysis estimated that nearly 20% of the Bitcoins created have been lost, based on stagnant addresses dating back to first day of the cryptocurrency. Back then, a Bitcoin was practically worthless, and few could have envisioned what it would ultimately become today.[14] When the price of Bitcoins goes up, any loss can cost a fortune. The most mysterious Bitcoin owner is its inventor, Satoshi Nakamoto. Since the early days of Bitcoin, he was one of the few miners. It is estimated that he owns 1,100,000 Bitcoins, which is worth of $33 billion at the Bitcoin price of $30,000. This places him as one of the richest men on Earth. However, he has not yet claimed his Bitcoins.

The place to safeguard a private key is called a *wallet*, which is a digital wallet created using the same concept of the physical wallet that holds your money. Bitcoin wallets come in many forms, but there are two basic types of wallets: on-line (hot storage) and off-line (cold storage). In cold storage, you are the only one who is responsible for safeguarding your keys. Lost or stolen keys could compromise the entirety of the assets stored with the keys. It adds more responsibility to the holder of digital assets in the blockchain.

Since keys are being stored in a variety of places, such as USB drives, hard drives, and laptop computers, they are vulnerable to theft and misuse. Backed up keys suffer the same vulnerability.

From the point of view of physical locations of the wallet, there are

- Mobile wallets: These are apps for both Android and Apple phones, such as Muun, Samourai, Atomic, Guarda, Coinbase, and Trust.
- Desktop wallets: These are apps for PCs or Apple computers, such as Armory, Atomic, Exodus, Bitcoin Core, and Ethereum. These wallets reside on the hard drive of your computer.
- Hardware wallets: These are USB-like devices. They work with a PC, but can be removed from the PC. The most common ones are Ledger Nano S, Cabo Vault, and Trezor.
- Paper wallet: You print your private key or its QR code on paper.
- On-line wallet: Wallets are applications such as Nexo, FXT, and Coinbase; you can also store your Bitcoins on the exchange where you purchased them.

In addition to relaying transactions on the network, a wallet also enables you to create a Bitcoin address for sending and receiving the virtual currency and to store the private key for it.

All forms of wallets have risks. Mobile wallets, hardware, or paper wallets can be stolen or destroyed. Maintaining these disparate keys becomes time-consuming and unmanageable. Backup is advised to safeguard the keys. However, backup also creates either a risk of theft or risk of the third party if the backup is online. This is a basic dilemma faced by the holders of the digital assets. Deploying a high-assurance crypto management platform is the best way to protect your cryptographic keys.

A crypto management platform can generate, store, and securely manage these keys, so even if data is seized, it cannot be decrypted. Key management centralizes and supports cryptographic keys throughout their lifecycle.

Restricting access to these cryptographic keys is the best practice. The level of security surrounding the key storage container is also important.

There are many apps of mobile digital wallets. The wallet can hold multiple digital currencies and tell you the units you are holding and the amount in USD.

There are many choices of desktop wallets, as well. You can download and try them to see which one works better for you. The desktop wallets are, in general, more powerful than other types of wallets. They have more functions. Some wallets are for Bitcoins only. Other wallets can store several cryptocurrencies.

For example, Bitcoin Core Wallet is a full Bitcoin client and builds the backbone of the network. It offers high levels of security, privacy, and stability. However, it has few features, and it takes a lot of space and memory.

Armory Wallet offers backup and encryption features, and it allows secure cold storage on offline computers. Electrum Wallet emphasizes speed and simplicity, with low resource usage. It uses remote servers that handle the most complicated parts of the Bitcoin platform, and it allows you to recover your wallet from a secret phrase.

If the assets in protection are large, one should consider storing their keys in a hardware security module. A hardware security module (HSM) is a hardware wallet, specially designed for safekeeping cryptocurrency. It safeguards and manages digital keys for strong authentication and provides crypto processing. These modules traditionally come in the form of a plug-in card or an external device that attaches directly to a computer or network server.

HSMs serve as an isolated, tamper resistant, and responsive platform that acts as a root of trust for the entire encryption environment. By removing physical key storage devices from networks, you can add another line of defense against security breaches.

In each wallet setup, you can have multiple wallets, and you can store many private keys. These multiple wallets allow you to store Bitcoins for different purposes. You can have one wallet for petty cash and one wallet for a large deposit, such as the savings account. Of course, you can swap funds between different wallets at any time. When your petty cash wallet balance is low, you can transfer some funds from the saving wallet to the petty cash wallet with just a few clicks on your computer or mobile device if you have hot storage. If your fund is in a cold storage, you will have to move your fund online.

Most people prefer hot storage or online storage for simplicity. Hot storage is any storage connected to the network. Therefore, it can be accessed from the network. Instead of keeping the wallet on your computer, your wallet resides somewhere in the cloud of third parties. The process of accessing Bitcoin is easy and convenient. However, the downside is that you have to trust this third party for maintaining the integrity of your wallets and that it will allow you to access your Bitcoin whenever you want. They are like banks. However, banks are well established financial institutions, but the Web wallet services providers are not.

Almost all of the Bitcoin exchanges also function as wallets. They are like security brokers, where you buy and sell stocks and never bother to get the actual stock certificates from them. This is an advantage for frequent traders. However, you sacrifice your anonymity, since you have to give your identity to open an account with them.

The advantage of a Web wallet is the ability to bundle transactions together before pushing them onto the blockchain and therefore lowering transaction fees. They can also perform internal transfers for zero fees as an attraction to pull in customers and increase their user base. Some people also find the payment services, often offered by the Bitcoin exchanges, such as Bitpay, are quite useful.

Web wallets are prone to cyberattack. The most famous examples are the attacks on Mt. Gox, Bitstamp, and Mintpal. In addition, a network problem at a wallet site can prevent you from withdrawing your funds when most needed.

Since the private key is very long and impossible to remember, wallets allow you to associate a passphrase with your private key. You can enter the passphrase of your choice. For example, the passphrase could be "What is your favorite movie?" After you click "View," the program generates the address and private key. Your passphrase can also include spaces and symbols. Like a password, it is also case sensitive. Therefore, "What is your favorite movie?" is different from the one used in the example. Every time you enter the same passphrase, the wallet gives you the same address and private key.

You can use this address to receive payments and this private key to make payments. As long as you remember the passphrase, you will have the public and private keys. Thus, instead of remembering the private key, you only have to remember the passphrase.

A passphrase does not have much security. However, it is convenient. It can be used for storing pocket change, such as $100 to $200.

A variation of the Web wallet is a *hybrid wallet*. It is similar to the hardware wallet in that the private keys are stored locally and under control of the individual, not the third party. The transaction is sent to the individual to be signed with the private key on their computer, rather than uploading the private key and signing online.

If you are concerned about the cost of the fees, some wallets give you full control over them. This means the wallet allows changing the fees after funds are sent or provides fee suggestions based on current network conditions so that your transactions are confirmed in a timely manner without paying more than you have to. As a security measure, most of the wallets also provide a two-factor authentication login.

Wallets are platform specific. That means if you have a wallet on your cell phone and a wallet on your laptop, even if you use the same wallet app (in this example, we will use *copay*), they are not the same wallet. You will see different balances of your coins in each wallet. The coins you receive in one wallet will not show in the other wallet. It is not a good idea to synchronize the wallets by copying the wallet files, such as wallet.dat. Many things can go wrong, and you will lose your coins. Even changing a directory where your wallet resides can have a certain risk. However, you can share wallet with yourself. For example, you can share your desktop wallet with your cell phone wallet. It will serve the same purpose. Another way to do it is to transfer the coins between your wallets.

2.6 TWO-FACTOR AUTHENTICATION (2FA)

Two-factor Authentication (2FA) and Multi-Factor Authentication (MFA) grant a user access to an object of value (e.g., online account or a digital wallet) only after the user produces two or more pieces of evidence of ownership. Two-factor authentication requires two pieces of evidence, and multi-factor requires three or more pieces of evidence.

Obviously, 2FA or MFA is more secure than the simple one-factor authentication. We often use 2FA without even knowing it in our daily life. When you use your bank card and PIN to get access to your account at an ATM, you are using 2FA. In this simple act, you show two pieces of evidence – your card and PIN. A thief with either the card or the PIN cannot access your account – they need both. More sites are requiring 2FA to sign in. Many financial institutions also require you to enter a PIN into their apps that is texted to your mobile device as a form of 2FA.

There are three types of factors to prove that you are the owner of the object of value: something only you know, something only you have, and who you are.

A password or PIN is something only you know and the ATM card is something only you have. In 2FA, you need to show a second authentication factor: something only you have. A key is a typical example of something only you have – you open a door with a key.

This something only you have is usually referred to as a *token*, which can be a hardware device issued to the user for the purposes of authentication. For example, a bank ATM card is a token. For you to withdraw money from ATM, you need to have both the ATM card and the PIN. Likewise, hotels issue a card key to you for your room. The card key is something only you have. The key does not have the room number and address on it – that is the information only you know.

In the digital world, there are different kinds of tokens:

- Data token: A "one-time password" is a data token that only you have, because it is generated at your request (when you sign into an account using a normal password) and sent to you only (to your phone or email on record); it is good only for a short period of time, or can only be used once.
- Hardware token: These are physical devices that only the user possesses and is also known as the *disconnected token*. The hardware token offers the most secure two-factor (token-based) authentication mechanism.

- Soft token: These rely on a software component present on the client's computer, e.g., a cookie or a software token application. It is also known as a *connected token*.

The soft token is the most sophisticated type of token. One example is the Google Authenticator, a mobile app developed by Google. Google Authenticator uses the Time-based One-time Password Algorithm (TOTP) and/or the hash-based authentication code called Hash-based One-time Password Algorithm (HOTP) for authenticating users of mobile applications. TOTP is an algorithm that computes a one-time password from a shared secret key in current time. HOTP is one-step further of TOTP. It uses the hash algorithm on TOTP to generate HOTP. Please refer to Figure 2.5 for the flow chart of the TOTP and HOTP mechanisms.

To use Google Authenticator, you have to install the app on your phone and then follow the instructions to set up two-factor authentications. You have to set up the accounts, which accept Google Authenticator, to provide you with the one-time-use password. Once it is set up, each time you try to log into these accounts, it will prompt you to enter the temporary password generated by the Google Authenticator. This is a two-factor authentication because you provide your own password to your account and a Google Authenticator generates a one-time-password.

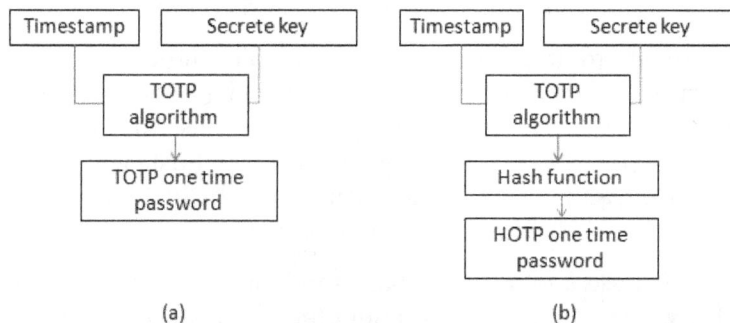

FIGURE 2.5 Flow chart of TOTP and HOTP mechanisms.

The 2FA system, which combines encryption with something only you know and something only you have, is already secure enough for most of our daily life needs. If this is still not secure enough, then we can add a third factor: who you are. This factor refers to some form of biometric authentication, based on a measurement of some personal characteristics (which may or may not be physical).

Multiple forms of biometric authentication are widely available today, all of which may enhance the level of security in the authentication process. The most common factors are fingerprint, voice, and facial recognition.

2.7   HASH

Hash is a cryptographic function that has a very important role in the blockchain. Once the miner validates the transaction, it time-stamps and produces a hash of the transaction using the SHA-256 algorithm.

The idea of hash was first proposed by C. Dwork and M. Naor in 1993.[15] Adam Back invented the Hashcash algorithm in 1997.[16] Hashcash is a cryptographic hash-based algorithm that requires a selectable amount of work to compute, and it was originally developed for screening spam email.

In the email system, a hashcash stamp is added to the header of an email. The hashcash stamp is characterized by the amount of time that sender spends to prepare the email – an email prepared by an algorithm, which generates an email in a fraction of a second, has a very different stamp from an email generated by a human. By using Hashcash, it is easy to tell emails composed by people or by algorithms. Microsoft used the Hashcash algorithm for email spam prevention in Hotmail, Exchange, and Outlook.

Hashing produces a unique, reproducible, and yet simple, data string that represents a record or dataset. A hash can identify the integrity of a dataset, but it cannot reconstruct the original dataset. Hash to data is like a fingerprint to a person (Figure 2.6). Any change in the input data will generate a different hash. Since hash is a simple data string, it can be verified easily and the data is thus tamper-proof, which is essential to many blockchain applications.

We will use a very simple hash function to illustrate the concept. Let us say that we want to hash a document (e.g., a contract), which contains 15,630 characters. We want the hash to be 30 characters long. We divide 15,630 by 30 and get 521. We then select every 521st letter of this document and form a string of 30 bytes long. This hash uniquely represents the original document since any alteration in the document will produce a different hash. It does not matter how long the document is, you can always create a hash of 30 letters long. Of course, this hash function is too simple for any practical use. For example, if we change a letter not included in the hash, it will produce the same hash and yet the document changes. This is called *collision*.

A person is identified by his finterprint.

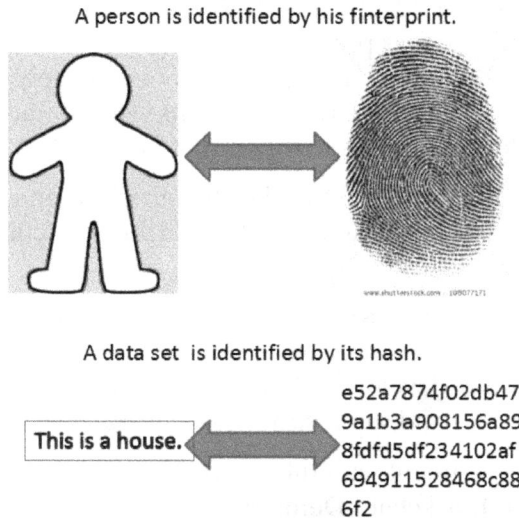

A data set is identified by its hash.

This is a house.

e52a7874f02db47
9a1b3a908156a89
8fdfd5df234102af
694911528468c88
6f2

FIGURE 2.6 Hash and fingerprint.

Let us look at another hashing example: To take the square root of a number, 43,122 (answer 207.6583732961). We then take the string of numbers from the fifth to ninth digits after decimal point: 73296. We call 73296 the hash of 43122, and if we change the number slightly, we will get a different result.

$$\sqrt{43122} = 207.658\underline{373296}$$

$$\sqrt{43123} = 207.6607\underline{81083}$$

$$\sqrt{43124} = 207.663\underline{188842}$$

$$\sqrt{6402} = 80.012\underline{499024}$$

$$\sqrt{342} = 18.493\underline{42009}$$

We thus have a simple hash function that consists of two steps: 1) the square root, and 2) the string number from the fifth to ninth digits after the decimal point of the square root number. If we change 43122 to 43123, the hash changes from 73296 to 81083. Or,

HASH(43122)=73296

HASH(43123)=81083

Please note that 43122 and 73296 form a pair. We can use 73296 as the public key, and 43122 as private key. The public key 73296 is generated from the private key 43122. From the public key one can never guess the private key. This is, in fact, how many password systems work. In this simple hash example, it works only for the positive numbers, but not negative numbers or text.

The hash algorithm used in the Bitcoin platform is the SHA-256, which includes the checksum, randomization, error-correction, ciphers, and cryptographic functions.

Historically, the first SHA, SHA-1, was developed in 1993 and it produces a 20-byte hash value.[17] Over time, improved versions of SHA, such as SHA-2 and SHA-3, were developed. SHA-256, used in the Bitcoin blockchain, is much more secure and sophisticated than its predecessors.

You can experiment with the SHA-256 hashing function by using a demo program at the Blockchain Demo site.[18]

We used the demo SHA-256 hash program to generate hashes from three pieces of data, as shown in Figure 2.7. We produced three hashes using short-, medium-, and long-length data. The hash strings are generated in the box below the data, and all hash strings are the same size regardless of the data size. You can hash a dataset many times and as long as the data are the same, the hash string is always the same. In the bottom box, we can clearly see that the hash is much shorter than the input data. This illustrates the point that the hash does not contain enough information to restore the original input data. Independent of the size of the original data that generates the hash, the hash is always of the same length. This is the beauty of hashing. You can hash one paragraph, one chapter or one book and the size of the hash is always the same. If you use the same algorithm and input the same data, you will get an identical hash string. You can hash text as well as a picture or any digital data.

In the Bitcoin platform, all transaction data is hashed. At the bottom level, two transactions produce a hash of the second level and each two hashes in the second level produce a new hash at the third level. In this way, the hash of hashes produces a pyramid-shaped structure, called a Merkle Tree. The hash at the top represents the hash of all transactions and is known as the *root hash*. Altering any individual transaction will inevitably alter the combined hash, so that the Proof of Work can verify Bitcoins involved in the transactions without verifying each transaction individually.

A hash generated using SHA-256 on the header of the block represents a block. This hash embeds itself inside of the header of the next block in the

SHA256 Hash

SHA256 Hash

SHA256 Hash

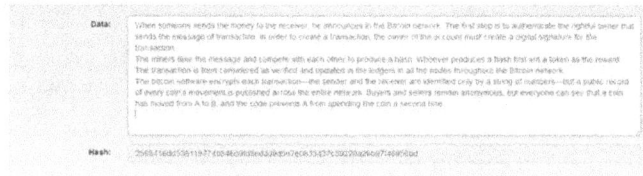

FIGURE 2.7 Examples of hashing using the demo program.

blockchain. In this way, the blocks form a chain. (One way to think about this is to compare it to how a child's DNA contains his/her parents' DNA.)

SHA-256 is also used for other crypto coins, such as NameCoin (NMC), Devcoin (DVC), and IxCoin (IXC).[19,20] So far, SHA-256 is the most widely used hash algorithm for cryptocurrency. However, there are cryptocurrencies using other hash algorithms. For example, the Scrypt hash algorithm is used in for Litecoin (LTC), DogeCoin (DOGE), FeatherCoin (FTC), WorldCoin (WDC), and Reddcoin (RDD). Scrypt Adaptive-N is used for Vertcoin (VTC), ExeCoin (EXE), GPUcoin (GPUC), ParallaxCoin (PLX), and SiliconValleyCoin (XSV).[21] Scrypt-Jane (Scrypt-Chacha) is used for YaCoin (YAC), Ultracoin (UTC), and Velocitycoin (VEL). SHA-3 (Keccak) is used for MaxCoin (MAX), Slothcoin (SLOTH), and Cryptometh (METH).

2.8 MERKLE TREE AND BLOCK HEADER

The miner makes hashes of two transactions, say hash(tx1) and hash(tx2), and hashes them again into a new hash called hash[hash(tx1), hash(tx2)], and then repeats the process for more transactions. The result is a tree of hashes called a Merkle tree (see Figure 2.8).[22] In such a process, the miner builds a pyramid-like hash structure for all the transactions that can be fit into a block – roughly 3,000 transactions. Eventually, all the hashes merge into one hash, called the *root hash*. The root hash further merges with the hash of the last block and the nonce (a random number implemented when mining) to produce the Block Hash. This is all done within that 10-minute interval.

The newly created transactions in the Bitcoin network form a pool of un-verified transactions. Miners pick up the transactions to validate them according to their own preference and priority, and hash into their blocks to begin construction. The miner who completes the block first announces to the Bitcoin network and all other miners to stop the construction of their own blocks.

The root hash contains the hashes of all the transactions because any change in one of these transactions built into the Merkle tree will alter the root. The intermediate hashes do not need to be stored, which greatly saves the disk space in the miners' nodes.

After having a valid Merkle root, the miners build the block's header. The header includes a hash of the previous block, thus making a chain of blocks, Merkle root, timestamp, a representation of the network's current difficulty, and finally, the *nonce*, a number incremented when mining.

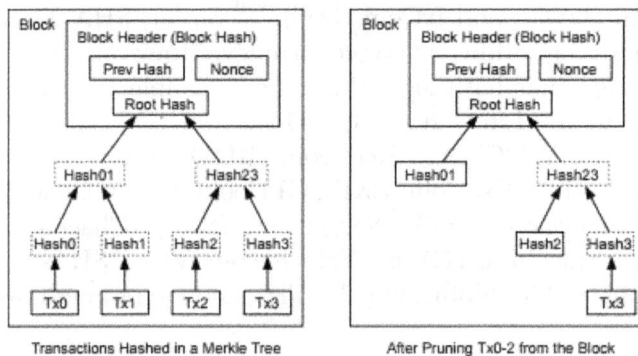

Transactions Hashed in a Merkle Tree · After Pruning Tx0-2 from the Block

FIGURE 2.8 A Merkle tree.

The block header contains all the essential information about the block. The structure of the header is shown in Figure 2.9.

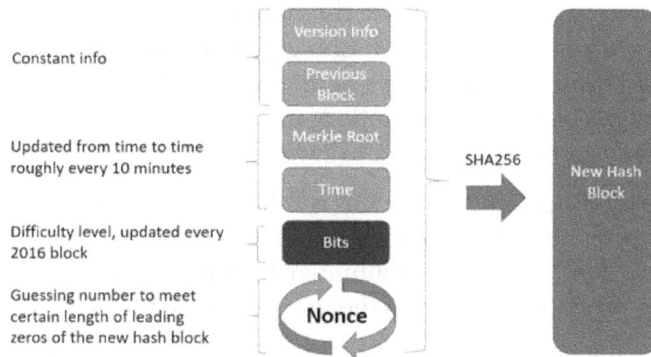

FIGURE 2.9 Block header.

2.9 NONCE

Even though SHA-256 is complex to generate, modern computers are powerful enough to produce an SHA-256 hash in microseconds. A block can, in theory, be constructed in a fraction of a second. The more powerful the computer, the faster it constructs blocks. This would make the miner with the most powerful computer in the Bitcoin network always win the construction of new block, thus collecting all the rewards of building the blocks. Such a system would not be decentralized, however. In addition, the time needed to construct the block would be seconds instead of 10 minutes. All 21 million Bitcoins would be mined in a few months instead of over decades. To address this issue, Nakamoto introduced another concept: "difficulty and nonce." Here, "difficulty" means the amount of work that needs to be done to build a block.

The purpose of introducing difficulty is to increase the challenge for producing the required hash by demanding the hash produced meet certain criteria. This requires multiple iterations to produce the hash, therefore increasing the difficulty of obtaining a valid hash.

Not only does it make hashes more difficult to produce, but it also acts as an equalizer. The miner with the highest hashing power will not always be the first to build a new block each time. This is because the nonce is random and the transactions picked up by the miners are also random. A miner with more hashing power may randomly encounter the situation in which he will have to do more work. In this way, the miner's chance to win the block-building game is in proportion to its hashing power. But the miner with the highest hashing power will not always be the winner. This is the same as the lottery. The chance of winning the lottery increases as you buy more lottery tickets, but there is no guarantee you will win.

On the Bitcoin platform, this is achieved by requiring the valid hash begin with certain number of zeroes. A nonce is incorporated into the message. If the hash does not meet the number of zeroes requirement, it continues the hashing process by changing the nonce number.

The following example illustrates the procedure. In this case, we require that the hash must start with a zero. The SHA-256 hash of "My name is John. 00000001" is 841286639d940470cec3951322fd3502bf1a21488f28327bb5d-15f044b5df8f7, which does not begin with a zero. We continue to hash by increasing the nonce by 1.

TABLE 2.1 Hashing with nonce

MESSAGE	NONCE	HASH
My name is John.	00000001	841286639d940470cec3951322fd3502bf1a21488f28327bb5d15f044b5df8f7
My name is John.	00000002	ccd546f9d30552cbe0cb2ba17f74faf99eda1f94e339b7d68b1c55622ce64f27
My name is John.	00000003	0abde8823f988ccdccf7db44d3f75466158b85143f2b6aa217b6f9801bf03d16

It takes three trials to obtain a hash beginning with a zero. If we require that a valid hash must begin with, say 3 zeroes, it will take more iterations. Therefore, the difficulty increases. When the difficulty increases, the demand for hashing power, or the computing power, increases proportionally. Since the transactions are randomly picked up by the miners, there is no telling what combinations of transactions will require few hash iterations. Thus, on average, the chance of producing a block will be proportional to the hashing power of the miner. The miner with the most powerful hashing power will not always be the first to produce a block, however.

The difficulty is calculated from the formula:

$$Difficulty = \frac{genesis\ block\ hash\ value}{current\ target\ hash\ value}$$

In the prior example, the difficulty is

$$Difficulty = \frac{841286639d940470cec3951322fd3502bf1a21488f28327bb5d15f044b5df8f7}{0abde8823f988ccdccf7db44d3f75466158b85143f2b6aa217b6f9801bf03d16}$$

Apparently, the smaller the target value (that is, more zeroes in the first digits), the larger is the difficulty. An acceptable hash must be smaller than the target. All Bitcoin clients share the same target value. The difficulty adjusts itself every 2,016 blocks, based on the network's recent performance, with the aim of keeping the average time between new blocks at 10 minutes. When the hash rate of the Bitcoin network increases, the difficulty also increases. The level of difficulty has been increasing ever since Bitcoin mining began (Figure 2.10).[23] In 2009, the difficulty was near 1, that is, no zero is required. As of January 2022, the difficulty has hit 21 trillion, that is, a valid hash starts with 12 zeros.

We also noted that the price of Bitcoin is in line with the difficulty. This is expected because if the difficulty increases much more than the price, miners will lose money by paying more for the energy consumption than the Bitcoin is worth. This would discourage mining and the construction of new blocks. For Bitcoin investors, this chart may be very inspiring. When the Bitcoin price is lagging behind difficulty, Bitcoins are cheap. The price will catch up, as it did in mid-2015 and the end of 2018. In January 2022, at $43,000, the Bitcoin price already fully reflected the difficulty. Further appreciation will push the difficulty even higher than 21 trillion.

Readers can go to the Blockchain demo website to mine a hash for any data to further understand the concept of the nonce.[24] As the difficulty increases, it requires more computer computing power to mine the Bitcoins or to do the Proof of Work. Running more powerful computers for longer times consumes more electricity, in addition to the depreciation of more expensive equipment, therefore, the cost of mining Bitcoin increases over time. Unless the value of a Bitcoin can catch up with the cost of resources, it does not pay to mine Bitcoins anymore. Miners have the discretion of choosing transactions randomly from a pool of unprocessed transactions that were broadcast to the Bitcoin network. To make up the higher cost of mining, miners seek to maximize their profits by processing transactions, which pay higher fees.

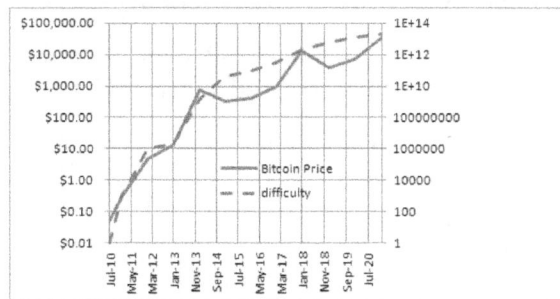

FIGURE 2.10 Difficulty of the Bitcoin network and Bitcoin price.

Each block contains the hash of the preceding block; thus, each block has a chain of blocks that together contain a large amount of work. Changing a block requires regenerating all successors and redoing the work they contain. This protects the blockchain from tampering.

One can imagine that before a block is formed and added to the blockchain, there are many versions of the block, because the competing miners pick up random transactions from the pool of unverified transactions. This is called *forking*. Only the first block accepted by the consensus of nodes becomes the official block to be added to the blockchain. Forking disappears when a block is added to the blockchain.

2.10 BITCOIN SUPPLY

One interesting aspect of Bitcoins is that the supply is limited. The creation of new Bitcoins slows down approximately every four years – the limited supply of Bitcoins is built into the software by design. Eventually, the total Bitcoin supply will be limited to around 21 million coins.

Bitcoins are created every time a new block is mined. The network allows a new block to be created every 10 minutes; six blocks are mined in an hour. For the first 210,000 blocks, miners were rewarded with 50 Bitcoins for each block mined, and the reward decreased by 50% for every 210,000 blocks mined thereafter, or approximately four years at the rate of 10 minutes per block. So, in the first four-year cycle (from 2009 to 2012), 210,000 (blocks) times 50 Bitcoins were mined, or 10.5 million Bitcoins. For the next 210,000 blocks mined (2013 to 2016), 210,000 times 25 Bitcoins were mined, or 5.25 million Bitcoins. Every 210,000 blocks (or roughly four years), the number of Bitcoins mined will be halved. Currently, in 2022, the reward for a block is only 6.25 Bitcoins, and that will halve in 2025. The result is that the total number of Bitcoins will not exceed 21 million. Figure 2.11 shows the details of the Bitcoin supply.

Note that the actual number of Bitcoins available in the marketplace will be less because of lost and destroyed coins and keys.

One may think that 21 million Bitcoins is not possibly enough to support Bitcoin transactions in the future. Fortunately, a Bitcoin is divisible: 1/1000th of a Bitcoin is 1 MBTC. If the value of a Bitcoin is at $60,000, one MBTC is $60. The smallest Bitcoin unit is a Satoshi. A Satoshi is one-hundred-millionth. (The unit has been named in homage to the original creator of Bitcoin, Satoshi Nakamoto.)

total blocks mined	time required in years	reward per block	Bitcoins generated per period	total Bitcoins generated
210,000	4.0	50	10,500,000	10,500,000
420,000	8.0	25	5,250,000	15,750,000
630,000	12.0	12.5	2,625,000	18,375,000
840,000	16.0	6.25	1,312,500	19,687,500
1,050,000	20.0	3.125	656,250	20,343,750
1,260,000	24.0	1.5625	328,125	20,671,875
1,470,000	28.0	0.78125	164,063	20,835,938
1,680,000	32.0	0.390625	82,031	20,917,969
1,890,000	36.0	0.195313	41,016	20,958,984

FIGURE 2.11 Bitcoin supply.

2.11 BITCOIN ADDRESSES

A Bitcoin address is a secure identifier to accept Bitcoin payments, just like an email address to receive emails. Since the address must be publicly known for anyone who wants to send funds to it, it is also known as the public key. The owner of the address is the only one who can unlock the address to exclusively access the funds by using the private key associated with the address (the public key). This is akin to the email system that the owner must use a password to log into the account to see his emails.

There are three kinds of Bitcoin addresses:

- Legacy address P2PKH
- SegWit compatible legacy address P2SH
- SegWit address Bech32

Pay-To-Public-Key-Hash (P2PKH) is the standard Bitcoin address. It has a 34 letter/number combination. You can create P2PKH address by using any wallet app. For example, in the Armory wallet, you get an address to receive Bitcoin as soon as you click the "Receive Bitcoin" icon on the page. Only the person holding the private key can sign a transaction with the cryptocurrency token assigned to this address – while everybody who knows your address can verify the validity of your signature.

A typical P2PKH address looks like 15Cytz9sHqeqtKCw2vnpEyNQ8teKtrTPjp. It starts with "1." To spend Bitcoin in a P2PKH address, the payer must use the private key associated with the public key hash to create a digital signature. The flow chart of the procedure is shown in Figure 2.12.

Another type of Bitcoin address is called P2SH or Pay-To-Script-Hash. A transaction using P2SH sends payment to a scriptPubKey instead of the public key address. The script locks the output. A P2SH address always begins with a 3, instead of a 1 as in P2PKH addresses. The purpose of P2SH is to move the responsibility for supplying the conditions to redeem a transaction from the payer to the payee. In fact, P2PKH is a special case of P2SH. Its data contains only the hashed public key.

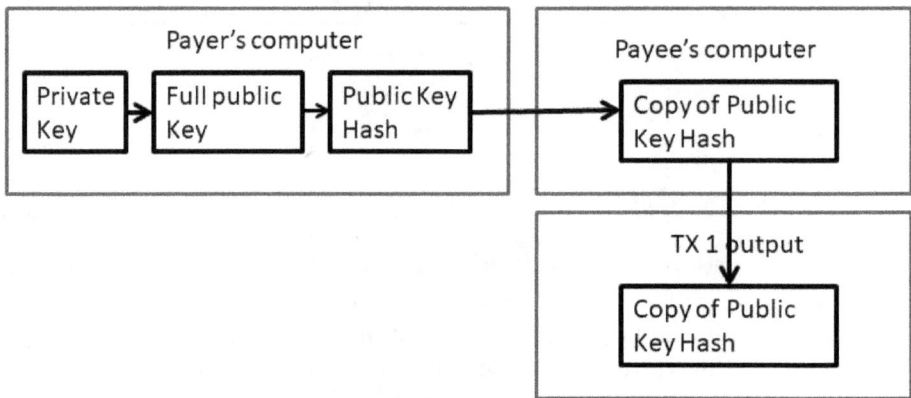

FIGURE 2.12 P2PKH payment flow.

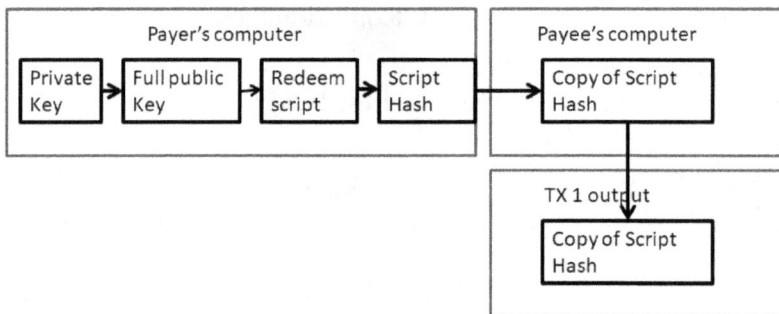

FIGURE 2.13 P2SH payment flow.

The script hash is shorter (20-byte), therefore is more efficient in the data usage and results in lower transaction fees. Also, P2SH allows users to send

Bitcoin without having to worry about how a recipient unlocks access to the payment.

If you want to use a P2SH address instead of the P2PKH address, you can do so by selecting the address type in the wallet. The scriptPubKey contains a script with instructions defined by the receiver describing how he wants to gain access to the Bitcoin. It is also called the *redeem script*. For example, the instruction may ask the receiver to provide a public key that yields the destination address embedded in the script, and a signature to show evidence of the private key. Or the instruction may dictate who needs to sign to spend this Bitcoin. The signature party can be one or more. We discussed this multisig scheme previously.

Payment by P2PKH is sent directly to the payee's public address, while in the payment of a P2SH scheme, the payer sends the funds to a payee-designated location, and the payee retrieves the funds from the location by using scriptPubKey.

To spend Bitcoins sent via P2PKH, the recipient must provide a Private Key to match the Public Key. However, to spend Bitcoins sent via P2SH, the recipient must provide a scriptPubKey (2.12) instead of the public key.[25] The scriptPubKey then reproduces a redeem script hash and is checked against the redeem script hash in the signature. If they match, the transaction is verified. P2SH transactions were standardized on BIP 16.

When SegWit was activated in August of 2017, a new type of address specified by BIP0173 was created that is more efficient with the use of block space.[26] The new address format is called Bech32, and more about SegWit will be discussed in the next chapter.

2.12 ZERO KNOWLEDGE PROOF

Zero Knowledge Proof (ZKP) means that one can prove something is true to others without giving away any information. An excellent example is Sudoku. You can prove to your friend that you successfully completed a Sudoku puzzle without revealing how you did it. Your friend will not learn from you how you solved it, but they can verify that you did it correctly.

Another example is when a magician plays a trick by putting a rabbit in his hat and then shows you that the rabbit is not in the hat. You can say that magician performs a ZKP, because you indeed verified that the rabbit was gone, but you do not know how.

In our daily life, we use ZKP methods all the time. For example, when you pay by debit card, the cashier asks you to input your PIN to prove that you are the card owner. The cashier does not know your PIN because you do not reveal it to him or her. By entering the number, you prove your identity without revealing it.

In the ZKP protocol, the person who verifies challenges the person who proves. However, the challenge is in such a way that the person who verifies does not learn the knowledge required to do it. Otherwise, it cannot be called a ZKP. Using ZKP, a person can verify the end result, even though he does not how to do it.

A ZKP program is a cryptographic system that lets a person run an arbitrary program with a mixture of public and secret inputs and prove to others that this specific program accepted the inputs, without revealing anything more about its operation or the secret inputs.

In the cryptocurrency and blockchain world, ZKP is very useful. It can be used in an authentication system where one party wants to prove its identity to a second party via some secret information but doesn't want the second party to learn anything about this secret. A ZKP can be as simple as a PIN, but it can also be very sophisticated to provide an extremely secure environment.[27]

In February of 2016, Bitcoin Core integrated Zero-Knowledge Contingent Payment (ZKCP) on the Bitcoin network. This made Bitcoin transactions even more secure as ZKCP is a protocol that allows transactions to be private, scalable, and secure. The parties to the transaction do not need to trust one other or depend on arbitration by a third party, since the blockchain accounts for all of it. Using a ZKCP avoids the significant transactional costs involved in a sale, which can easily go wrong otherwise.

2.13 DIVISIBLE BITCOIN

Each transaction has a different number of Bitcoins. How do you divide the Bitcoins, if you have received five Bitcoins as one transaction in the past, but you want to spend two Bitcoins? This issue is resolved by using multiple inputs and outputs, which allow the Bitcoins to be split and combined.

Transactions can have multiple inputs combining their amounts, and multiple outputs: one for the payment and one return the change to the sender if any. The difference between the total input and output amounts of a transaction goes to the miner as a transaction fee. The transaction fee depends on the priority of the transaction set by the sender and on the data size of a transaction. In this way, Bitcoins become divisible. You can send any fraction of a Bitcoin.

For example, in Figure 2.14, John is to be paid 6.9 Bitcoins, using the Bitcoins received in three previous transactions. These three transactions combined total more than 6.9 Bitcoins. Therefore, there are three inputs for the current transaction. However, the sum of these three inputs is larger than the amount that needs to be paid, so there will be change back. Therefore, an output of 0.7 Bitcoin is generated as change after paying a transaction fee to the miner. This output is called the Unspent Transaction Output (UTXO). The sum of Bitcoins in the Inputs must be equal to the sum of Bitcoins in the Outputs, like a financial balance sheet.

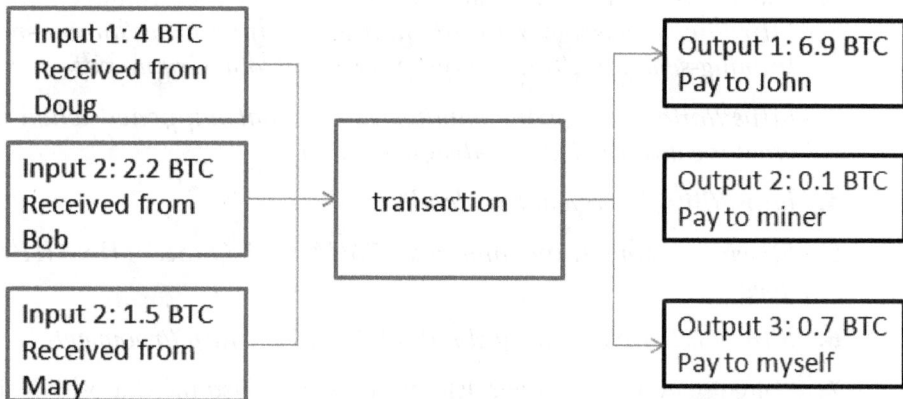

FIGURE 2.14 Multiple inputs and outputs of a Bitcoin transaction.

Miners tend to pick the transactions paying the highest fees to maximize their profit. This means that low-fee-paying transactions could experience an extremely long confirmation time or never be confirmed at all. These low-fee-paying transactions can be floating in the network for a long time. Most likely, the number of these transactions will increase rather than decrease. To solve this problem, Bitcoin Core introduced opt-in replace-by-fee. If a transaction is sent using opt-in replace-by-fee, users can replace their own transaction with a newer transaction by including a higher fee.[28]

The transactions shown in the figure are the relevant transactions. For the lightweight nodes (also known as partial nodes), they need only to download the relevant transactions instead of all transactions for the verification. This is called the Simple Payment Verification (SPV).

Since each input came from a different previous transaction, they will have to be signed individually. (For example, imagine there are three checks from Doug, Bob, and Mary that will need separate endorsements.) However, please note that this is different from the multisig, or multi-signature, which refers to the requirement of more than one person to sign the transaction for security purposes.

REFERENCES

1. Wei Dai (1998) "B-Money", *http://www.weidai.com/bmoney.txt*

2. Satoshi Nakamoto, Bitcoin: A Peer-to-Peer Electronic Cash System. *https://www.ussc.gov/sites/default/files/pdf/training/annual-national-training-seminar/2018/Emerging_Tech_Bitcoin_Crypto.pdf*

3. *https://bitcoinmagazine.com/technical/what-happened-when-bitcoin-creator-satoshi-nakamoto-disappeared*

4. *https://Bitcoin.org/en/download*

5. *https://miro.medium.com/max/775/1*Jk_IicQuaRUrHNRHRrMpDQ .jpeg*

6. *https://web.archive.org/web/20071222072154/http://rpow.net/*

7. "Bitcoin: A Peer-to-Peer Electronic Cash System", Satoshi Nakamoto, *https://www.ussc.gov/sites/default/files/pdf/training/annual-national-training-seminar/2018/Emerging_Tech_Bitcoin_Crypto.pdf*

8. *https://en.Bitcoin.it/wiki/Script#Opcodes*

9. "The year of multisig: How is it doing so far?" by Thomas Kerin, Coindesk. *https://www.coindesk.com/markets/2014/05/17/the-year-of-multisig-how-is-it-doing-so-far/*

10. *https://www.cnbc.com/2021/01/15/uk-man-makes-last-ditch-effort-to-recover-lost-Bitcoin-hard-drive.html*

11. *https://www.ccn.com/190m-gone-how-canada-biggest-Bitcoin-exchange-lost-it/*

12. *https://spreadshare.co/spreadsheet/dormant-Bitcoin-addresses*

13. *https://bitinfocharts.com/Bitcoin/address/1FeexV6bAHb8ybZjqQMjJrcC rHGW9sb6uF*

14. *https://Bitcoinist.com/lost-and-found-man-recovers-Bitcoin-from-hard-drive-burned-in-a-fire/*

15. *https://www.metaco.com/digital-assets-glossary-hash/*

16. *http://www.cypherspace.org/adam/*

17. *https://en.wikipedia.org/wiki/SHA-1*

18. *https://anders.com/blockchain/hash.html*

19. "List of SHA-256 coins", *https://Bitcointalk.org/index.php?topic=482002.0*

20. "SHA-256 coins", Bitcoinnational, Steemit., *https://steemit.com/sha256/@Bitcoinnational/sha-256-coins*

21. "Cryptocurrency mining on Scrypt algorithm", *https://bitmakler.net/scrypt___mining*

22. "Merkle tree Bitcoin", Crudden Research Group, *http://simlamagto.cakedecoratingpro.info/jixuj/merkle-tree-Bitcoin-3153.php*

23. "A guide to Bitcoin (part 1): a look under the hood", Alex Barrera, *http://tech.eu/features/808/Bitcoin-part-one/*

24. *https://anders.com/blockchain/block.html and http://Bitcoin.sipa.be/*

25. "Bitcoin-multisig-the-hard-way-understanding-raw-multisignature-Bitcoin-transactions", *https://www.soroushjp.com/2014/12/20/bitcoin-multisig-the-hard-way-understanding-raw-multisignature-bitcoin-transactions/*

26. *https://ambcrypto.com/Bitcoin-segwits-adoption-levels-what-you-need-to-know/*

27. "Efficient Zero-Knowledge Contingent Payments in Cryptocurrency Without Scripts": Waclaw Banasik et al. *https://pdfs.semanticscholar.org/5cbf/e46f4b026f8dee4afb1e788236b3fdf08b81.pdf*

28. *https://Bitcoin.org/en/release/v0.12.0*

CHAPTER 3

BITCOIN ISSUES

The Bitcoin platform, although elegantly designed, has fundamental and circumstantial technical limitations and difficulties. Over time, the Bitcoin community has resolved many of these issues, but as the number of Bitcoin transactions has grown, so have the problems.[1]

These issues have sparked heated debates as to how to quickly respond. Without solutions, Bitcoin may run into a bottleneck. Some of the proposed solutions may undermine Bitcoin's fundamental principle of decentralization.

Satoshi Nakamoto designed Bitcoin with a very lofty goal – no central authority or decentralization. To many, Bitcoin's decentralization is extremely important. Others believe that without compromise, Bitcoin may find itself unable to achieve its next lofty goal – a cryptocurrency to replace the fiat currency.

One problem is Bitcoin's block size. Any attempt to increase the block size or attach a sidechain to allow faster transactions is bound to make the blockchain more centralized. The most fundamental debate is philosophical: does Bitcoin want to become a store of value or a global payment system? In other words, should Bitcoin behave more like gold or like a currency? After all, people do not use gold for daily shopping, and yet it still holds value.

3.1 BITCOIN BLOCK SIZE

Bitcoin's popularity has grown tremendously over the last few years. The user base increased the number of transactions per day tenfold from 34,000 in January 2013 to 350,000 in January 2022.[2] The rate of transactions has stabilized since then. The Bitcoin network finds itself congested due to the software design, which has remained the same since its creation in 2009.

In August 2017, the congestion issue was partially addressed by a technique known as SegWit, explained later in this chapter. In January 2022, the total number of transactions per day was maintained at around 310,000, out of which half were SegWit transactions.[3] Figure 3.1 shows the number of transactions per day for SegWit and non-SegWit transactions.

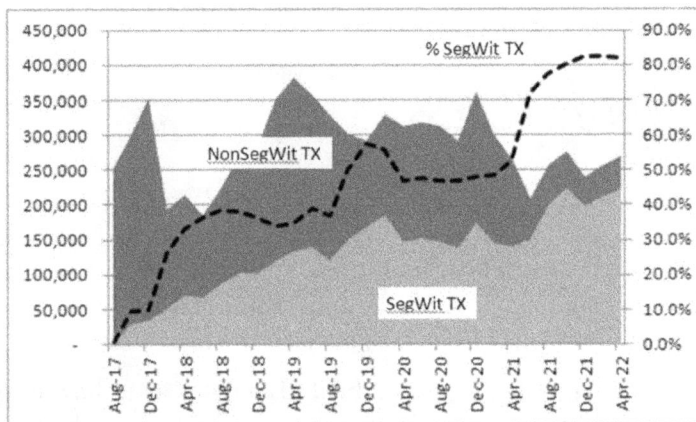

FIGURE 3.1 Number of SegWit and Non-SegWit transactions per day since the implementation of SegWit

Newly-created transactions are broadcasted to the Bitcoin network and received by miners. The miners compete to validate and confirm the transactions before including them in a new block. Whoever completes the task first will have their block attached to the blockchain after other nodes confirm the block.

Every 10 minutes, the mining process creates a new block. The block size is 1 MB by design so that each block can only contain a finite number of transactions. In 2017, when SegWit was introduced, the witness data was excluded in the transaction. Bitcoin's block size limit was replaced by a block weight limit of 1 million "virtual bytes." The actual data byte did not change, but how the data was counted changed: SegWit witness data weighs less than transaction data. A non-SegWit transaction of the size 400 bytes is 300 bytes using SegWit, so Bitcoin blocks can now contain more transactions. Therefore, the average block size today is 1.3 MB, which is larger than the theoretical limit of 1 MB. (More about SegWit later.)

The average data block size of the transactions is around 400 bytes, so 1 MB can fit only 2,500 transactions. A block is created every 10 minutes by design. Therefore, the Bitcoin platform can handle only 2,500 transactions every

10 minutes, or 4.17 transactions per second. If the incoming rate of the new transactions is higher than 4.17 transactions per second, the queue of transactions waiting for validation will grow and the transaction confirmation time gets longer. The overflowed transactions remain in the memory pool of the mining nodes and flock to the next block to, hopefully, be included. This is what happened in early 2017, and the Bitcoin blockchain became overwhelmed.

The faster the new transactions come, the longer the queue of the unconfirmed transactions becomes. These unconfirmed transactions reside in the memory pool of the miners' computers. The *blockchain.info* website continuously updates the size of the queue in memory size.[4] In early 2022, the size was about 80 MB or 80 blocks. Considering the platform generates each block every 10 minutes, 80 blocks takes 800 minutes or 13 hours for the miners to process.

The average transaction confirmation time before May 2016 increased from less than 20 minutes to more than 400 minutes by June of 2017. The daily average reached an all-time high of almost 500 minutes, or roughly nine hours. The slowest transactions took as long as 2,500 minutes or two days to be confirmed during June 2017. This became unacceptable.

The transaction time eased off in August 2017 due to the Bitcoin hard fork, when Bitcoin Cash was split from Bitcoin. However, such relief was only temporary, and the confirmation time shot up to more than 10 hours by January 2018. The implementation of SegWit seemed to be effective in reducing the Bitcoin transaction confirmation time. By early 2018, when the percentage of SegWit transactions exceeded 20%, the transaction confirmation time drastically came down, but started to creep up again in 2020. Since then, the transaction time has been greatly improved, thanks to the adoption of the Lightning Network. There were more than 2,500 nodes with 7,800 payment channels operating on the Lightning Network in early 2022. More details about how Lightning Network works will be discussed in Chapter 7.[5]

The transaction delay is a serious problem because the coins received cannot be spent until the transaction is confirmed. This is a scaling issue due to the limited scale of the Bitcoin platform.

Transaction data size varies depending on the amount of data it contains. The transaction involving multiple inputs and outputs is apparently larger. Figure 3.2 shows the typical distribution of the transaction data size in 2021. The transaction data size also tends to increase slightly over time (see Figure 3.3). This is because when Bitcoins become more valuable, most transactions tend to be a fraction of a Bitcoin and therefore involve more inputs and outputs.

Not only do the overflow transactions cause a delay in the transaction confirmation time, but they can also crash the system of nodes if the backlog of transactions grows too big and the system runs out of memory. Full node operators can configure their limits to prevent the crash. Bitcoin Core 0.12.0 set the default maximum size to be 300 megabytes.

As a reference, Visa (the credit card company) can handle 24,000 transactions per second, which is 6,000 times faster than the Bitcoin platform. If the Bitcoin platform does not scale up, it will have no chance to become a mainstream transaction platform. It needs the capability to handle, at its slowest, the transaction speed of Visa today, considering that Visa is a major credit card. It seems that the future of Bitcoin, or any other digital currency for that matter, depends on finding a solution to this problem.

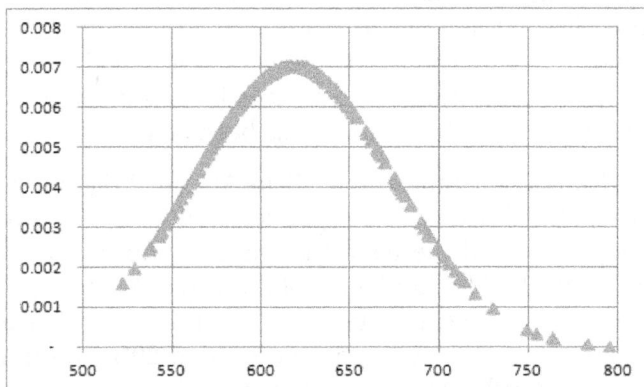

FIGURE 3.2 The distribution of transaction data size in 2021 (in bytes).

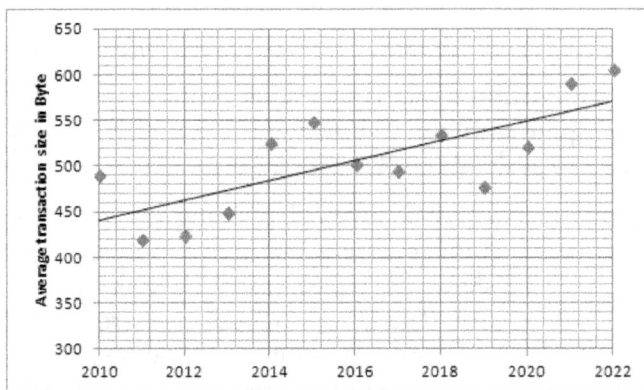

FIGURE 3.3 The average transaction size in bytes increases over years.

We discuss some of the proposed and hotly debated solutions in the next section. However, none of these solutions can improve the transaction rate to the 24,000 transactions per second rate of major credit card companies.

The blockchain consists of blocks chained together, one after another. It records the history of all Bitcoin transactions. New transactions form new blocks, and new blocks are attached to the tip of the blockchain. The number of blocks in the blockchain continue to grow. Figure 3.4 shows the size of the blockchain over time.[6] In early 2022, the blockchain size was around 400 GB.[7] There are many copies of the blockchain residing on all nodes of the Bitcoin network. You can also download a copy of the Bitcoin blockchain. Increasing the block size will improve the transaction rate, but the blockchain size will grow even faster. This will require significantly more resources from the Bitcoin nodes. Unless the cost of computing power can match the block size demand, fewer nodes will be full nodes. There have been attempts to reduce the size of transactions so that more transactions can squeeze into a block.

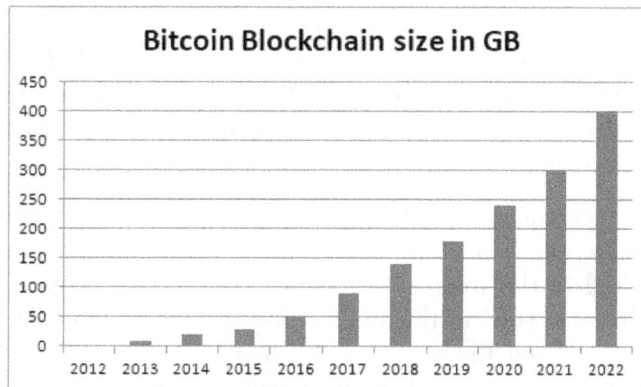

FIGURE 3.4 Size of the Bitcoin Blockchain over time.

3.2 SEGWIT AND THE CHANGE OF BLOCK SIZE

The Bitcoin issue related to the transaction congestion is also known as the "Bitcoin scaling issue" because it is caused by the limited block size of 1 MB in the original Bitcoin software design. Each transaction is about 400 bytes in size; the number of transactions per block is limited to around 2,500 by the 1 MB block size. The transaction byte size is larger if it has more inputs and outputs. Since only one new block is generated every 10 minutes, Bitcoin cannot handle more than 250 transactions per minutes, on average. This barrier must be broken to solve the scaling problem. There are two approaches: make the transaction data smaller or increase the block size.

Each transaction contains inputs and outputs. The signature, as part of the input, consists of roughly 60% of the data size. By removing the signature from the transaction data, the size can be greatly reduced. The most prominent proposal to do so was SegWit, short for Segregated Witness. It is a software update developed by Bitcoin Core to fix the Bitcoin scaling and malleability issues in December 2015, which was implemented in August 2017.

SegWit separates the digital signature (also known as the *witness*) from the transaction data by stripping it off from the input and moving it towards the end of the transaction separated by a marker. Once the signature is removed from the transaction data, the data become smaller. In general, SegWit data is 25% of its original size. The original megabyte can contain 4 times more transactions. Even though the actual block size remains 1 MB, the decreased data size makes 1 MB work like 4 MB. The new equivalent byte is called a *virtual byte*, or vByte. Each vByte is divided into 4 units, called Weight Units (WUs). Four WUs make up one virtual Byte (vByte). When counting the transaction size by vByte, each byte of the witness field is counted as 1 WU. A simplified transaction data structure is shown in Figure 3.5.

The post-marker signature data is considered a different layer from the transaction. This additional layer is called the *sidechain*. The sidechain is attached to the main chain by a two-way peg. SegWit also has an additional benefit: solving the malleability problem. Since the digital signature is detached from the input in the SegWit transactions, there is no way of changing the transaction ID (also known as a transaction hash, TXID) without also nullifying the digital signature. The proposal includes fraud proofs and Simplified Payment Verification or SPV.

Before SegWit						
version	mrk	input	(signature)	output		

After SegWit						
version	mrk	input	output		mrk	signature
					separate layer	

FIGURE 3.5 Transaction data structure without and with SegWit.

Nevertheless, the upside of scaling with SegWit is limited. In 2022, just over 50% of transactions had adopted SegWit. That means the number of transactions in a block has only doubled, which is far away from the transaction capacity of any credit card. Therefore, many people think that SegWit is only a temporary fix.

In May 2017, the miners that represented 80% of the Bitcoin hashing power got together in New York and signed the "New York Agreement." In this agreement, in addition to the SegWit implementation, they also proposed to double the block size to 2 MB in six months following the implementation of SegWit. This effort was dubbed SegWit 2X. With SegWit 2X, the block size was doubled again, but that was still not nearly enough.

Many people are against SegWit because it can potentially degrade decentralization. The third party running the sidechain can potentially become the centralized authority of the blockchain. It defeats the original purpose of the blockchain to be a completely decentralized system. Therefore, not all miners support SegWit, and not all wallets support SegWit transactions.

In summary, the SegWit solution does not solve the long-term scalability issue because it potentially undermines the decentralization of the Bitcoin network. Nevertheless, SegWit brought an immediate relief of the transaction congestion problem, which buys time for the community to find a permanent solution. The SegWit soft fork was implemented in August 2017, and another useful feature was found almost accidentally. SegWit helped to improve the Bitcoin network capacity, making it possible to process a larger number of transactions per second, which led to a decrease in the transaction confirmation time, as discussed earlier in the chapter.

3.3 BITCOIN SPLIT

After ongoing debates over how to scale Bitcoin, Bitcoin was officially split into Bitcoin and Bitcoin Cash after a hard fork on August 1, 2017. Bitcoin Cash (BCH) started trading on August 3, 2017. It was the first Bitcoin hard fork, and owners of Bitcoin then received two coins: Bitcoin and Bitcoin Cash.

The dissident group, mostly miners and some developers, initiated the hard fork (also known as the User-Activated Hard Fork). Upon the UAHF, a copy of Bitcoin's blockchain from block 478,558 was transferred to the BCH blockchain.[8]

After the Bitcoin split, SegWit was activated in the Bitcoin blockchain and subsequently gained significant support from the mining industry.[9]

Bitcoin Cash did not implement SegWit. Instead, the block size limit became adjustable, with an initial increase to 8 MB. It can be further increased depending on future needs.[10] In fact, the Bitcoin Cash developer makes it easier for a future block size change by using a full node implementation of the Bitcoin Cash protocol, called Bitcoin ABC.[11] ABC means Adjustable Bitcoin Cap.

With a future roadmap of massive scaling, Bitcoin ABC allows an immediate block size increase with a simple, sensible, adjustable block size cap resolving the scaling problem once and for all. It paved the way for Bitcoin Cash to be a cryptocurrency for payment.

There are other changes as well, such as the new transaction type using the SigHash type signature, which provides replay and wipeout protection, improves hardware wallet security, and eliminates the quadratic hashing problem. This essentially minimizes user disruption and permits safe and peaceful coexistence of the two chains. There is a new PoW Difficulty Adjustment Algorithm (DAA), which allows miners to migrate from the legacy Bitcoin chain as desired.

Bitcoin Cash attracted support from users who want a block size increase, as well as developers of other proposals, such as Bitcoin Classic and Bitcoin Unlimited. Most importantly, Bitcoin Cash has the support of some big miners. Many think that if Bitcoin had failed to implement the 2X part of the SegWit 2X, which happened on November 16, 2017, as scheduled, many more miners would likely have defected to Bitcoin Cash. There are also mining companies, like Bitmain, which support both SegWit 2X and Bitcoin Cash. Like Bitcoin, no single entity controls Bitcoin Cash. Only coordinated efforts across independent development teams can make changes.

The Bitcoin split created two very different cryptocurrencies: one for payment and transactions, and one for storing the value (Figure 3.6). The Old Mutual Gold and Silver Fund is the first traditional precious metal mutual fund to invest in Bitcoins.[12]

As a store of value, many financial derivative products, such as futures and options, can be applied to Bitcoin. After all, if gold can be traded in the futures market, why not Bitcoin? Some financial institutions are trading Bitcoin on the futures market. On December 1, 2017, the U.S. Commodity Futures Trading Commission (CFCT) approved Bitcoin for the listing of such products from CBOE, CME Group, and Cantor Fitzgerald.[13] Others have followed, and futures trading is active, but Bitcoin prices are already volatile enough; its futures contracts are not for the faint of heart.

However, futures trading for Bitcoins should be an interesting experiment, which may evolve. CME Group already has a blockchain project for gold trading.

3.4 KEEP YOUR COINS SAFE DURING FORKING

A forking event represents a risk to Bitcoin holders. The two primary risks are the replay attack and the loss of coin value. There are several contingency measures to secure your wealth during the period preceding a potential hard fork and immediately after it.

The *replay attack* is a form of attack on a freshly split network when the two blockchains are barely different from each other. When a person sends Bitcoins to someone, an attacker may replicate the same transaction on the other blockchain and the network will accept it. Thus, unknowingly and unwillingly, the user may lose their coins on the alternative blockchain just by sending transactions across the first one.

To prevent this, refrain from conducting any transactions at all until the normal transaction volume returns. Of course, the new version of the software causing forking does implement preventive measures against a replay attack.

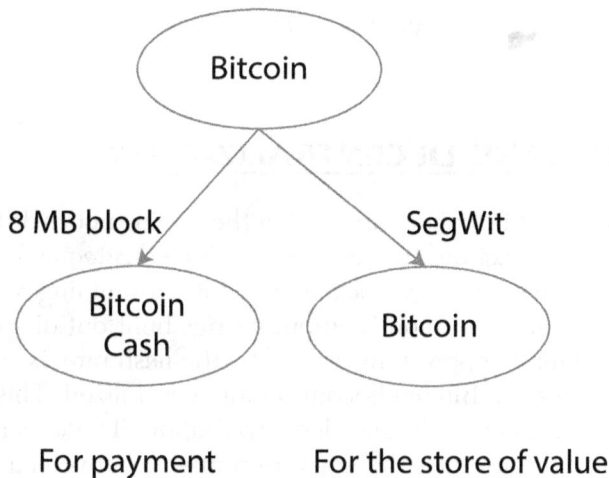

FIGURE 3.6 Bitcoin split.

Another important safeguard is to always have control of the private keys to your funds. The best way is to withdraw your coins from an online exchange or wallet to a software wallet stored on your PC. Any third party, even one you deem trustworthy, such as an exchange, or a Web wallet service, may present unnecessary risk to your coins. The risk is even greater during a contentious hard fork. When users are not in control of the key to their funds, they are at the mercy of the decisions made by the company holding the keys.

A hard fork split is like a stock split. The moment a hard fork takes place, all the people holding Bitcoins receive the equivalent number of coins on the alternative blockchain. That is because all the records on both blockchain are identical up until the point of the fork. Since they are left with two sets of coins, some people will want to dump the ones they find less promising. That may cause people to panic, and so they rush to sell before the price drops too much. The commotion creates a lot of uncertainty and volatility in the market, which is bound to last for some time after a hard fork takes place.

For a short while after the split, the combined value of two new coins may be less than the value of the old coin. Under such conditions, the least risky strategy is to just hold onto your coins on both blockchains and wait it out. It is impossible to predict which one of the alternatives will be more successful and taking sides may result in a massive loss if you choose wrong.

A much safer solution is to wait for the market to calm down, see which coin increases in value, and go from there. In other words, if you truly believe in the eventual success of Bitcoin, your best bet is to keep holding it. No matter how dire the short-term consequences of a fork can be, the community will eventually sort it out, like it always does.

3.5 BITCOIN AND DECENTRALIZATION

The concept of Bitcoin mining is that the mining nodes do the complex work of validating transactions to receive newly issued Bitcoins as a reward. Any node in the Bitcoin network can be a miner, but most mining is done by professional miners running enormous computing rigs built out of specialized hardware. When the mining power, measured by the hash rate, is controlled by a handful of big miners, Bitcoin becomes more centralized. This is the fundamental trade-off between scale and decentralization. The decentralization factor is important because it is the key differentiator between a cryptocurrency and fiat currency. As such, Bitcoin is more than just a financial instrument, it is also an ideology. If the market deems decentralization important, it will push up the Bitcoin price to make the Bitcoin platform more decentralized. So far, after more than 10 years of the existence of Bitcoin, we have seen that the market indeed has the faith to push up the Bitcoin price to an unthinkable level – reaching as high as $60,000 twice in 2021.

With the total number of Bitcoins approaching the theoretical limit of 21 million, the Bitcoin supply is dwindling, so it is foreseeable that the Bitcoin price will continue to increase.[14] Like anything else, Bitcoin's price is dictated by supply and demand.

However, because all transactions need to be validated, if miners and nodes do not have enough incentives to validate the transactions, the circulation of Bitcoins may slow down. Bitcoin will lose its competitive advantages and eventually collapse.

Since its creation in 2008, Bitcoin has been regarded as a radically different kind of currency that works independently of central banks and the established financial system, with no single centralized source of power or control. Satoshi Nakamoto believed that if the majority of the computing power was controlled by nodes that are not attacking the network, they will generate the longest chain and outpace the attackers

As miners get more powerful by amassing mining power, Nakamoto's basic assumption has become less valid. Increasing the block size effectively weeded out small miners and gave large miners control of the Bitcoin network. Today, the Bitcoin platform is more centralized than it was 10 years ago. When miners get control of the Bitcoin blockchain, they can act in their own favor by, for example, setting higher transaction fees. Eventually, Bitcoins will become no different than today's fiat currencies and miners will become bankers. This defeats the noble intention of Bitcoin.

However, from the miners' perspective, the mining fee is an important source of income when the Bitcoin reward decreases. Because the lifetime supply of Bitcoin is limited, when the end of Bitcoin mining is attained, there will be no more mining reward. Miners will have no income to support the work for the PoW, which consumes a large amount of electricity. At that point, no one will verify the transactions, and the Bitcoin platform could collapse. The transaction fee will be the only way to keep Bitcoin platform going. The bitterness of the debate on transaction fees sparked a 20% collapse in Bitcoin price in early 2017 because people thought that the future of Bitcoin was bleak.

While the centralization and decentralization discussion on the Bitcoin platform is still largely in favor of decentralization, the blockchain technology can be centralized or decentralized (or anywhere in between). The irony of the blockchain technology is that when used as a permissioned blockchain, its centralization power can reach an unprecedented level.

The entire decentralization concept lies in the distribution of the mining power. Mining power resides in the miners who contribute resources to mine. For the Bitcoin platform, the mining resources needed to do the PoW process, or validation, are quite intensive. Even with today's Bitcoin price, individuals or small miners who do not deploy the most efficient mining rig will most likely lose money.

As the blockchain technology evolves, less resource intensive validation techniques are being adopted by the *altcoins* (alternative cryptocurrencies). It is, therefore, possible that one centralized entity, such as a single company or an organization, can afford all the mining resources required, and thus control the blockchain.

A centralized blockchain application can wield tremendous power over its users, more so than any other tool available today. Such a vision is quickly becoming a reality, as is in the case of the digitization of the Indian currency, the rupee, by the Reserve Bank of India.[15] The project can track every single rupee spent.

Even Bitcoin, regarded as a truly decentralized system, is built on the premises that the system is secure so long as honest nodes collectively control more CPU power than any cooperating group of attacker nodes. Such premises may not hold.

3.6   THE MT. GOX INCIDENT

Although Bitcoin is supposed to be un-hackable, its private keys are not. Because of the small file size of the key, it is extremely portable, and can be easily stolen or lost. Because a private key is the only proof of ownership of the underlying asset, when one loses the private key, one loses the asset.

This is what happened in 2013 when an estimated 740,000 Bitcoins were stolen from the exchange Mt. Gox.[16] With a Bitcoin price of $60,000, the stolen Bitcoins were valued at a staggering $42 billion; at the time of the theft, the Bitcoin price was approximately $480.

The security breach was first discovered in June 2011. Mt. Gox was likely inexperienced or did not realize the extent of the vulnerability, and the company did not take a strong enough action to patch the problem. The hacker continued to steal the compromised wallets unnoticed by the exchange. By 2013, Mt. Gox was handling 70% of worldwide Bitcoin transactions, and its trading volume reached 150,000 Bitcoins per day – masking the volume of the stolen Bitcoins.

When CoinLab, Mt. Gox's partner in the U.S., filed a lawsuit against Mt. Gox for breach of contract, the problem was gradually unearthed. The U.S. Department of Homeland Security (DHS) was alerted of the problem and seized the money from Mt. Gox's U.S. operation because it was considered an unregistered money transmitter. As a result, Mt. Gox suspended the U.S. dollar withdrawals. Soon afterward, Mizuho bank in Japan closed Mt. Gox's accounts. From that point on, it became extremely difficult for Mt. Gox to operate normally. In February 2014, Mt. Gox had to halt all Bitcoin withdrawals and filed bankruptcy protection. All the Bitcoins held by Mt. Gox were frozen. Hundreds of millions of dollars were, as well. The Bitcoins stored in Mt. Gox's hot (online) wallets were stolen, while the Bitcoins stored in the cold (offline) wallets were safe. After years of litigation, investors may finally see the light at the end of tunnel to recover their Bitcoins. At the end of 2021, a Japanese court approved a "final and binding" resolution in which creditors would receive 90% of the value lost.[17]

In July 2017, a Russian national named Alexander Vinnik was arrested by U.S. authorities in Greece and charged with the laundering of Bitcoins stolen from Mt. Gox. Investigation shows that Vinnik was the owner of the wallets into which the stolen Bitcoins had been transferred. In December 2020, Vinnik was sentenced to 5 years in prison in connection to the crime.[18]

It is a painful but valuable lesson concerning the theft of Bitcoin (or any cryptocurrency, for that matter). As Bitcoins become more valuable and as many other cryptocurrencies proliferate, the online security risk becomes greater.

3.7   FULL NODES VS. PARTIAL NODES

To run a node, a computer needs to download and run the Bitcoin Core's node software. Anyone willing to invest in the equipment can do so.[19] There are two kinds of nodes in the Bitcoin blockchain network: a full node and a partial node.

A full node stores the complete blockchain, which contains the entire history of the Bitcoin transactions. The Bitcoin blockchain is growing 50 gigabytes per year under the current 1-megabyte block size limit. Besides the memory capacity requirement, the bandwidth required for the full nodes is also significantly larger, because they need to download and upload all the blocks in the blockchain.

To allow more nodes to participate in the Bitcoin network, the Bitcoin development eases the resources required. Bitcoin Core 0.12.0 allows nodes to download the relevant data only. The opted nodes are downgraded to partial nodes or lightweight clients' status. Partial nodes do not have all the blockchain data. Bitcoin Core 0.12.0 introduces a data cap and a priority for upload traffic.[20] When the data cap is full, the node will skip uploading blocks that are older than a week.

Partial nodes run in the Simplified Payment Verification (SPV) mode. The transaction data unrelated to the transactions in the current block do not download. They connect to full nodes and use filters to decide what data to download. Partial nodes get the Merkle branch to the link to be verified transactions by going to the location of the chain that shows that a network node had previously accepted it.

Full nodes have consensus power, but partial nodes do not. Full nodes represent the Bitcoin community and can exercise economic power. Each full node has the complete blockchain date. The nodes with the same and newest block in their blockchain are said to be in *consensus*. The validation rules followed by these nodes to maintain the consensus are called the *consensus rules*. When a fork happens, the branch that has more participation from the full nodes wins. In other words, the branch that has the most, full nodes', votes wins. This is the consensus mechanism at work.

In this way, Bitcoin establishes a consensus based on voting among the nodes. These full nodes accept validated blocks and reject blocks that they cannot validate. Validation means to check the transactions against the consensus rules, such as the Bitcoin address in a transaction not previously used (without a double-spending issue). Since partial nodes do not have the complete blockchain, they do not have the data to perform validation. Thus, running the full node is the only way to ensure Bitcoin can provide trust without involving a third party.

Still, SPV performed by partial nodes has an important function. It enforces a subset of the validation rules by checking on block headers. For example, they check the validity of the work included in those headers, but do not verify all the transactions, only the transactions relevant to them. Partial nodes act as pre-screen of transactions, thus alleviating full nodes from validating invalid transactions.

When the blockchain becomes longer, it is more resource intensive. More nodes choose to run as partial nodes. Since partial nodes validate only the most recent transaction history of a Bitcoin, they create forks. Such forks propagate until a full node rejects it. However, when there are more partial nodes in proportion to the full nodes in the network, there will be more invalid transactions in the network and the risk increases.

3.8   IS BITCOIN TRULY ANONYMOUS?

Even though the Bitcoin network is claimed to provide anonymity, when it connects to the outside world, the user's identity can be revealed in many ways. For example, the identity of Bitcoin users can be revealed from the IP address where a transaction originated. To protect users' privacy, Bitcoin Core 0.12.0 automatically connects to the Bitcoin network through the Tor browser – if the Tor browser is installed on the same computer. Tor encrypts data and routes it through several nodes across the world before broadcasting it. This makes it hard to trace where a Bitcoin transaction originated.

Bitcoin is best described as pseudo-anonymous in the following way:

Bitcoin addresses are not tied to the identity of users on a protocol level. When you create a new Bitcoin address, you do not need to submit any personal information.

Transactions do not link to the identity of users. One can transfer Bitcoins from any address to which it controls the (private) keys to any other address, with no need to reveal any personal information. The payee does not need to know the identity of the payer.

Bitcoin transaction data is transmitted and forwarded by nodes to a random set of nodes on the peer-to-peer network.

When the Bitcoin platform interfaces with the real-world environment, the user's identity can be revealed. Therefore, if one trades Bitcoins in an account linked to their bank account, they are not anonymous.

Even if you deposit Bitcoin from your cold storage (offline) wallet anonymously, since the Bitcoin platform is transparent and traceable to anyone, someone can trace your identity through one of the many non-anonymous transactions you have made. For example, you use multiple Bitcoin addresses as inputs (please refer to Chapter 2) of a transaction, if one of these inputs can be linked to your identity, all other inputs and outputs can be linked to you.

There are many other analytic techniques that can deduce the connection between non-anonymous addresses and anonymous addresses, such as taint analysis, amount analysis, or timing analysis.[21]

It is not easy to be truly anonymous. If you want more privacy, there are a few simple measures to take:

1. Use the Tor browser for any Bitcoin transaction to hide your IP address.

2. Use a new address for each transaction. Of course, no measure will help your anonymity if your Bitcoin exchange account is linked to your bank account.

3.9 TRANSACTION FEES

Bitcoin miners have incentives to do PoW because of the Bitcoins they receive as a reward. However, by design, the reward is halved for every 210,000 blocks mined, even though more resources are required for mining due to the greater difficulty.

To compensate for a more resource-intensive problem, miners resort to increasing fees for the transaction. We can see in Figure 3.7 that the transaction fee increases over time.[22] Because a miner's cost of mining is related to the amount of data in the transaction, not to the transaction amount, the incentive is to charge each transaction by a fixed Bitcoin amount. For small amounts of Bitcoin transactions, the fixed fee structure, rather than fee as a percentage of the transaction amount, becomes excessive. For example, the fee for sending 1 Bitcoin or 0.01 Bitcoin are the same if their transaction size in a byte is the same. The transaction with many inputs and outputs will have a higher fee. It is not reasonable to pay a fee of 0.1 BTC when spending 0.5 BTC.[23]

This discourages the use of Bitcoins for small transactions. Paying for a cup of coffee with Bitcoins may result in a higher fee than the coffee itself. The problem gets worse over time because the mining reward decreases while the resource requirement increases.

Of course, cheaper computing power, greater data storage and Internet speeds, and an increasing Bitcoin price partially offset the increasing transaction costs. However, the higher transaction fee makes Bitcoins less competitive.

In most wallets, you can set your own fee. When you set a higher fee, your transaction will be processed at a higher priority and your transaction will be confirmed sooner.

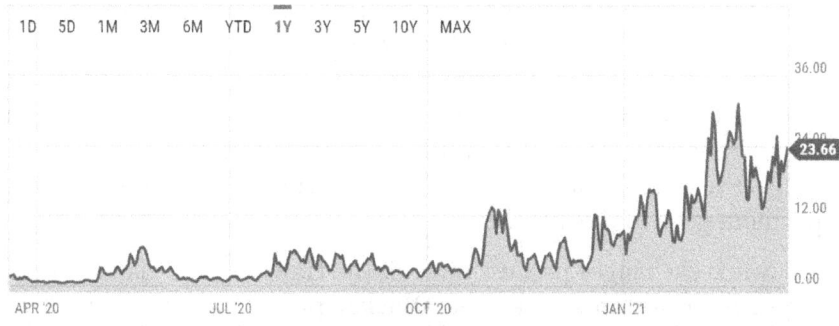

FIGURE 3.7 Bitcoin transaction fees.

3.10 TRANSACTION MALLEABILITY

Malleability is the ability to be shaped. In the Bitcoin world, transaction malleability means that the transaction can be altered. This can happen to the unconfirmed transactions. The unconfirmed transactions are transactions that are broadcasted, but not yet confirmed, or incorporated into the blockchain. Further transactions created from the Bitcoin of an unconfirmed transaction also become unconfirmed. There are many unconfirmed transactions at any given time.[24] In early 2021, there were approximately 24,000 unconfirmed transactions in the Bitcoin network at any given time. This number updates itself constantly. Because the number of transactions is created faster than the Bitcoin platform can handle, the number of unconfirmed transactions increases. We have discussed that the Bitcoin platform can only handle four transactions per second (TPS), which is much, much less than Visa or Mastercard.

Since the unconfirmed Bitcoin transactions are in the Bitcoin network memory pool until picked up by a miner for confirmation, anyone can pick up unconfirmed transactions. This exposes the unconfirmed transactions to the risk that someone can hijack the transaction, alter its data, or even spend the Bitcoins again. Some transactions remain longer in the memory pool as unconfirmed because they pay a small transaction fee. Miners are less inclined to process the low fee transactions. In 2016, BIP 125 was implemented to allow users to change the transaction fee in case they find that their transactions are unconfirmed for long time. However, BIP 125 opens the door for the Replace-By-Fee (RBF) attack. What if someone catches a transaction and changes the payee's address to their address or duplicates the transaction? Such interference creates two transactions involving the same Bitcoin. If a miner confirms a mutated transaction before the original transaction, the original transaction becomes invalid. Bitcoin transactions are identifiable by their Transaction ID or TXID, the hash of the transaction data and signature. If the transaction data is altered, the TXID will be different. In effect, the payment goes to the attacker.

Since exchanges process most of the transactions, malicious software can target them for an attack. The attacker picks transactions from the Bitcoin network and modifies the signature data, creating two different TXIDs circulating on the Bitcoin network for the same transaction. The system has no way of telling the right TXID from the wrong TXID. In addition, since a specific transaction can only be confirmed once, just one of the TXIDs will be included in a block, while the other will be rejected. Moreover, the transaction with the altered TXID would be included in the block instead of the original TXID.

The lower the fee that a transaction pays to the miner, the lower the priority to be confirmed and included in the block, and therefore, the wait is longer for confirmation. This results in risk: the longer a transaction is unconfirmed, the higher its risk of malleability. Furthermore, if you try to spend the unconfirmed transaction, your outbound transaction will have an "unconfirmed parent." If the parent transaction has been tampered with, then your outbound transaction will not be able to be validated.

If you make payments to many parties in a short period, you may split up outputs ahead of time. When the parties receive a 100 BTC output, they might break it into four 25 BTC chunks paying themselves, which will allow them to pay four people without needing to attempt to spend unconfirmed change. Some delicate balancing is required here. If you have too many outputs in your wallet, the fees increase dramatically, and the confirmation becomes slow.

The immediate effect of the malleability attack is that it appears as though the transaction did not go through – though it did with an incorrect TXID. In addition, the attack also impedes chained transactions even though the attacker cannot steal the funds. This is because only the TXID can be changed, not the transactions themselves.

BIP 62 has a remedy to prevent malleability attacks by narrowing down the types of data that can be included in Bitcoin transactions. BIP 62 has been implemented as a soft fork, which means that it is up to miners to adopt the software changes; it is also backwards compatible.[25] However, BIP 62 does not address all possible malleability issues. Signatures can still be changed by anyone who has access to the corresponding private keys.

SegWit provided the fix to the malleability problem by removing the signature from the transaction data into the segregated sidechain. It is no longer possible to change the transaction ID.

3.11 BIPS, HARD FORKS, AND SOFT FORKS

Bitcoin blockchain is still a relatively young technology. From its early theoretical concept and framework to its real-world implementation, many shortcomings have arisen, especially when the scale is getting bigger. As the Bitcoin platform evolves, it encounters deficiencies that require improvements. Otherwise, the Bitcoin platform runs into a bottleneck.

Along the way, there have been many proposals to improve the Bitcoin platform. A proposal is different from an idea. A proposal must be implementable. There are wide implications to the Bitcoin operation and monetary properties when the Bitcoin platform is modified. Therefore, the Bitcoin community imposes a strict procedure for a proposal to become a BIP (Bitcoin Improvement Proposal). Once it becomes a BIP, it acquires a serial number, and is thereafter referred to as BIP {number} by the community. Because the Bitcoin platform has no central authority, its implementation or adaption must go through the approval of a Bitcoin community consensus.

So far, there are a several hundred BIPs.[26] Some BIPs are for information only. Others are to change the network protocol, transaction validation, and measures affecting the platform operation. When the change is more dramatic, its implementation is more controversial. Such was the case of SegWit.

Any implementation of the changes to the Bitcoin platform will inevitably run into compatibility issues. After all, the Bitcoin platform has a set of strict rules. When the rules are changed, there is a new version of the blockchain software that adapts the new rules. However, the blockchain can only run one version of the software.

The blocks formed by the new version will deviate from the existing blockchain. The blockchain will have two heads or a fork. A *fork* in software development means a spin-off project from the original software project for the improvement of certain aspects of the original software. A fork in the blockchain terminology means two branches of the blockchain growing out of the existing blockchain due to the divergence of software versions used by different miners.

Here, a consensus is at work. The fork of the blockchain runs the new version against that of the old version. The fork of the blockchain, which wins more hash power or economic power, becomes the majority fork of the blockchain. The other branch of the blockchain is the minority fork. Since the blocks generated by the minority fork will be rejected by the majority fork, the minority fork will either fade away (because no more transactions will come their way) or join the majority fork by giving up their version of the software. When this happens, the minority fork will disappear, and the majority fork continues as the only blockchain. The new blockchain can run either the new version or the old version of the software depending on whichever wins the consensus.

However, if the minority fork persists and does not fade away because there is enough support, then both forks can run in parallel to each other, but each follows a different set of rules. These two parallel blockchains are not compatible and cannot send transactions to each other because the transaction passing the validation of one fork does not pass to the other fork. In other words, the coins are not transferrable across these two blockchain. Two blockchains grow from one. Each blockchain has its own coins.

In some cases, the new rules are backwards compatible. Backwards compatibility exists when the new rules are a subset of the old rules (Figure 3.8). This type of fork is called a *soft fork*. If the old rules are a subset of the new rules, it is a *hard fork*.

Figure 3.8 illustrates the difference between two blockchains, one with a soft fork and the other with a hard fork. The backward compatibility is outlined in the drawn boundaries. The blocks in the drawn boundaries are backwards compatible but not with the blocks outside of the boundary.

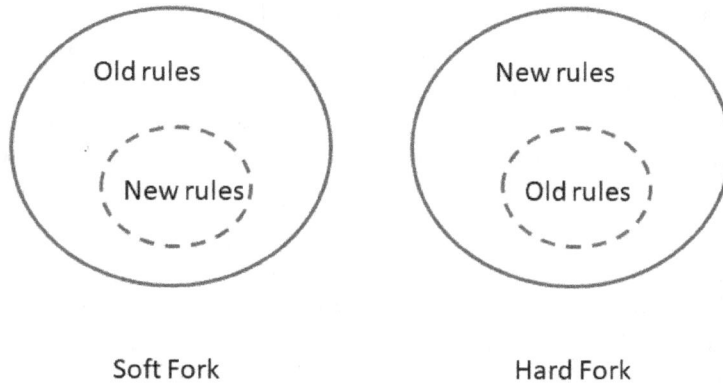

FIGURE 3.8 In a soft fork, new rules are subset of old rules. In a hard fork, the opposite is true.

In the case of the soft fork on the left of Figure 3.8, both Fork A and Fork B are validated by the original blockchain. However, in the case of the hard fork shown on the right, the blocks formed by the new rules (Fork A) are rejected by the original blockchain; therefore, it breaks off from the original blockchain.

3.12 UASF AND UAHF

The Bitcoin software has a built-in mechanism to reject the transactions that break the consensus rules or reject the blocks containing such transactions. This prevents the miner from including any invalid transactions. The forks resulting from invalid transactions dissipate quickly and are normally not an issue. However, if most miners decide not to adopt the change of software that is mandated by the Bitcoin developers and approved by the Bitcoin community, it will cause a problem. The fork arising because of such a situation is called a *User Activated Fork*. A User Activated Soft Fork and a User Activated Hard Fork are types of User Activated Forks.

In the Bitcoin world, the developers hold the key to the software upgrade. They are the ones who develop a new version of the software from BIPs. It is up to the Bitcoin community to upgrade the software to the new version by consensus. When the Bitcoin developer imposes a mandatory software version change supported by part of the Bitcoin community, and yet the dissidents are comparable in size, the Bitcoin community splits itself and the User Activated Fork happens.

In a UAHF case, the nodes running the new version will accept the blocks generated by the miners using old rules. The fork of new rules will grow. After the flag date, UAHF will even make certain invalid blocks under old rules valid under new rules. This is seen as a voluntary departure of the dissident nodes from the majority blockchain. The old blockchain will continue as if nothing happened. It has a minimal impact on the existing blockchain.

However, for a UASF, the story is very different. The nodes running new rules will not accept the blocks generated by the miners using the old rules. Only the miners, who upgrade the software, will be able to generate the blocks for the nodes of new rules. That means, without miners' support, the nodes running new rules will soon be starved of new blocks. This is because the economic power has very little hashing power. If most of the hashing power does not go along with the new version, the hash rate will not be enough to process the transactions. Therefore, even if the economic power wins a UASF, it can be sabotaged by the hashing power.

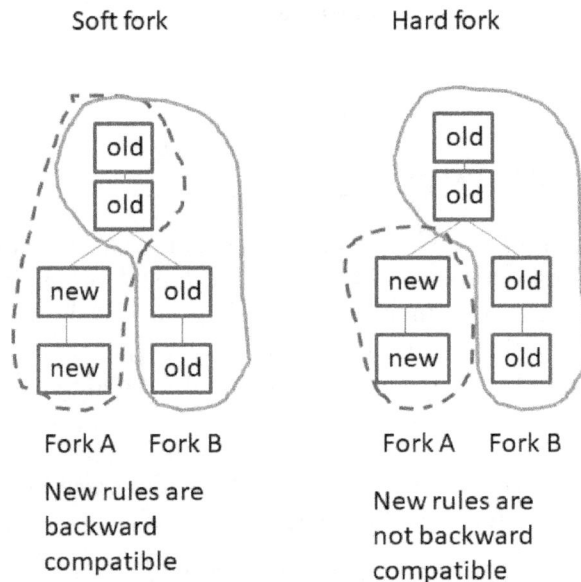

FIGURE 3.9 Difference between soft forks and hard forks.

A UASF, which wins the economic power, still needs miners' support for the attack to be successful. Nevertheless, if the hashing power and economic power are in harmony, UASF can be carried out smoothly. A successful example of the UASF is the implementation of P2SH (BIP16). A fearful UASF example is the BIP 148 activation (SegWit activation).

The most notable hard fork cases are when Ethereum forked into the new Ethereum (ETH) and Ethereum classic (ETC) in 2016, and Bitcoin forked into Bitcoin (BTC) and Bitcoin Cash (BCH) in 2017.

3.13 OTHER PROPOSED FIXES

Beyond SegWit, there are many other interesting but less visible proposals, such as the Invertible Bloom Lookup Tables (IBLT) scheme, P2Pool, Weak Block, and other non-bandwidth scaling schemes.[27, 28, 29]

There are many non-bandwidth solutions to fix malleability issues, such as proposals of the bidirectional payment channel and transaction cut-through. There are also proposals for a flexible block size that allows miners to produce larger blocks at some cost.[30] These proposals preserve the alignment of incentives between miners and general node operators and prevent defection between the miners from undermining the fee charging market behavior.

Bitcoin Unlimited (BU) is the alternative software client for the Bitcoin network. It is a big proponent of the flexible block size. Bitcoin Unlimited was the first client to provide the tools that node operators and miners need to remove the 1 MB block size limit. Its software allows users to find the majority consensus limit and set their block size limit to that value. The node operators running BU client can easily adjust the size of blocks their node accepts, without having to restart their node or recompile new executables from source code.

By giving miners the option to configure the size of blocks they will validate, Bitcoin Unlimited is doing things very differently from Bitcoin Core. The default size is still one megabyte, yet the maximum generation size is a fully customizable option.

Network nodes have a similar option to determine which blocks they will validate and how large they can be. As one would expect, Bitcoin Unlimited has gained some support from mining pools. However, the mining community is only a part of the overall network. Service providers, exchanges, and wallet operators are not pleased with what Bitcoin Unlimited proposes. Without that critical support, the chances of BU succeeding are limited.

Another interesting solution to the Bitcoin scaling problem is the micropayment. Micropayments provide a radically different solution than the SegWit or larger block sizes to achieve the transaction rate faster than the credit card transaction rate. This over 30,000 per second rate would be done by moving the payment mechanism outside of blockchain.

Micropayments involve setting up a pending transfer by dividing a large payment amount into many small payments. For instance, instead of sending a $100 bill for a payment; you send 100 $1 bills in 100 separate envelopes. The payment channel is off the blockchain, so the transaction data in the blockchain is minimized. Then, a block can fit in many more transactions.

Such a micropayment method already exists on the Bitcoin platform. Satoshi Nakamoto himself disclosed it in an email on January 1, 2009. It is implemented by offloading the transactions to a third-party custodian, which creates counterparty risk. The current micropayment channels in the Bitcoin platform still use real Bitcoin transactions, only electing to defer the broadcast to the blockchain for both parties to guarantee their current balance on the blockchain. Therefore, it is slow and expensive. However, there are other micropayment solutions in development, which will be discussed later.

3.14 GOVERNMENT ATTITUDE

Governments around the world look at Bitcoin with suspicion because of its anonymous nature and free flow across the national boundaries.

As of early 2022, nine countries have completely banned Bitcoin: Algeria, Bangladesh, China, Egypt, Iraq, Morocco, Nepal, Qatar, and Tunisia. Other countries set strict rules to deal with Bitcoin. China banned financial institutions from dealing in the virtual currency in December 2013, although trading volume in Chinese Yuan persisted. Germany, France, South Korea, and Thailand have all looked unfavorably on Bitcoin at times. The European Banking Authority, Switzerland, Poland, Canada, and the United States continue to deliberate about different Bitcoin-related issues and regulation.

In early September 2017, China banned Bitcoin and drove the price down from $4,500 to $3,700. However, one month later, the price bounced back to $4,500, and since then, it went above $60,000 in 2021. The action taken in China has had a big impact, because the country mined 80% of the worldwide Bitcoin.[31] Even so, the government can do little to slow down the momentum of Bitcoin.

In 2021, China cracked down on Bitcoin mining again because it consumes a large amount of energy and does not contribute to the GDP. As a result, many miners moved their rigs elsewhere in the world: central Asia, North America, Europe, and Latin America.[32] It is estimated that 25% of the hash rate will be relocated to the United States. In September 2021, China banned all cryptocurrency transactions and mining.

China is not alone in its focus on the $2 trillion blockchain sector, nor is it the only country to have restricted access to unregulated cryptocurrency exchanges. U.S. officials have also expressed concern about users gaining access to offshore crypto exchanges. The exchanges are required to block access to U.S. users.[33]

Countries try to match Bitcoin to their existing regulatory structures, but often find that the cryptocurrency does not quite fit. Countries then ultimately conclude that new legislation is required. However, new legislation takes time. Blockchain technology is evolving fast; there is no telling how it may be in a few years. Blockchain technology is also branching out as more financial industries are embracing fintech, and so hasty legislation may become obsolete as soon as it becomes effective.

At present, some countries, like the U.K., have classified Bitcoin as a currency, whereas other countries treat Bitcoin as an investment in the same category as stocks and bonds. While some cryptocurrency may become currency, others may become the store of value, just like gold.

Even different agencies in the same country may treat cryptocurrencies differently. For example, in the U.S., the Internal Revenue Service treats Bitcoin like stock, so it is subject to capital gains taxes on transactions. The IRS requests that cryptocurrency exchanges report annual transactions over $20,000.[34] However, there are other U.S. government agencies—including FinCEN (Financial Crimes Enforcement Network), banking regulators, and the CFPB, SEC, CFTC, and DOJ—who regulate Bitcoins as a currency. In March 2014, the IRS issued a guidance (IRS Notice 2014-21) labeling cryptocurrencies, including Bitcoin, "intangible property." Investors and traders should report the capital gains or losses from cryptocurrency trading just like stock trading.

Due to the centralized nature of the permissioned blockchain, many countries also either contemplate or plan to issue digital currency. With Internet access widely available and the improvement of encryption technology, the conditions are ripe for digital currencies, which can reduce operating costs, increase efficiency, and enable a wide range of new applications. China's central bank, the People's Bank of China (PBOC), expressed the desire to supervise private digital currencies and develop its own national digital money. Its intention is to maintain financial stability, innovation, and proper supervision on the issuance and circulation of its legal digital tender. Digital currency can co-exist with cash for quite a long time before it eventually replaces cash.

In fact, most central banks in the world are experimenting with a central-bank-issued digital currency in different stages. The countries studying digital currencies include Canada, Denmark, U.K., Sweden, Germany, Netherlands, Russia, Ukraine, India, Ecuador, and South Korea. Countries like Cambodia, the Bahamas, and China already have digital currencies in circulation.[35, 36] We will discuss this in more detail in Chapter 6.

3.15 THE FUTURE OF BITCOIN

Predicting the future of Bitcoin is like predicting the stock market. Nothing can be guaranteed. Despite government crackdowns, such as the case in China, Bitcoin is still viable. Each time a government takes a severe measure to outlaw Bitcoin, the price is inevitably depressed, but not for long. When it bounces back, it does so with much vigor.

For the next few years, the future of Bitcoin seems to be bright. The reason is that more large institutions are utilizing Bitcoins. For example, Tesla, the largest EV Company in the world, bought $1.3 billion worth of Bitcoins in 2021.[37] Many other companies are buying Bitcoins as part of their company assets, such as Square, Coinbase, and MicroStrategy.[38] As of April 2021, public companies hold 1.4 million Bitcoins. At a price of $40,000, this holding amounts to $56 billion dollars. Instead of buying Bitcoins directly, some companies and institutions are investing into Bitcoin mining companies, such as the New Jersey Pension Fund and California Pension Fund. Pension funds normally only invest in safe assets.

Bitcoin investment is also entering mainstream institutions. Many Wall Street investment firms offer Bitcoin ETFs. This has the effect of broadening the market for Bitcoins. Until now, to buy Bitcoins, you needed to open an account with a Bitcoin exchange. To safeguard the Bitcoin addresses, many people used cell phone wallets. If you lost your cell phone, you lost your Bitcoins. Bitcoin security was a constant worry, especially when the price was high: and the possession of Bitcoins can represent a small fortune for many people. Now that institutions offer Bitcoin ETFs, which have Bitcoins as the underlying assets, you can buy and sell ETFs just as you buy and sell stocks in any brokerage account. There are no more complicated Bitcoin transactions and security issues to worry about. This will dramatically broaden the market for Bitcoins. These funds not only invest in Bitcoins, but also in other cryptocurrencies such as Ethereum. This provides some diversification. Some of these funds are Ark Next Generation Internet ETF, Simplify U.S. Equity Plus GBTC ETF, and Grayscale Bitcoin Trust. More investment companies are seeking SEC approval of Bitcoin or other cryptocurrency ETFs.

REFERENCES

1. "What is BIP? Why do you need to know about it?," Sudhir Khatwani, *https://coinsutra.com/bip-Bitcoin-improvement-proposa/*

2. *https://blockchain.info/charts/n-transactions?timespan=all*

3. *https://Bitcoinvisuals.com/chain-tx-day*

4. *https://blockchain.info/charts*

5. *https://www.bitdegree.org/crypto/tutorials/lightning-network#what-is-the-lightning-network*

6. *https://bitcoinvisuals.com/chain-tx-size*

7. *https://www.statista.com/statistics/647523/worldwide-bitcoin-blockchain-size*

8. *https://bitinfocharts.com/comparison/bitcoin-size.html*

9. "Bitcoin vs. Bitcoin Cash: What is the difference?", Jake Frankenfield, *https://www.investopedia.com/tech/Bitcoin-vs-Bitcoin-cash-whats-difference/*

10. "Segregated Witness Activates on Bitcoin: This is What to Expect", Bitcoin Magazine, *https://Bitcoinmagazine.com/articles/segregated-witness-activates-Bitcoin-what-expect/*

11. *https://www.Bitcoinabc.org/*

12. "A gold fund is investing in Bitcoin", Ryan Browne, CNBC, *https://www.cnbc.com/2017/11/24/a-gold-fund-is-investing-in-Bitcoin.html*

13. *https://www.cryptoeq.io/coreReports/bitcoincash-abridged*

14. "Bitcoin price above $10,500 on US future listings", Omkar Godbole, Coindesk, *https://www.coindesk.com/Bitcoin-price-pushes-above-10500-on-u-s-futures-listings/*

15. "India's Central Bank Considering Creating Digital Rupee, Dislikes Bitcoin", Lisa Froelings, *https://cointelegraph.com/news/indias-central-bank-considering-creating-digital-rupee-dislikes-Bitcoin*

16. "The inside story of Mt. Gox Bitcoin's $460 million disaster", Robert McMillan, Wired, *https://www.wired.com/2014/03/Bitcoin-exchange/*

17. *https://decrypt.co/54366/mt-gox-victims-can-now-recoup-some-their-Bitcoin*

18. *https://en.wikipedia.org/wiki/Alexander_Vinnik*

19. *https://Bitcoin.org/en/download*

20. *https://Bitcoin.org/en/release/v0.12.0*

21. "Is Bitcoin anonymous? A complete beginner's guide", by Aron Van Wirdum, Bitcoin Magazine

22. *https://localBitcoin.com/blog/rising-tx-fees/*

23. *https://ycharts.com/indicators/Bitcoin_average_transaction_fee*

24. *https://blockchain.info/unconfirmed-transactions*

25. "How much of the BIP62 has been implemented?", *https://Bitcoin.stackexchange.com/questions/35904/*

26. "Bitcoin in Bloom: How IBLT allows Bitcoin to scale", Alex Gorale, *https://www.cryptocoinsnews.com/Bitcoin-in-bloom-how-iblts-allow-Bitcoin-scale*

27. "IBLT and Weak Block propagation Performance", *https://scalingBitcoin.org/hongkong2015/presentations/DAY1/3_block_propagation_1_rosenbaum.pdf*

28. *https://en.Bitcoin.it/wiki/P2Pool*

29. "IBLT and Weak Block propagation Performance", *https://scalingBitcoin.org/hongkong2015/presentations/DAY1/3_block_propagation_1_rosenbaum.pdf*

30. "A flexible limit: trading subsidy for larger blocks", Mark Friedenbach, *https://scalingBitcoin.org/hongkong2015/ presentations /DAY2/3_ tweaking_the_chain_2_friedenbach.pdf*

31. "The electricity to mine Bitcoin this year is bigger than the annual usage of 159 countries", Oscar-Williams Gruts, Business Insider, *http://www. businessinsider.com/Bitcoin-mining-electricity-usage-2017-11*

32. *https://www.msn.com/en-us/money/markets/why-china-s-crypto-crackdown-is-creating-tremendous-opportunities-for-miners-in-other-countries-according-to-industry-execs/ar-AAMvPjM*

33. *https://www.nytimes.com/2021/09/24/business/china-cryptocurrency-bitcoin.html*

34. "IRS blinks in Bitcoin probe, exempts Coinbase transactions under $20,000", Fortune Magazine, *http://fortune.com/2017/07/10 /Bitcoin-irs-coinbase/*

35. *https://bakong.nbc.org.kh*

36. *https://www.sanddollar.bs*

37. *https://news.yahoo.com/elon-musk-tesla-holds-1-201240876.html*

38. *https://www.coingecko.com/en/public-companies-Bitcoin*

CHAPTER 4

CONSENSUS MECHANISMS

Consensus in a network is the process of reaching an agreement on the subject in discussion by the participants in the network. Reaching or achieving the consensus means most of the nodes agree on the subject. Once a decision is reached, it is final. The democratic election process is a consensus process. The population places trust on the elected officials, and it is a trust model without a third party or higher authority figure. Simply, a consensus means that the answer is right if the majority thinks it is right.

For network applications, there are many consensus protocols. They are different for public, private, and federated networks. Public networks belong to the public and private networks have an owner. A federated network consists of several distinct, disconnected networks with a standardized operation so that a user from one network can send a message to the user in the other network, such as Yahoo! Messenger and MSN Messenger.

The same concept applies to databases, as well. A federated database system consists of several independent databases that can allow users to store and retrieve data from multiple noncontiguous databases with a single query. This is possible through a common standard, such as the user interface. Obviously, the consensus protocols for the public, private, and federated networks are very different. Even within the same type of network, there are many consensus protocols.

Blockchain is a specialized database. It uses special consensus mechanisms to establish trust. Bitcoin, a public blockchain, uses Proof of Work (PoW) as consensus mechanism for validation. PoW is a resource-intensive mechanism. According to some estimates, the Bitcoin network consumes power at an annual rate of 32 TWh—about as much as Denmark.[1,2] This is clearly not sustainable in the long run. In fact, the choice of using PoW as the Bitcoin consensus mechanism may not be a good choice for blockchains of other applications.

There are many other options of generic consensus mechanism that can be used as a trust model. The choice of consensus mechanism will not affect blockchain properties like distribution, cryptographic immutability, and transparency. Indeed, many other consensus/validation mechanisms available are equally effective and less energy intensive than PoW. They have received the attention of blockchain platform developers.

In a permissionless blockchain, such as Bitcoin and Ethereum, transaction validation and consensus formation work inherently together. In a permissioned blockchain protocol, one could separate the consensus formation from the validation of transactions.

Building consensus protocols belongs to a discipline of computer science. Consensus protocols evolved from cryptosystems and other security mechanisms. Their assumptions, security models, and logic/reasoning must endure serious challenges. Developing consensus protocols is like engineering cryptographic systems, which requires experience in cryptography, security, and the theory of distributed systems. All aspects of their performance and their resilience to actual attacks or network failures are important.

Building a consensus protocol is a difficult task. Among the recent flurry of blockchain-consensus protocols, many have not progressed past the stage of a paper-based description. A consensus protocol must perform under a wide range of adversarial conditions on the nodes and the network, including malicious attacks.

There are many possible consensus models. In fact, no single consensus model can fit all the applications. Some most discussed consensus models are PoW, PoS, Synchronous or Asynchronous Byzantine Agreement, Byzantine Altruistic Rational Fault Tolerance, and Federated Byzantine Agreement.

Different cryptocurrencies use different consensus protocols. It is safe to say that the fate of the cryptocurrency depends largely on the success of its consensus protocol. A protocol may look great on paper, but when put into practice, it does not perform as expected. Detailed analyses and formal argumentation are necessary to gain confidence that a protocol achieves its goal. In fact, many cryptocurrencies may fail because their consensus mechanism may not endure the real-world challenges.

For the private blockchain applications, such as blockchain applications offered by financial institutions, where the trust already exists, the traditional trust mechanism is preferred over the cryptographic consensus mechanism. The traditional trust mechanism can be an easier way to integrate blockchain applications into the existing financial system. A combination of the traditional trust mechanism and the cryptographic consensus mechanism can offer the advantages of both worlds.

4.1 PROOF OF WORK VS. PROOF OF STAKE

The Bitcoin blockchain uses Proof of Work (PoW) as the consensus protocol, which is an elaborative process that the miners do to validate the transactions. It requires significant computing power, thus requiring considerable electricity resources and making it ecologically unfriendly. This process is one of the major downsides of Bitcoin mining, but it provides security to the Bitcoin system. In Chapter 2, we discussed the reason why the PoW uses so much energy. Because PoW requires large resources, an attacker also needs to have comparable resources to launch an attack. In this sense, any method to reduce the resources is not compatible with the security using the basic PoW methodology.

To overcome the energy consumption problem in PoW, some modified PoW systems allow transactions to include a hash of a recent block known to a transaction sender. The nodes will reject the transaction without the hash of reference block.

A popular alternative consensus mechanism is the Proof of Stake (PoS). In PoS, the user's ownership stake in the system is used as a security deposit in the validating process instead of using the brute force of computing power in the PoW mining process. The rationale is that one is unlikely to attack something of which he himself is the biggest stakeholder.[3]

PoW and PoS are two opposite mechanisms on validating the blocks. *Block mining* is the process of solving a computational challenge imposed by a PoW protocol. *Block minting* is the process of collateralized validation in a PoS protocol. The word "minting" implies that you need to have currency reserve as a backup to mint your coins. It is the same concept that some central banks have a gold reserve to back up their printing of the national currency. In the PoS system, the minter put an ownership stake in the system as a security deposit.

Sometimes, PoS is also called *virtual mining*. PoS miners do not receive new coins as a reward as an incentive, but rather transaction fees.[4] They are virtual miners or validators. If they do not follow the rules, they can lose their deposits. The downside of PoS implementation is that it is more vulnerable to attacks than PoW.

The PoS consensus is not as objective as the PoW consensus. In an objective consensus protocol, a new node equipped with only the knowledge of the protocol definitions must arrive at the same state as the rest of the network. While this is true in the PoW consensus, it is not true in the PoS consensus. This is because, in the PoW consensus, the new node will always regard the blockchain with the highest computational difficulty as the valid chain. Forks pose no threat to PoW because they cannot pass the consensus rules.

In the PoS system, it is possible that two or more nodes can come to two different but equally valid conclusions due to the asynchronous nature of the network because the arrival order of the transactions varies among the nodes.[5] In addition, because of the low amount of resources required, miners can mine multiple blocks simultaneously to make sure that one of the blocks will win. No matter which fork prevails, the miner always gets the reward without any penalty. This is the "Nothing at Stake" problem. In this sense, the PoS system is more chaotic.

In addition, the PoS genesis block members can always launch a fork with an alternate transaction history and take over the original fork, no matter how long the blockchain is. Therefore, the PoS scheme weakens its decentralization and mathematical soundness. To prevent long-range forks from occurring, a PoS system needs to implement subjectivity by combining protocol rules with the social-driven security.

However, some may argue that in the PoW scheme, as the mining process becomes more resource intensive, the nodes with a high hashing power will always dominate. Eventually, a few miners with a high hashing power will mine all the blocks. This is a form of centralization in a decentralized system. Therefore, PoW is not perfect either.

PoS is a viable alternative to PoW for certain applications, although it has not been proven as trustworthy in the field as PoW. PoS cryptocurrencies take precautionary measures to prevent the "Nothing at Stake" vulnerability. A recent development in PoS is the so-called Delegated PoS system or DPoS.[6] It provides a solution to the "Nothing at Stake" problem and prevents short-range attacks on the system.

In the DPoS system, only the elected delegates can earn PoS revenue from running a full node. They vote for the consensus instead of the delegates themselves. The voting power of the delegates depends on their stake in the network, measured by how many coins they own. The idea is that the nodes with a high stake have the best interest to maintain the functionality of the system. The voting is in real-time to achieve consensus. The elected delegates can create blocks and prevent non-trusted parties from participating. Each time they generate a block, they receive rewards as payment. The delegates can also vote out elected delegates if they do not do their job. In this way, the delegates who try to take advantage of the "Nothing at Stake" will be voted out soon enough. Like the miners in Bitcoin, they are unable to change transaction details. However, they can prevent specific transactions from being included in the next block. Such a consensus mechanism is extremely fast. To produce a block takes mere seconds.

The downside is that DPoS makes the network more centralized. The nodes with higher stakes can assert more control over the network. Currently, several digital currencies using PoS consensus include Peercoin, Nxt, Novacoin, BlackCoin, and BitShares.[7]

4.2 PoW AND PoS HYBRID

A compromise solution is to develop a scheme with the combined advantages of the PoW and PoS schemes and to avoid their pitfalls. There are many ways to combine PoW and PoS. In one of the proposed PoW/PoS hybrid schemes, PoW is used for the distribution of new coins, while PoS is used to secure transactions. This type of blockchain is called a *hybrid blockchain*.

How to achieve the balance between the benefits and pitfalls of the two consensus mechanisms is the tradeoff between resources and security. A hybrid PoW/PoS solution is safe against long-range attacks provided there is enough hashing power in the network. This is because mining (creation of new coins) is for the long range, and minting (validation of transactions) is for the short range. The inclusion of PoW blocks into a blockchain can protect against attacks. However, when a blockchain is aged, there will be more minting and less mining. The weight of PoS will be heavier. Therefore, the best combination of PoW/PoS at one point may not be the best later. Currently, there are few cryptocurrencies using the hybrid PoW/PoS blockchain. Espers (ESP) and Swisscoin (SIC) are two examples.[8,9]

Another hybrid method is to alternate the use of PoW and PoS blocks. When forming a PoW block, the staking is deactivated, and when forming a PoS block, the staking is activated. The PoS blocks work as "checkpoints."

This is a check and balance system. The high stakeholders check and balance the PoW miners with high hashing power. To mine PoS blocks, the stakeholders need to sign using their private keys. If there are several blocks at the same height, they can only sign one of them. To finalize a block, two-thirds of the validators in the active validator pool need to commit for that checkpoint. Once a block finalized, even a majority of the validators working together cannot roll back the block without taking a substantial economic loss.

Ethereum developed Casper to change validation scheme from PoW to a hybrid PoW/PoS scheme. In the hybrid Ethereum system, Ethereum alternates between the PoW and PoS. In its first version, only every 100th block uses the PoS consensus as a checkpoint. The checkpoint utilizes the concept of block validators.[10] Anyone depositing Ether can become a validator who will be able to participate in the PoS consensus process. The size of a validator in the active validator pool refers to the amount of Ether that they deposited. Two-thirds of validators weighed by deposited amounts select one of the newly formed chains as the correct chain, rather than the longest chain. The selected chain is the chain containing the justified checkpoint of the greatest height. To resist majority attacks, Casper punishes deviations from the protocol by withholding rewards and locking funds from misbehaving validators. The valuator's entire deposit can be lost. Such a penalty is greater than the mining reward, thus PoS provides stronger security incentive than PoW.

Once the checkpoint is in place, the blocks before the checkpoints are all frozen. PoW does not have to validate the blocks before the last checkpoint. This greatly reduces the resources required for the PoW. PoW becomes less resource intensive and can produce blocks faster. This also allows the network to scale more efficiently by partitioning a large database into smaller parts. The PoS checkpoints also make the 51% attack more difficult. Since the PoW is less resource intensive, the block reward is reduced from 5 ETH to 3 ETH. This has an added benefit of reduced inflation, which can make ETH more valuable.

If Ethereum uses PoW, it still has a scaling problem. Ethereum can process 10 - 30 transactions per second; although faster than the 4 transactions per second of Bitcoin, this still pales in comparison to the processing power of VISA. It is still far from sufficient for large-scale applications. Ethereum is testing a sharding technique to improve the transaction speed.[11] *Sharding* splits the network into small partitions known as *shards*, with each piece containing its own independent state and transaction history. The performance of the transaction speed of sharding still remains to be seen.

4.3 dBFT, AN ALTERNATIVE TO PoW, AND PoS

There are different ways to power the blockchain besides PoW and PoS, which have their advantages and drawbacks. PoW is resource-intensive in terms of both electricity and computing power. PoS requires far less electricity and less powerful computer hardware. However, the wallet staking coins needs to be always online, which could be vulnerable to hackers. Furthermore, many people think that it is not a fair system because whoever owns more gets more rewards.

We have already discussed the fork problem of PoW and PoS. If blockchain technology becomes widely adopted in the financial sector with large-scale applications involving billions of dollars, such as a national digital currency and stock trading, the fork problem will be amplified, able to disrupt the financial system and cause disasters. The financial system will not be able to tolerate this ever-lurking possibility of the blockchain splitting into two alternative versions. Furthermore, even the fastest PoS blockchain out there can accommodate a few hundred transactions per second, very different from today's credit cards' transaction rate; the need for an alternative is clear. That is why some developers are searching for better solutions.

The Delegated Byzantine Fault Tolerance (dBFT) algorithm is one of these solutions. Consensus protocols for tolerating Byzantine faults provide attractive alternatives. While consensus is easy in the absence of faults, it becomes complicated when faults are present.[12]

The name of the dBFT is derived from a paper published by Lamport et al. in 1982, entitled "The Byzantine Generals' Problem," which is a game theory in computer science.[13,14,15] A real-life example of the Byzantine Generals Problem is the nine Supreme Court Justices during Obama administration, split 4–5 between being conservative and liberal. To achieve a consensus in the Supreme Court can be a Byzantine Generals' Problem.

Leslie's paper discussed the reliability of a computer system to handle the fault caused by the Byzantine Generals' Problem that gives conflicting information. A fault is a failure or error. Failure tolerance means the system is tolerant of failure or error. In a distributed system, faults can happen in the network, crashed servers, delays in transmission, and malicious attacks. When a fault happens, the outputs can give conflicting information.

There are many ways to tolerate faults. Early isolation of the fault in a containment zone or a built-in redundancy can prevent the fault from propagating and eventually breaking down the system. The way to avoid this is early detection and possibly the early correction of the fault.

Several algorithms have been developed to make the system Byzantine fault tolerant. By using the dBFT to achieve consensus, the relationship between different blockchain nodes is rearranged so that the entire network becomes almost invulnerable to the Byzantine Generals' Problem, while still being able to achieve consensus if a malicious node attempts to cause harm.

To do so, the nodes are divided into two categories: professional nodes and ordinary nodes. The professional nodes run a node to gain extra income (equivalent to miners in the Bitcoin blockchain). The user nodes are ordinary nodes. A delegated voting process by ordinary nodes appoints the professional nodes. Therefore, the term "delegated" is used.

The professional nodes have the responsibility of block verification. First, a professional node builds a block and broadcasts its version of the blockchain to the network. If two-thirds of the other nodes agree with the information, the consensus is achieved, and a block is verified. Otherwise, a different professional node is appointed to broadcast its blockchain version. This process repeats itself until a consensus can be established. This process effectively blocks the propagation of Byzantine fault. For the safety and security critical systems, it is important to prove the effectiveness of blocking the fault propagation to an acceptable level.

In view of all the potential issues of PoW and PoS, dBFT presents an attractive alternative for the blockchain application. It provides swift transaction verification times, de-incentivizes most attack vectors, and upholds a single blockchain version with no risk of forks or alternative blockchain records emerging (regardless of how much computing power or coins an attacker possesses). Ethereum's upgrade, Casper, has incorporated Byzantine fault tolerance (BFT) into PoS. A Byzantine consensus is extremely fast: it can process about 80,000 transactions per second with very low latency overhead.

In reality, PoW is just a variation of the BFT design, with an emphasis on peer-to-peer networking and cryptographic authentication.

4.4 PAXOS AND RAFT: CONSENSUS PROTOCOLS FOR DISTRIBUTED SYSTEMS

In a distributed system, as the name implies, data processing is done on multiple servers. Servers may crash, and messages sent to the network may be lost or delayed so that they will arrive in different orders as they were sent. If most of the servers are up, the system is functioning. Each site of the data processing is considered as a replicated state machine. Even these state machines are replicated, and the same inputs fed into different state machines may give different outputs. There is a need to have a consensus mechanism to guarantee that the results are consistent.

A state machine takes inputs to produce outputs. When a state machine is replicated, it is known as a *replicated state machine*. State machine replication is a fundamental approach in distributed computing for building fault tolerant systems. A system of replicated state machines should consist of at least three state machines, the replicated log, and the consensus module. When several replicated state machines receive an input for execution, the log of each state machine records the output. When the program to execute the command is identical in each state machine, one can say that the same output will be produced. However, this is not always true. The job of the consensus model is to manage the logs to ensure that they are properly replicated. If one of the replicated state machines is faulty, the other two produce identical output. The identical output can be accepted by the consensus. The clients interact with the replicated state machine through the consensus module. The clients make requests to, and get responses only from, the leader server. This means that the replicated state machine service can only be available when a leader has been successfully elected and is alive.

Consensus used in the replicated state machines is different from the conventional idea of consensus. The conventional consensus is to reach an agreed single value. It is the single decree consensus. However, in a replicated state machine, the goal of consensus is to find the agreement to a replicated log. A replicated log contains a series of values of the outputs. In other words, such a consensus protocol must integrate several instances of single decree consensus within the replicated state machine to agree on a series of values forming the log.

Paxos has revolutionized the distributed systems by providing a functional fault-tolerant consensus protocol. Paxos was first introduced in 1989, long before the invention of Bitcoin. It provides a simple algorithm to deal with the challenges of asynchrony, process crash/recovery, and message loss in a distributed system. After the introduction of Paxos, there appeared other distributed consensus algorithms, such as Raft, with improvements over Paxos.

Both Paxos and Raft are asymmetric consensus protocols. That is, at any given time, one server acts as the leader and the others accept its decisions. In such a system, clients communicate with the leader.[16]

In the early 2000s, Google faced increasing service downtimes induced by fault in its cloud-computing platform, Google File System (GFS). GFS, a cloud-computing platform, deals mainly with big data storage, processing, and serving. Google was searching for a fault tolerant coordination solution for its GFS. It adopted the Paxos protocol and called it the Google Chubby. The Google Chubby project boosted interest in the industry about using Paxos protocols for fault-tolerant coordination. Since then, Paxos protocols quickly grew in number to become the protocol of choice of the consensus and coordination in the cloud-computing platform.

Other industry leaders, such as Amazon and Microsoft, also use the Paxos consensus algorithm for their cloud computing services, i.e., Amazon Web Service and Microsoft Azure Services (Windows Fabric).

As the first consensus protocol for the distributed system, Paxos is both hard to understand and difficult to implement. The reason is that the protocol is detached from real-world issues and use cases in the implementation. The proofs in theory may not hold in practice. This requires extensive proofs and verification during the Paxos implementations.

Over the time, many versions of improved Paxos appeared. Raft is one of the most notable improvements.[17] It is a consensus algorithm to enhance the understandability of the Paxos protocol. Consensus in a Raft system has a narrow definition of the assurance of the validity, agreement, and termination, which are the three important properties in a distributed system.

Raft uses decomposition to improve understandability. Decomposition is the process of separating functions like leader election, log replication, and safety. Raft also improves the ease of implementation of the Paxos protocol by embedding the module within the replicated state machines.[18] Facebook's HydraBase uses the Raft protocol.

Once a server becomes the leader, it becomes available to serve the clients requests. These requests are commands that are to be committed to the replicated state machine. For every received command, the leader assigns a term and index to the command, which gives a unique identifier within the server's logs and appends the command to its own log.

A fundamental difference between Raft and Paxos is that Raft implements strong leadership. Raft integrates leader election as an essential part of the consensus protocol. Once a leader has been elected, the leader will drive all decision-making within the protocol. Only one leader can exist at a single time and log entries can only flow from the leader to the followers.

4.5 PROOF OF CONCEPT

Microsoft announced yet another blockchain validation scheme called Proof of Concept (PoC). It is a framework for blockchain deployments in Microsoft's Azure cloud. Microsoft takes the burden of building the blockchain, including the hashing and signing, so that its customers can focus on developing desirable features through smart contracts without worrying about the inner structure of the blockchain itself. By doing so, Microsoft makes the task of building Web applications extremely simple. It is possible to create the blockchain application without writing any code.

The PoC framework provides users with the ability to publish the underlying code and Azure services using Azure Resource Manager (ARM) templates. Users can quickly prepare Application Programming Interfaces (APIs), Web applications, integrations, and SQL databases.[19] The SQL database can be configured to collect on-chain data. The blockchain data is replicated into an off-chain store so that users can leverage their existing skill sets to enable additional capabilities. Using Microsoft's Azure Event Hubs, users can also build additional Azure services like Azure Stream Analytics and Azure Data Lakes.

REFERENCES

1. "Bitcoin's insane energy consumption, explained", Timothy Lee, *https://arstechnica.com/tech-policy/2017/12/bitcoins-insane-energy-consumption-explained/*

2. "Bitcoin energy consumption index", *https://digiconomist.net/Bitcoin-energy-consumption*

3. "Proof of Stake", Bitcoin Wiki, *https://en.Bitcoin.it/wiki/Proof_of_Stake*

4. "PoW vs. PoS: Basic mining guide", *https://blockgeeks.com/guides/proof-of-work-vs-proof-of-stake/*

5. "Understanding the basics of a PoS security model", Terdermint, *https://blog.cosmos.network/understanding-the-basics-of-a-proof-of-stake-security-model-de3b3e160710*

6. "Delegated Proof of Stake consensus", *https://bitshares.org/technology/delegated-proof-of-stake-consensus/*

7. *https://coinsutra.com/cryptocurrency-dividends/*

8. "What is the hybrid blockchain? PoW and PoS explained", Chiboyanyki, *https://swisscoinhub.com/what-is-hybrid-blockchain/*

9. *https://espers.io/*

10. "What is Ethereum Casper Protocol", Ameer Rosic, *https://blockgeeks. com/guides/ethereum-casper/*

11. "Ethereum will soon test sharding tech to fix scaling issues, Vitalik Buterin hints", *https://thenextweb.com/hardfork/2018/02/23/ethereum-vitalik-buterin-sharding*

12. "The Swirlds hashgraph consensus algorithm: Fair, fast, Byzantine fault tolerance", L. Baird, Swirlds Tech Report, *https://www.swirlds.com/ downloads/SWIRLDS-TR-2016-01.pdf*

13. "The Byzantine Generals' Problem": Leslie Lamport et. al., *https:// lamport.azurewebsites.net/pubs/byz.pdf*

14. *https://medium.com/loom-network/understanding-blockchain-fundamentals-part-1-byzantine-fault-tolerance-245f46fe8419*

15. "The next 700 BFT protocols. ACM Transactions on Computer Systems", P. Aublin et al., 2015.

16. "Yet another visit to Paxos", C. Cachin, Research Report RZ 3754, IBM Research, Nov. 2009.

17. "Consensus in the Cloud: Paxos Systems Demystified". Ailijiang et. al. *https://www.cse.buffalo.edu//~demirbas/publications/cloudConsensus.pdf*

18. "Raft explained", Titus von Koller, *http://container-solutions.com/raft-explained-part-1-the-consenus-problem/*

19. *https://azure.microsoft.com/en-us/es/sql-database/*

CHAPTER 5

ALTCOINS

Bitcoin's market capitalization reached a whopping $2 trillion by early 2022. Nothing in financial history has seen such explosive growth of an asset in such a short period of time.

Bitcoin's success has inspired many competing cryptocurrencies called *altcoins,* or alternative cryptocurrencies. Today, there are over 2,000 cryptocurrencies. Altcoins try to distinguish themselves with some competitive advantages. Most of them are not popular and have small market capitalizations, volumes, and limited circulation. The top four cryptocurrencies in terms of the market capitalization are Bitcoin (~$800 billion), Ethereum (~$312 billion), Tether (~$80 billion), Binance Coin (~$61 billion), and U.S. Dollar Coin (~$52 billion) (as of March 2022).[1]

Altcoins differentiate themselves by using different hash algorithms, timestamping, and block sizes, or sometimes, different concepts and philosophies. For example, Litecoin was the first cryptocurrency to use Scrypt as a hashing algorithm. Ripple was designed as the first peer-to-peer debt transfer currency. Zcash uses Zero Knowledge-Proof for authentication. Antshares uses delegated Byzantine Fault Tolerance in place of PoW and PoS. Other Altcoins' designs tried to avoid or address Bitcoin's shortcomings.

Some of these altcoins have their merits and may have bright futures, but most of them may fade away over time. We will discuss some of the most important ones, not so much from the perspective of market capitalization, but from the technology point of view.

Some cryptocurrencies, like Ethereum and Ripple, are not intended to be cryptocurrencies alone but are tokens for enterprise solutions. They are software platforms intended for the development of new applications. Their creation opens a completely new branch of blockchain applications. In fact, their long-term impact may be much more than the cryptocurrency itself.

Cryptocurrencies are tokens in their blockchains. A *token* in a blockchain application is something of value that is held electronically and transferred at will without a third-party's involvement. Tokens are like coupons issued by stores or the tokens in the amusement park. Blockchain application's creator/owner or the consensus of the participants define the rules for the transfer of tokens. For example, the Bitcoin blockchain has rules to specify how many Bitcoins can be created, how many Bitcoins are rewarded to the miners executing validation of the blocks, and how the Bitcoin transactions are performed.

In a decentralized blockchain application, such as the Bitcoin blockchain, the consensus of most of the participants decides any change in the rules, and the miners control and execute the rules. In a centralized blockchain application, most of the participants and the owner of the application are usually the same. The participants/owners define, control, and execute the rules (such as the banks running the nodes).

5.1 LITECOINS – A LIGHTER VERSION OF BITCOIN

Charlie Lee, an MIT graduate, launched Litecoin in 2011.[2] It was one of the early cryptocurrencies following Bitcoin. In 2022, its market capitalization was around $8 billion. In every aspect, Litecoin is like Bitcoin: an open P2P digital currency not controlled by a central authority. The major difference is that Litecoin uses Scrypt as a Proof of Work, instead of the SHA-256 hash function as in the Bitcoin network.

Scrypt uses few resources, so that even consumer-grade computers are powerful enough to mine Litecoins. Other differences include it has a faster block generation rate and a faster transaction confirmation. The Litecoin platform generates a block every 2.5 minutes, instead of the 10 minutes required by Bitcoin. Therefore, the confirmation time is shorter for Litecoins. This also implies that miners receive Litecoins faster than do miners of Bitcoin. The downside is that the Litecoin blockchain grows faster and the miners need to have more storage space than Bitcoin miners.

The Litecoin mining equipment is less expensive than that of the Bitcoin. Anyone with a computer connected to the Internet can mine Litecoins. This makes the Litecoins more decentralized than Bitcoin because the barrier to entry is lower. For the same reason, the Litecoin network is more prone to attack than the Bitcoin network. It would also be easier for the attacker to double-spend Litecoins compared to Bitcoins.

Faster block generation means there are fewer temporary forks. When a block is attached to the blockchain, all the temporary forks dissipate. However, the faster transaction time allows some miners to take advantage by generating blocks with fewer transactions to be ahead of everybody else and win the mining rewards. Like Bitcoin, Litecoin's block mining reward halves every 840,000 blocks. It started with 50 coins per block. In 2018, the coin reward is 25 coins per block. It decreased to 12.5 coins in 2019, the number still given in 2022.

The faster block rate also has implications for the miners' incentive in the difficulty retargeting. It can lead to instability in difficulty adjustment. The difficulty and hash powers of the current network are two levers to control the overhead of blocks. It can mean more monetary inflation and a slower transaction time.

The total number of Litecoins ever to exist is 84 million, four times the number of Bitcoins. Since Litecoin generates blocks four times faster than Bitcoin and the maximum number of Litecoins is four times that of Bitcoins, the monetary inflation of Litecoin follows the same trajectory as that of Bitcoin – halving the mining rewards every four years.

5.2   ZCASH – A TOKEN WITH PRIVACY

Zcash (ZEC) is a decentralized and open-source altcoin launched in late 2016. Zcash offers privacy, extra security, and selective transparency of transactions.[3] It claims to have the best privacy among cryptocurrency by using the Zero-Knowledge-Proof (ZKP) construction called a zk-SNARK.[4]

Zcash derives its name from ZKP authentication. (Please refer to Chapter 2 for the discussion on ZKP.) The privacy option allows businesses and consumers to control who can see the details of their transactions. ZKP construction has the advantage of ensuring the validity of transactions and securing ledger of balances without giving out any other information. Bitcoin lacks this feature.

Most cryptocurrencies do not hide the amount of the transaction and the parties involved in the transaction. The parties involved are represented by their addresses. However, in the exchange, your addresses are linked to your bank accounts. Therefore, privacy is not guaranteed.

Some cryptocurrencies, such as Bitshares, can hide the transaction amount, but not the receiver and recipient. Others, such as Monero, create many dummy addresses as well as inputs and outputs for each transaction to hide the identity. However, it is not 100% private.

Zcash uses cryptographic Zero-Knowledge Proofs to protect both the amount and recipient of shielded transactions. Zcash also allows for transparent transactions, which do not provide any privacy protections at all.

5.3   RIPPLE – A DIGITAL EQUIVALENT OF SWIFT

Ripple is not a cryptocurrency in the traditional sense. Ripple Labs, the creator of Ripple, created 100 billion XRP (Ripple's currency) at Ripple's inception in 2012.[5] It releases XRP over time according to its release strategy. As of early 2022, there were 30 billion XRPs in circulation. It operates based on a Ripple Transaction Protocol (RTXP), a real-time global settlement network that offers an instant, secure, and low-cost international payment system.[6]

The development of the Ripple payment protocol predates the development of Bitcoin. Ryan Fugger proposed the system in 2004.[7] He intended to create a decentralized monetary system that could empower individuals to create their own money.

All money in Ripple is either in the debt or credit line. Transactions simply consist of shifting balances from the payer account to the receiver account. This works in the same way as gift cards. You buy a gift card to create credit. Only the people who have credit in the Ripple system can join the network, and so everyone can trust each other.[8]

Ripple also works like the SWIFT, an acronym for the Society for Worldwide Interbank Financial Telecommunications, which is a system that handles the transfer of money internationally.[9,10] SWIFT is a messaging network that financial institutions use to transmit instructions for money transfers through a standardized system of codes.

When you want to wire money to another person in a different country, you go to the bank to deposit the money. In doing so, you create credit. You then give the instruction for the money transfer, such as the transfer amount, and the recipient's name, address, and bank account information. The bank then sends a message to the destination bank to advise of such a wire. Then, the recipient can withdraw the money from the destination bank. The bank does not actually transfer the money. The bank only sends a message describing the transfer. The two banks settle their transactions later. Ripple works the same way. The party who interfaces with the customer is the gateway, equivalent to the bank in the real world. Ripple records the transactions in its distributed ledger.

Obviously, this type of transaction requires trust. In the Ripple system, there are agents of trust. In the SWIFT system, the banks work as the agents of trust. In the gift card system, the gift card issuing party works as the trust agent. In the Ripple system, if the transaction parties do not have a mutually known trust agent, Ripple will find a trust agent acceptable by the parties of the transactions. The Ripple algorithm tries to find the shortest trust path between the gateways. Ripple recruited a list of organizations to work as trust agents who validate the transactions. Among them are Microsoft, MIT, the Swedish ISP Bahnoff, CGI, WorldLink, and ST Corporation. Currently, there are roughly 166 validators in Ripple's validator registry, which lists their public keys. The non-validator nodes are called the *monitoring nodes*. Even so, because of the large number of validators, Ripple is still considered a decentralization system. There is no truly central authority running the system.

By using a chain of trust, money can be exchanged between people who do not know each other at all. For the first few years, only a very small community used the Ripple system. This is because, without a blockchain type of technology, the system allowed only trusted people to join the network. In 2012, when the system adapted the blockchain technology with Ripple (XRP), the trust problem was resolved, and the system expanded worldwide.

Ripple introduces the concept of the *gateway*, which is a link between the XRP ledger to the outside world. Ripple enlisted financial institutions to be the gateways. The gateway also serves as the link in the trust chain to make a transaction. Since there are many gateways to choose from, the system still preserves a measure of decentralization comparable to mining pools. Only when the assets move in and out of the Ripple network do the gateways convert XRP to the fiat currency and vice versa. Within the Ripple network, all transactions take place in XRP. In this way, Ripple operates like a national domain, where XRP is its currency. The gateways are like money exchanges. Only when the external transactions are involved is XRP converted into other currencies.

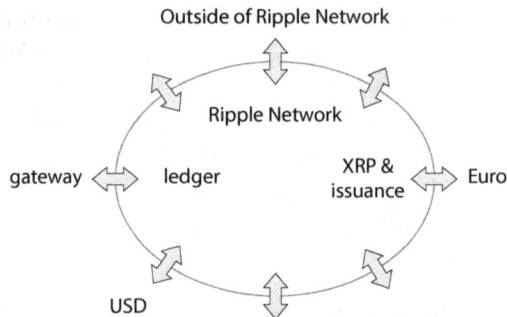

FIGURE 5.1 A Ripple network.

The Ripple network keeps a public ledger of accounts, balances, and IOUs. The network constantly updates the ledger and distributes to all the servers in the Ripple network around the world. There are two kinds of assets in the Ripple network: XRP and issuance. *Issuance* is the digital balance that represents assets held by an issuer. A gateway sends the issuance to the address of the customer, the issuer, who deposits an asset or money to the XRP Ledger from outside of Ripple network. Thus, issuance is like a receipt of a deposit of an asset. XRP is a coin to trade the issuance in the Ripple network. When the issuer decides to send the asset to someone outside of the Ripple network or withdraw it, the process goes through a gateway. Figure 5.1 shows the Ripple network, its gateways, and assets in the network. So, in the Ripple network, there are only two ways to create credit: buying XRP using fiat currency at the gateway or receiving XRP from someone. One can send XRP from one Ripple address to another over the Ripple network, just like Bitcoin in the Bitcoin network.

Transactions in XRP are settled immediately, and the Ripple network instantaneously updates the ownership of the actual asset changes. The transaction verification is by consensus among members of the network. Transactions in Ripple incur smaller transaction fees, paid in XRP. The servers agree on changes by consensus. Any computer can be a server by running the free software, and the Ripple rules govern the transactions.

Ripple's mechanism for keeping track of balances is like Bitcoin. Transactions are done using addresses, public and private keys, and modifications to the database through digital signatures. Ripple private and public keys use the same elliptic curve cryptography (ECC) as Bitcoin. ECC is a cryptography based on the algebraic structure of the elliptic curve over finite fields.[11] One can use the same private and public keys to sign transactions and messages in the Bitcoin and Ripple networks.

Ripple does not use PoW or PoS for its consensus. Individual nodes decide which version of a new ledger to accept by polling the nodes around them to see what the majority opinion is, allowing the network to settle on a single choice. The process is much faster than Bitcoin's block confirmation.

This consensus approach has a risk of causing chain fragmentation where two parts of the network settle on irreconcilable transaction histories. It is vulnerable to attack, which employs various forms of proxy and IP address spoofing techniques that pretend to be a million separate nodes that overwhelm the opinion of the rest of the network through sheer numbers.

To avoid this risk, Ripple introduced a Unique Node List (UNL).[12] Instead of taking the consensus from the wider, unknown network, the UNL of a node provides the consensus. The Ripple Protocol Consensus Algorithm (RPCA) makes the UNL flexible. Each node can choose its own trusted nodes in its UNL. Different nodes have different UNLs. A typical UNL contains 100+ nodes (i.e., their public keys). Ripple provides a recommended list of nodes that can serve in a UNL.

There is a requirement that the pairs of validating nodes need to have a minimum number of nodes in common. Otherwise, the ledger would fork. Ripple states that the overlap should be at least 1/5 of the size of the larger list. Since Ripple is a trusted public network, most nodes will connect to probably 10 to 100 large organizations running validators, and these organizations will connect to each other. This makes a split reasonably unlikely.

By using UNLs, Ripple essentially duplicates the original confined trust environment a million times over the Ripple network. To ensure the trustworthiness of the UNLs, Ripple's platform runs auditing software to analyze the UNLs and report on potential degenerate lists so they can be corrected.

A node chooses to accept the ledger, which is validated by the consensus of its UNL, under the assumption that the nodes are not likely to work together to push a fraudulent ledger by consensus. Once the nodes reach the consensus, all nodes update their ledgers to the consensus ledger.

The UNL system also ensures that the network is tightly linked. Every node connects to every other node in millions of ways, so all nodes are only, at most, a few hops away from each other. Thus, any fragmentation would rapidly resolve itself.

Ripple builds its ledger in a ledger chain differently from Bitcoin's block in the blockchain. Instead of keeping all the transaction history, the Ripple ledger consists of a transaction tree and a state tree. The transaction tree shows the transactions that have taken place since the last ledger. The state tree contains all the information of the account balances and credit limits in the Ripple system.

The Ripple ledger does not carry the transaction history beyond the last ledger. This greatly simplifies the information to be stored in the ledger chain. The node also needs to deposit a minimum balance of 200 XRP to create an address and an additional 50 XRP to create a credit line. This is a strong incentive against bloating the ledger state with many addresses. As a result, most Ripple clients are fully participating nodes, as the cost of full participation is small enough to be negligible for most computers. This ensures a greater degree of decentralization.

The lack of mining in Ripple is both a strength and weakness in the system. Without mining, nodes cannot receive a reward by doing the work. Instead, the Ripple platform started with all 100 billion XRP that will ever exist. The developer of Ripplepays transaction fees out of the 55 billion XRPs it is holding in reserve.

Without mining, XRP is deflationary, since the existing XRP unit can only decrease. The number of XRPs starts at 100 billion and then gradually decreases as some XRPs are lost. This means the XRP coin price can increase over time.

One can trade anything, e.g., USD, CAD, gold, or even airline miles in the Ripple network. For example, a seller of airline miles can deposit a miles' credit at a gateway. A buyer deposits USD at another gateway. The trade is carried out in the Ripple network.

Transactions on a distributed network with public ledgers is faster, cheaper, lower risk, and much better in almost every way possible than centralized, pre-Internet correspondent banking messaging networks such as SWIFT.

Ripple also has the potential for greater integration with the existing banking system, as its currency exchange is a service that even existing financial businesses will quickly be able to benefit from. Many large banks are testing XRP in a blockchain trial.[13] For those who are afraid of the prospect of gateways defaulting or disappearing, or who wish the greater privacy that Bitcoin's trust-free anonymity offers, Bitcoin continues to be the best bet.

Regardless, the fact that Bitcoin now has a strong and compelling alternative makes it clear that the idea of cryptocurrency is here to stay. Ripple's technology can connect the world's ledger and networks without replacing the existing systems. It gives financial institutions full control and privacy over their transactions through RTXP.

5.4   ETHEREUM: THE SMART CONTRACT BLOCKCHAIN

Ethereum deserves more attention because it is the second most popular cryptocurrency behind Bitcoin.[14] It also distinguishes itself for being the first blockchain platform to run smart contracts. A *smart contract* is the coding on the blockchain that allows transactions to take place according to the rules defined in the contract. It can help deal with the uncertainty and complexity of the real world, while enhancing the reliability of transactions.

Today, Ethereum is the largest and most well established open-ended decentralized software platform. It has the second largest market capitalization of crypto currencies, after Bitcoin, at $312 billion in early 2022.

Vitalik Buterin and the Ethereum Foundation launched the Ethereum platform on July 30, 2015. Ethereum is a distributed blockchain platform that enables users to build and run Distributed Applications (Dapps).[15] Dapps execute smart contracts in the Ethereum blockchain. They are secure and free from downtime, fraud, control, or interference from third parties. The smart contracts automate many of the procedures that require human intervention today.

The cryptographic token Ether pays the service of execution of Dapps on Ethereum. In 2014, Ethereum launched a pre-sale of Ether with great success. The blockchain also allows people to carry out transactions in Ether.

Despite Bitcoin and Ethereum's commonalities in the concept of distributed ledgers and cryptography, they are different in many fundamental ways. The major difference is their purposes: Ethereum is not just a platform, but also a blockchain-based programming language, which allows developers to build and publish Dapps. Dapps for the Ethereum blockchain are like apps for cell phones.

Ethereum, as a platform, facilitates peer-to-peer contracts and applications via its own token. Anyone can go to *MyEtherwallet.com* and click the tab "Contract."[16] There, you can deploy a contract by entering your own code. This is not possible with Bitcoin.

The applications of Ethereum are not limited to the peer-to-peer network; they run in the cloud-computing environment as well. This has immense commercial applications. Ether can codify, decentralize, secure, and trade just about anything. This capability created a software foundry business. Like a semiconductor foundry that uses IPs to build application-specific circuits for customers, a software foundry uses Ether to build application-specific software for its customers. Companies interested in building Ethereum applications but without know-how or resources can outsource the project to software foundries.

The startup ConsenSys,[17] based in New York, offered Ethereum Blockchain as a Service (EBaaS) in early 2015 as a software foundry to develop decentralized services and applications that operate on the Ethereum blockchain both in the cloud and in peer-to-peer networks.

Software giant Microsoft formed a partnership with ConsenSys to offer customers of the Microsoft cloud-based enterprise computing service platform, called Azure, to develop cloud-based blockchain applications using EBaaS.[18]

The combination of cryptocurrency with distributed applications drastically differentiates Ethereum from Bitcoin. Ethereum brings blockchain technology to cloud computing. In doing so, Ethereum has created a massive, decentralized computing platform that merges the cloud with a peer-to-peer network, and many people call it a "world computer."

Ethereum is also a utility token, meaning it trades like any cryptocurrency yet powers the creation and execution of smart contracts. In real life, you can find many analogs. For example, petroleum can be traded as a commodity, but it can also power automobiles. In fact, Ether works as any kind of commodity. You can buy and sell Ether the same way as you can buy and sell coal. Coal can power steam engines, as Ether can power smart contracts.

Ethereum has created a rapidly growing ecosystem of software startups vying to build Dapps. These Dapps create markets, store registries of debts or promises, move funds in accordance with instructions given long in the past like a will or a futures contract, and many other things that have not been invented yet, all without a middleman or counterparty risk.

The programming language used by Ethereum is the Ethereum Script, also known as EtherScript. It writes agreements without ambiguity and is more precise than the agreements written in words. A smart contract written in the script can precisely define the terms and conditions governing the transfer of value and assets and automatically enforce the execution of the contract with the same script. The cryptocurrency Ether serves as the transfer media.

There are other less notable differences between Bitcoin and Ethereum. For example, the block time in Ethereum transactions is seconds rather than ten minutes as in Bitcoin. Their hash algorithms are also different.

Microsoft is not the only large company interested in working with Ethereum. Other large companies across different industries, such as JP Morgan Chase, Cisco, Bank of New York Mellon, Red Hat, CME Group, and Banco Santander, are working with Ethereum in one way or another, as are the Chinese Internet giants: Alibaba Cloud,[19] Tencent, and Wancloud. In fact, the Enterprise Ethereum Alliance (EEA) boasts a membership of over 150 companies and organizations and is becoming the largest open source block-chain initiative in the world.

Ethereum and Bitcoin are at the two opposite ends of the centralization and decentralization axis. Ethereum Foundation, the creator of the Ethereum platform, guides and controls the development of Ethereum applications. This is opposite from the creator of the Bitcoin platform, the Bitcoin Core, which cannot force any change in the Bitcoin platform to the Bitcoin community.

In the Bitcoin platform, most of the Bitcoin community needs to reach a consensus to implement any change. As a result, the Bitcoin community rarely reaches an agreement on many technical issues. This is probably also the reason that Ethereum, having a shorter history, has already implemented more hard forks than Bitcoin.

Less decentralization, however, does not diminish Ethereum's importance because the applications built using the Ethereum platform are still decentralized. In a way, decentralization takes a different meaning when referring to Ethereum.

In 2016, Ethereum had a hard fork. The token split into Ether Classic (ETC) and Ethereum (ETH). We will discuss the hard fork event in more detail later. The cap for the Ethereum Classic (ETC) issuance is roughly 230 million ETC, a much larger supply than that of Bitcoin. The block reward reduces by 20% for every 5,000,000 blocks created.

Ethereum (ETH), on the other hand, takes a different approach to control the ETH reward. Instead of reducing the mining reward, as in the case of Bitcoin, it increases the block time by design. The block time started to increase in mid-2017, and the increase has been exponential. Starting from Block 3.5 million, the next 100,000 blocks will have an average block interval of 25 seconds. Thereafter, the block interval increases to 35 seconds, 55 seconds, 95 seconds, and so on, for every 100,000 blocks created.

However, the mining reward does not change. This has the same effect as capping the supply because it takes longer to mine Ethereum. When the block time is doubled, the supply of ETH through mining per fixed period is halved.

In this way, the total supply of ETH will be capped around 100 million. However, Ethereum Foundation reserves the right to change the cap in the future. As of mid-2022, the total supply of ETH is above 120 million.[20] The Bitcoin supply change requires votes from the Bitcoin community, while in Ethereum, it is more centralized and can be decided by the Ethereum Foundation. This is another difference between Bitcoin and Ethereum in terms of decentralization. When Ethereum Foundation decides to make a change in the protocol, and if part of the Ethereum community does not agree, they can depart the Ethereum blockchain and cause a hard fork.

Ethereum is still using PoW for mining in 2022 but it is moving to PoS. Like Bitcoin, it also consumes a lot of energy, 4.2 TWh per year. Although this is not as much as Bitcoin mining (32 TWh), it is still substantial. By moving to PoS, Ethereum becomes more scalable, secure, and sustainable. However, such a move is a big technical challenge. PoS requires users to stake their ETH to become a validator in the network. Validators are responsible for maintaining system efficiency, participating in voting, and forming new blocks. PoS mining is based on the percentage of coins held by a miner. Please refer to Chapter 4 for more details of PoS. The transition to PoS will take place in three phases, with the last phase to be implemented in the first half of 2022.

It is also speculated that the switch to PoS could lead to an increase in the ETH price because fees will be reduced and the barrier to entry will be lowered. Ethereum's DeFi network will have the potential to grow significantly, and Ethereum's price will likely increase with it.

PoW is secure because an attacker needs to have significant hash power. Some wonder about the security level of PoS. However, PoS has a similar kind of safety guard to prevent attacks. An attacker needs to have a large stake to launch an effective attack. If the attack fails, he could lose his entire stake.

In Ethereum's short history, there have already been numerous hard forks and there are more changes to come. According to Ethereum's roadmap, the development of Ethereum has four stages: Frontier, Homestead, Metropolis, and Serenity. Each stage adds new features and improves the user-friendliness and security of the platform.[21]

Out of these changes or upgrades, Metropolis has received the most attention. Metropolis offers significant improvements to the Ethereum ecosystem. The implementation of Metropolis occurs in two phases: Byzantine and Constantinople. Some of the improvements are for the developers. The major improvements include ZK-SNARK (Zero-Knowledge Succinct Non-Interactive Argument of Knowledge), PoS/PoW hybrid, Revert, Returndata, and Account abstraction.

Zk-SNARKs are meant to improve transaction privacy. This feature is already available in the altcoin called Zcash. Ethereum developers are working together with the Zcash team to implement zero-knowledge proofs. We have discussed the PoW/PoS hybrid scheme in Chapter 4.

The Revert and Returndata options allow the smart contracts to go back to the original state without eating up all the *gas*, which is the cost of running the Ethereum Virtual Code (EVC) or commands to execute a transaction or contract.[22] The gas system is akin to the KWh for the electricity used to run an engine. The necessity of using gas instead of Ether to pay the cost of running EVC is that the price of charging the service of running the EVC will not inflate if Ethereum increases its value. When the ETH price increased by over 1,000% in 2017, running EVC became highly profitable (if it was priced in ETH).

A miner needs to obtain a certain amount of gas to perform an operation for a smart contract according to the amount of work. The amount of gas used depends on the smart contract. The exchange rate of gas to Ethereum also fluctuates. The gas system is similar to a household electricity bill that changes due to electricity usage and the unit price of a KWh. In the gas system, the smart contract (or the user) sets the amount of gas rather than the miner. Bitcoin miners prioritize transactions with the highest mining fees. The same is true of Ethereum. If the user sets the gas price limit too low, no miner will be interested in picking up the smart contract.

The gas price per transaction or contract is set up to deal with the Turing Complete nature of Ethereum and its Ethereum Virtual Machine Code (EVM). If there is not enough Ether in the account to perform the transaction or smart contract, then the transaction will not be processed. This can prevent attacks from infinite loops, encourage code efficiency, and make an attacker pay for the resources they use (such as the bandwidth, CPU, and calculations for storage.

Before the Metropolis upgrade, if the gas limit was set too low and not acceptable to the miner, the gas would still be used. This is like hiring a contractor to repair your garage door. If you find that the quote is too high and decide not to use the service, you will still have to pay for his visit. With the upgrade, the visit does not cost anything. Best of all, the Returndata option allows the contract user to know exactly why his contract fails.

Account abstraction allows users to define their wallet address, or the private key, in the form of a smart contract. By doing so, private keys controlling external accounts would be less susceptible to attacks against the signature scheme. It also adds other security schemes, such as hash ladders. Abstraction also allows contracts to pay for gas. A more complex contract pays more gas for execution. For example, the price to pay for a SHA-3 (Secure Hash Algorithm 3) operation is 20 gases. However, this price is not fixed. It can change due to supply and demand.

There are many other improvements. For example, light clients are important to many users who do not want to run a full wallet. Some prefer fast blockchain synchronization. Metropolis makes light clients more secure.

Casper is the software update for Metropolis. Its developers publish the smart contract on Ethereum, creating an official Casper account where anyone can deposit Ether if they want to engage in the virtual mining process.

Since the Ethereum blockchain is more an application platform than a cryptocurrency, it has multiple development tools: a Python-based Ethereum client called Pyethereum, C++ based Ethereum client called Cpp- Ethereum, and Go-based Ethereum client called Go-Ethereum or Goeth. The client allows one to communicate with the Ethereum network to create accounts, perform transactions, and more. Using these tools, developers can quickly develop Dapps for their particular use.

5.5 DAO HACKS AND ETHEREUM FORKS

A German company called Slock.it (the name is derived from the term "smart lock") used the Ethereum platform to create an app called the DAO (short for Decentralized Autonomous Organization). To connect the IoT to blockchain technology, Slock.it builds smart locks that let people share their properties (such as cars, boats, or apartments) in a decentralized version of Airbnb, called the Universal Sharing Network.

DAO, an Ethereum app, was the company's first project. It runs on the Ethereum platform and uses Ether as its transaction currency. At that time, DAO was the largest app on the Ethereum platform. Therefore, it gained substantial support from the Ethereum Foundation. Slock.it designed the DAO to automate organizational governance and decision-making. Individuals can work collaboratively on the DAO platform. A registered corporate entity can also use DAO to automate formal governance rules contained in corporate bylaws or imposed by law.

The vision of DAO is to create organizations in which the participants maintain control of the contributed funds and the governance rules are formalized, automated, and enforced using the software. Think of DAO as an automated tool to run venture capital. DAO raises funds from investors through crowdfunding events,[23] and also solicits startup companies seeking investments to present their projects. The crowdfunding participants then vote for the projects they want to invest in. The whole process is conducted on the DAO's Ethereum-based blockchain using smart contracts.

A DAO project becomes active by its deployment on the Ethereum blockchain. Once deployed, a DAO contract requires Ether to engage in transactions on the Ethereum network. Like Bitcoin, DAO is open source. The code runs across a network of independent machines, and anyone can change the code if approved by a majority of the DAO's "voting power," which is in proportion to the money a voter has invested.

In the first DAO project, 50 project proposals were voted on for funding. The money raised by a crowdfunding event organized by DAO funded the projects selected by the vote. DAO passed an audit by Déjà vu Security on April 5, 2016, in preparation for the crowdfunding event.

On April 30, 2016, Slock.it launched its crowdfunding campaign with a 28-day funding window. It was a phenomenal event. By May 27, 2016, the deadline for investing in the DAO, over ten thousand people had anonymously poured more than $168 million into this new online creation.

The way it works is that an investor buys DAO's tokens with Ethers he owns. In effect, investors invest in DAO's crowdfunding event by their Ethers. The price of the token in Ethers fluctuates with supply and demand. Think of Ether as money and the token as the stock price. DAO's token grants its holder voting and ownership rights.

When voting starts, the investment fund is frozen or locked-in. Token ownership is freely transferable on the Ethereum blockchain only after the crowdfunding event. Each account has one vote. The weight of the vote is proportional to the token held in the account.

However, DAO's voting process has an inherent flaw in its logic. Instead of allowing each account owner to allocate his tokens to each individual project he would like to invest in, all the tokens in DAO are lumped together. The only control an investor has is to cast his vote for each project. If the project is approved, the investor's fund will go to the project, even if he voted against it. Investors do not have control over how much of the funds go to each project or whether they want to commit to the project because the funds are allocated to the projects by DAO. In this sense, the token is more like the stock price of an Exchange Traded Fund, which consists of a basket of stocks. Buying a token is like buying a basket of projects.

In June 2016, a security bug was discovered and disclosed to the public. One week later, on June 17, DAO was hacked, most likely due to the disclosure. The hacker drained 3.6 million Ethers to a child DAO. The market value of the siphoned Ethers was over 70 million dollars. It caused a panic in the market and the price of the Ether dropped to half.

The attacker did not break into the code, but exploited a weakness in the DAO rules to transfer the funds to another DAO controlled by the hacker. To the Ethereum platform, it merely executed a contract.

Fortunately, per DAO coding, there is a waiting period of 28 days before the fund can be spent, so that the fund was temporarily safe for 28 days. To protect the fund after the waiting period, the Ethereum Foundation froze it. The owner of the Ethers still could see their Ethers in their accounts, but could not withdraw them.

On June 24, 2016, the Ethereum Foundation released a soft fork client intending to censor transactions from the hacker, however, because of its hasty development, the software contained a flaw and miners decided not to implement it. It seemed that a hard fork solution was necessary, and hot debates began in the Ethereum community.

The hard fork spec was finally announced on July 15, 2016. The hard fork effectively reversed the hack from occurring and returned all funds to the original investors. However, not everyone was happy about the hard fork decision. Some felt that the hard fork violated the spirit and intent of a truly decentralized system adhering to the virtues of irreversible transactions.

By July 20, 80% of the nodes voted to approve the new fork, while the remaining 20% did not. The dissidents decided to continue to validate the old version of the blockchain, with the hack still present. Ethereum was therefore split into Ethereum Classic (ETC) and the new Ethereum (ETH). The ETC community left the Ethereum Foundation and is now run by a team called IOHK.

ETC started trading on the exchanges on July 23, 2016. As Ethereum Classic is a replica of the original blockchain, except for a few key changes regarding the DAO transaction reversals, everyone who owned tokens on Ethereum at the time of the fork now had the same number of tokens on Ethereum Classic. This is the same as a stock spin-off. Ethereum token holders should be aware that they can be affected by "replay attacks" if they don't properly "separate" their addresses to differentiate them on each blockchain.

By August 31, 2016, the Ethereum Foundation unlocked the DAO frozen funds and started to refund some Ethers to the owners. After the hard fork, three DAO refunds took place for investors who still held DAO tokens. The last refund was the DAO to ETC contract that gave balance holders until April 15, 2017, to claim their reimbursement. After the deadline, there were still 1,717,513 Ethers remaining to be withdrawn.

The DAO hack may be a setback for Ethereum. However, the incident was not due to bugs in the Ethereum network. The Ethereum network, which supports around $1 billion worth of Ethers, has never been hacked. However, by strongly supporting DAO, Ethereum's name has been tainted by the hack. At the time of the hack, DAO had roughly 15% of all Ethers. This fact alone was enough to crash the price of Ether. Ethereum's action is akin to a bail-out. Regardless of the Ethereum Foundation's actions, it still suffered serious consequences.

5.6   LEGAL ISSUES

The use of blockchain, DAOs, and smart contracts raises significant legal questions. As the technologies are more widely used, it becomes urgent for legislators, regulators, and courts to provide a proper legal framework for the blockchain applications. However, to establish the legal framework for blockchain contracts is overwhelming. Many unprecedented circumstances can occur. What are the jurisdictional and applicable laws to address a breach or failure occurring in a server located in a remote country? DAO is self-governing software engaging in commerce: what legal status, or liability does it or its creator have? Can the law legally enforce the smart contracts, or more specifically, their codes? What if a software bug in the codes causes the fault? After all, the coding may suffer from errors or the hosting platforms may fail.

The impacts of fraud at any point in the DAO's creation or operation can be very real. Courts and regulators across the world are unlikely to allow the wholesale adoption of technology before establishing the legal framework. There are several possible ways to approach the issues. The easiest solution is to embed DAO into a real contractual agreement spelling out the prevailing terms for the linked DAO. A contract can spell out provisions to include or exclude certain potential faults. In this way, the contractor has the responsibility for a certain fault caused by DAO. The contracting parties can also adopt a free-to-use platform with an agreed code. The legal framework can treat DAO itself as a tool, like an instrument such as a lathe machine, in which the creator is responsible for certain accidents but not all accidents. This would essentially separate the blockchain infrastructure from the contractual agreement and regards the DAOs or smart contracts as tools of the execution, but not the contract itself.

The adaptation of common law to technological changes is not a new event. Legislatures will have to consider what legal status to grant to DAOs before the wholesale adoption of this technology.

5.7 DAPPS – DECENTRALIZED APPS

Ethereum is the most popular platform to build Dapps. As of 2022, there are thousands of Dapps in existence and development.[24] Its growth is quite astonishing considering its short history. Here is a list of a few "live" ones:

- Storj: a decentralized cloud storage
- Numerai: a hedge fund
- Pick 3: a lottery draw
- Share & Charge: a platform for sharing electric vehicle refueling station
- Icebox: a cold storage for Ether
- VDice: on chain Ethereum betting game

Creating a Dapp does not require copyright or patent. Anyone can create a Dapp if they know how to do so. Creating Dapps in the Ethereum blockchain ecosystem is like the creation of apps for the smartphone. However, Dapps can issue tokens while apps in a cell phone cannot. Through tokens, Dapp developers can directly monetize their development effort.

Dapps have certain characteristics. The application must be completely open source. It must operate autonomously, with no entity controlling most of its tokens, and its data and records of operation must be cryptographically stored in a public, decentralized blockchain.

The application generates tokens according to a standard algorithm or set of criteria and distributes some or all of its tokens at the beginning of its operation. The participants need tokens to use the application and earn tokens for their contribution as reward payment. There are several ways to obtain tokens:

- Crowd-sale: buy tokens during the initial Dapp crowdfunding
- Participation in the Development: earn tokens by doing the development
- Mining: receive tokens by contributing resources

Any improvements or changes due to market feedback are decided by the majority consensus of its users. These contributors, whether miners or developers, benefit from the exchange of the tokens and from the possible appreciation of their value. Therefore, Dapps are self-sustaining because they empower their stakeholders to invest in the development of the Dapp.

Over time, Dapps will improve and have increased functionality. By relying on crowd "wisdom," many Dapps may become even more powerful than the services provided by large corporations today.

5.8   CREATE YOUR OWN COINS OUT OF BITCOIN

The Counterparty is a platform for creating peer-to-peer financial applications on the Bitcoin blockchain. It brings the smart contract capability of Ethereum to the Bitcoin blockchain. It established the world's first functioning decentralized digital currency exchange, as well as the ability to create their own virtual assets, issue dividends, and create price feeds, bets, and contracts for difference.

Unlike Ethereum, another smart-contract platform, Counterparty does not have its own blockchain. Counterparty's developers built a distributed financial system on top of the already existing Bitcoin blockchain. Since it does not have its own blockchain, it cannot create its own token by mining or minting. Rather, its token, called XCP, is created by "burning" Bitcoin. In January 2015, Counterparty announced the Proof of Burn concept to create XCP. XCP is used to pay for the execution of smart contracts in the Counterparty network.

The process is similar to the following. You take fifty $20 dollar bills to the U.S. Treasury Department; the U.S. Treasury Department burns it and mints ten $100 dollar bills for you.

In the Bitcoin situation, the burnt Bitcoins are sent to the address provided by the Counterparty, 1CounterpartyXXXXXXXXXXXXXXXXXUWLpVr, which is guaranteed to have no matching private key because the middle "X" values are left to chance. These "burned" Bitcoins, like the burnt $20 dollar bills, are eliminated from circulation forever.

Counterparty issued XCP to whoever submitted the Proof of Burn. Counterparty itself also burned 2,125.63 Bitcoins in January 2014 (worth roughly $1.8 million at the time). Until September 2015, only 2,673 Bitcoins have been lost for 2,648,755 XCPs. It is a small fraction (0.02%) of the total 21 million Bitcoins that will ever exist. It does not have any impact on the supply of Bitcoin. This ensured that all 2,648,755 XCPs that will ever exist were created and distributed in a fair, transparent, and public manner.

Like Bitcoin, the Counterparty community operates in a decentralized manner where everyone has an equal say in the project. The Counterparty is a second-level protocol that runs on top of the existing Bitcoin network and pays Bitcoin miners small fees to register Counterparty transactions in the Bitcoin blockchain. In this way, Counterparty benefits from having a trusted and secure mining network without spending any resources for its operation. At the same time, Counterparty developers eliminated any speculation that they planned to get rich quick or redistribute risk unequally.

The Counterparty was the first protocol to have a working distributed exchange, built in record time despite having no outside funding of any kind. Since then, Counterparty has built a new and exciting level of functionality in the form of a distributed financial system and exchange on top of Bitcoin. That is many potential benefits for the Bitcoin community as a whole in return for those burnt coins.

The protocol specifications and all Counterparty software are open source. To ensure the success of Counterparty, they have developed Counterwallet, a secure Web wallet for managing all transactions on the world's first peer-to-peer digital asset exchange. Counterwallet is based upon an escrow system to keep all transactions safe and secure and to eliminate the intermediary, a necessary part of a typical market system. It provides a secure, safe, and open-source way to manage the money you use in Counterparty.

Counterparty allows users to create and issue assets. User-created tokens are just as real as XCP or BTC. With the asset issuance function, every user can create a new currency project inside the Bitcoin and Counterparty ecosystem. They are separate from the Bitcoin currency itself but exist entirely inside ordinary Bitcoin transactions.

These tokens work the same as Bitcoin. Any Bitcoin address can receive, store, and send these tokens. Likewise, Bitcoin cold storage can also store these tokens. However, Counterparty tokens do not count as BTC balances in the Bitcoin address. This means that sending/receiving Bitcoins has no effect on the balance of tokens and vice versa. Among other features, Counterparty adds the ability for users to create, send, trade, and pay distributions on assets, in a fully decentralized and trustless manner.

While Counterparty has its own internal currency (XCP), trading and creating assets does not require anything apart from regular Bitcoin transaction fees. To transfer assets to the Counterparty, it must contain four important parts: the source of the asset, name of the asset, quantity of the asset, and asset destination.

Counterparty protocol allows the source to transfer issuance rights of the asset. Moreover, an asset can also be locked, so that there can be no further issuances of it. Beyond creating the most basic asset, it is also possible to make assets either divisible or callable. If an asset is deemed to be divisible or callable upon its initial issuance, it must always be divisible or callable with every issuance thereafter. A divisible user-created asset is, like Bitcoin and XCP, divisible up to 8 decimal places. A *callable asset* is an asset which the issuer can call back (i.e., repurchase) from its owners at a date (call-date) and for a price (call-price) specified at the initial issuance.

It is possible to distribute funds proportionally among asset holders using the distribution function. This feature is like dividend payments, depending on their desired purpose. Distributions are paid in any distribution asset to everyone who holds the asset in proportion to how many units they hold. Distributions can be paid out to any assets that one owns and controls. One can freely select the currency in which distributions are to be paid out: BTC, XCP, or any other user-created asset.

5.9   ANTSHARES OR NEO – A MULTI-USE TOKEN

Antshares is a cryptocurrency developed by a Shanghai-based company, founded in 2014, called Onchain. It is another cryptocurrency built on blockchain technology as a decentralized and distributed network protocol. AntShares provides users the ability to implement smart contracts/Dapps in many more languages than Ethereum currently supports.

Onchain runs Antshares as an open-source project without owning it. It can be used to digitize assets and accomplish financial business such as registration of assets, issuing certificates, making transactions, settlement, and payment through the P2P network. Its platform targets mainstream users. By sharing some commonality with Ethereum and Counterparty, Antshares intends to build a financial system bridging real-world assets and cryptocurrency.[23] It has some high-profile partners, including Alibaba and Microsoft.[25]

On June 22, 2017, Antshares developers rebranded the Antshares into NEO and converted Antshares coins (ANS) into Antcoins (ANC). So far, ANS is only traded on the Chinese exchanges and Bittrex. Like Ethereum, Antshares is a smart contract platform.

The similarity between Antshares and Counterparty ends at the asset digitization platform. Their differences are more significant. Antshares developers put particular emphasis on compliance. Antshares has built-in KYC and AML APIs. Third-party payment providers, banks, and other financial institutions may utilize the Antshares protocol with compliance.

Currently, the system is compliant with rules set out by the Chinese Ministry of Industry and Information Technology (MIIT), as are 38 digital certificate companies in China that provide digital certificates of personal identity. When used in other countries, local rules may require local digital certifications.

Like Ethereum, Antshares runs smart contracts using the Mainnet client. Mainnet promises a much better ecosystem to issue and trade smart contracts. The Mainnet platform also had some advanced personal identity features, allowing for instant authentication with the existing banking infrastructure, much like digital certificate companies do today.

The first token to run on the open-source Antshares blockchain was the platform's gas, a token named "Antcoins." The cap of Antcoins is set at 100 million Antcoins, generated over the next 22 years. There is the same amount of Antshares, the token used for asset transfer. All Antshares tokens were created at once in the first block.

Antshares smart contracts are very simple contracts. They are for smart financial products and can be used for recording titles and assets like equities, creditor's claims, securities, financial contracts, credit points, bills, and currencies. They can also be used as equity crowdfunding, equity trading, employee stock ownership plans, peer-to-peer financing, loyalty programs, private equity funds, and supply-chain financing.

To prevent the DAO-like hack, the Antshares contracts are less interactive. The most important difference between Antshares and other cryptocurrency is the use of delegated Byzantine Fault Tolerance (dBFT) (discussed in Chapter 4) instead of PoW or PoS to secure its blockchain. By using dBFT, the block verification is by consensus vote rather than mining. Other blockchain developers that use dBFT are IBM and Chain.com.

dBFT is a far more efficient way to achieve a security like the Bitcoin blockchain, without all the cost of mining. The current version of dBFT used in the Antshares requires the consensus nodes to maintain a state table to record current consensus status.

So far, Antshares has two partners in China, Bitrees, and WeLand. Both are startups. Bitrees is the first Big Data analysis service of blockchain/cryptocurrency in China. WeLand does the Return Crowdfunding of physical products. *Return crowdfunding*, a new business model, collects funds from the crowd to purchase physical products and promises to return the profit from the sales of these products to the investors.

In 2016, WeLand launched a "Landholder in Europe" crowdfunding on *Taobao.com* (not using Antshares), raising 4.1 million yuan from 19,000 participants to import European olive oil products and sell them in China, and returned the investment with profit to the participants. In WeLand's Return Crowdfunding last year, the average contribution from each participant was only $32, not a large amount. Most of these participants may not have cared about the outcome. However, for a larger contribution, the participant may have wanted a certificate or contribution agreement, such as a share registration. This is difficult to do with a traditional format. With digital registration on the Antshares Blockchain, this problem can be solved with ease. By using the Antshares platform, the future crowdfunding or Return Crowdfunding events will be able to implement digital registration of its return shares on the Antshares Blockchain. All participants will receive their copy of the smart contract.

5.10 BRIDGING BITCOIN & EVM

Being able to run smart contracts greatly increases the usefulness of a block-chain. Suddenly, the blockchain serves more than just creating and transacting cryptocurrency. It can be used for all sorts of financial applications that require pre-agreed terms and conditions between parties.

Ethereum is the de-facto leader of the smart contract blockchain system. However, PoW transaction validation imposes scalability limitations, so Ethereum is not feasible for most industrial applications. Ethereum is trying to solve the problem by gradually moving into a PoW/PoS hybrid system.

Imagine if one can run Ethereum-like smart contracts on the Bitcoin blockchain and reap all the benefits of a Bitcoin blockchain without any scaling limits. It would be like reinventing Bitcoin. Qtum, a Singapore-based foundation, developed such a technology.

Qtum is an open source, hybrid blockchain application platform. It builds an Account Abstraction Layer (AAL) between the Bitcoin blockchain and Ethereum Virtual Machine (EVM) to allow the two incompatible systems to communicate. The AAL extends the Bitcoin Script language to transport code to the EVM and allows the EVM to operate within a UTXO environment, which simplifies the payment verification so that it can support mobile devices and IoT appliances.

Qtum merges the reliability of Bitcoin's blockchain with the smart contract's capability of Ethereum. In addition, the PoS consensus protocol allows Qtum applications to be much more scalable than Ethereum.

Qtum is compatible with pre-existing Ethereum smart contracts. The Qtum platform can execute Ethereum smart contracts with little to no change to the code. Using Qtum, smart contracts and decentralized applications can run on a familiar platform with a robust environment. The target applications include mobile telecommunications, counterfeit protection, finance, industrial logistics, and manufacturing.

The Qtum project takes advantage of the best of the Bitcoin and Ethereum platforms and allows for a wide variety of applications not possible by Bitcoin and Ethereum alone.

5.11 ASSET DIGITIZATION

In June 2017, an organization called ACChain, operated by Guiyang Blockchain Financial Company in China, launched an ambitious blockchain project to develop a tool and platform to digitize assets on a global scale. ACChain is short for the Asset Collection Coin or Asset Collect Chain. This technology maps and segments all assets on a decentralized blockchain platform to realize tangible assets registration, issuing, and trading. It is essentially creating a unique digital copy of the asset in the blockchain platform. Such a digital copy of the asset can be tradable, just like a real asset.

The trading of digitalized assets uses ACC (Asset Collection Coin). In the ACChain, each node can create a new block by copying the general ledger to form an asset chain. ACChain distinguishes itself from other popular cryptocurrency in that ACC emphasizes commercial applications, assets digitization, and digital asset circulation, while Bitcoin focuses on value transfer and Ethereum focuses on smart contracts. Therefore, ACC takes the position as a digital asset interchange medium to allow the exchange of all digital assets through ACChain.

There are three steps to generate a token for a digitized asset:[26,27]

- It must meet certain criteria, such as being durable, verifiable, and traceable.
- Its published asset information must receive community recognition.
- It must receive approval from two-thirds of DAO.

On May 9th, 2017, ACChain launched an initial coin offering (ICO) to raise 100 million units of ACC. Twenty percent of the digital assets was used as an incentive for members and 80% of the digital asset was locked in an asset pool through a smart contract of the blockchain.

With this ICO, ACChain formed a DAO (decentralized autonomous organization) to manage the fund from the ICO. All members manage the capital; each transaction requires approval by 51% of the members.

The ACC ICO aimed to structure supernode networks of digital assets around the globe and establish a digital currency of "Special Drawing Rights" (SDR). The SDR digital currency has not received an endorsement by the IMF, the issuer of the SDR. It is not clear how this situation will unfold. It is quite possible that the IMF will not allow ACChain to issue SDR digital currency since it has global implications far beyond any commercial application.

The intention of ACChain was to use the SDR digital currency to spread the adoption of ACC. Each global node establishes a regional "general ledger token" (GLT) for regional circulation. Thus, ACChain envisions that the digital currency SDR will be the main exchange coin along with tokens of each international node's general ledger token in the international exchange.

In this ecosystem, each node's token can use GLT to realize regional circulation and each GLT and ACC to realize international circulation. Those who control the international supernodes win the market. This is like today's role of dollars and national currencies.

ACChain launched a commercial real estate deal using blockchain technology in Dallas Fort Worth two weeks after its ICO in collaboration with Serene Country Home Group, a home developer in Texas. Serene Country Home Group launched the ICO of its own digital asset, RET (Real Estate Token), with the help of the ACChain blockchain technology. RET is a token to buy and sell properties in a new real estate project: Sendera Ranch in Fort Worth, TX.[28]

A RET's applications are not limited to the trading of digital assets for Sendera Ranch. It will also serve as the general token for the U.S. region and is for sale through ACChain's P2P sales supernodes. NPC, which stands for Node Primary Coin, is the coin issued by the supernode. NPC is a standard digital token based on ACChain.

BTC, ETH, and ACC are the exchange subjects for the NPC. There are three types of tokens: the Equity token, application token, and commodity token. Different assets can have different tokens. Think of NPC as the certificate of the ownership of an asset and BTC, ETH, and ACC as the money. Money can be exchanged for a certificate of the asset, and vice versa.

Puer is a special Tibetan tea, produced in Tibet and southwestern province of China, Yunnan. This high-quality Tibetan tea is stored by the third party, evaluated, authenticated, and right authenticated. The holders of the tea NPC can redeem the specified amount of tea. Alternatively, they can also trade it for other tokens or exchange it for other fiat currency. The NPC token itself is a proof of the ownership of the tea. The price of NPC can rise or fall according to the market price of the underlying tea asset.

So far, ACChain has issued three different NPCs for three different qualities of the Puer tea via Fenghui International Finance in Shenzhen. They are the Daguan Qianxue, Daguan Qiaomu, and Daguan Jingong tokens. Likewise, Huayang, another company, has issued Jiangcoin for their product XiaoHongLiang Kunzi Pure Draft Liquor.

The growing number of institutions and companies joining ACChain to digitize their assets heralds a new stage in blockchain technology: the emergence of commercial applications, which will be useful to consumers across the globe. Pencil Blockchain Company joined the ACChain DAO community to be one of the ACChain super nodes in North America for advertising

ACChain and its commercial application implementation of the blockchain technology.

The company is in talks with a third-party fund management company to establish a mixed ETF Fund, the first building block of ACChain's financial services system. American Digital Asset Exchange Inc., a blockchain financial service institution, is also expected to join ACChain as a DAO member soon to establish a digital asset exchange transaction system for ACChain.

ACChain DAO offers different incentives to its members: the creation of block, asset issuing, and community voting. The ACChain DAO has an encrypted PBFT algorithm to address the issue of abuse of right by the delegates, which makes the delegate's ability of accounting become more controllable.

5.12 STABLECOINS

Stablecoins are cryptocurrencies backed by a reserve asset. The backup asset makes the price of stablecoins more stable, relative to other cryptocurrencies. Such price stability makes the stablecoins suitable for a store of value or medium of exchange. Because they are based on blockchain technology, they enjoy all the security measures of the blockchain technology. They are scalable and secure and can be used in payment transactions across the network with no trust, high speeds, and low transaction fees and without boundary restrictions. The most popular Stablecoins are Tether, USD Coin, Binance USD, and DAI, which had a combined market value exceeding $100 billion dollars at the end of 2021.

There are many ways to stabilize the price of the coin. Some stablecoins, like tether and USD coin, are pegged to the U.S. dollar, gold, or other real assets. Others, such as DAI, are backed by cryptocurrencies, such as Ethereum. They are known as the *crypto collateralized stablecoins*. There are also others using algorithms to stabilize the price of the coin.

Even the those responsible for the U.S. financial system are paying more attention to stablecoins for their use in the financial system to see if they can be regulated legally.

While altcoins are a still emerging and developing area of cryptocurrency, there is a tremendous amount of promise in the creative solutions they can provide in a digital world where commerce is done in ways that we cannot yet conceive.

REFERENCES

1. *https://www.bankrate.com/investing/types-of-cryptocurrency/*

2. *https://litecoin.com/*

3. *https://z.cash/*

4. "Zerocash: decentralized anonymous payments from Bitcoin", Eli Ben Sasson et. al., Zerocash white paper, *http://zerocash-project.org/media/ pdf/zerocash-extended 20140518.pdf*

5. Ripple: Overview and outlook." Proc. Trust and Trustworthy Computing", F. Armknecht, et. al., volume 9229 of Lecture Notes in Computer Science, Springer, 2015.

6. *https://ripple.com/*

7. *http://ryanfugger.com/*

8. Vitalik Buterin, "Introducing Ripple": *https://Bitcoinmagazine.com/ articles/introducing-ripple/*

9. *https://www.swift.com/about-us*

10. "The Society for Worldwide Interbank Financial Telecommunication", S. V. Scott, M. Zachariadis, *www.oapen.org/download?type=document& docid=623230*

11. "Elliptic Curve Cryptography: a gentle introduction"", Andrea Corbellini, *http://andrea.corbellini.name/2015/05/17/elliptic-curve-cryptography-a-gentle introduction/*

12. "Unique Node List", *https://wiki.ripple.com/Unique_Node_List*

13. "Global Banks Test Ripple's Digital Currency in New Blockchain Trial", Michael del Castill, *https://www.coindesk.com/global-banks-test-ripples-digital-currency-new blockchain-trial/*

14. *https://www.ethereum.org/*

15. "What are Dapps? The new decentralized future", *https://blockgeeks. com/guides/Dapps/*

16. *https://www.myetherwallet.com/#contracts*

17. *https://consensys.net/*

18. "Ethereum Blockchain as a Service now on Azure", Marley Gray, *https:// azure.microsoft.com/en-us/blog/ethereum-blockchain-as-a-service-now-on azure/*

19. "9 Brand-Name Companies That Have Joined the Enterprise Ethereum Alliance", Sean Williams, The Motley Fool, *https://www.fool.com/ investing/2017/07/27/9-brand-name-companies-that-have-joined-the-enterp.aspx*

20. *https://messari.io/asset/ethereum/chart/sply-circ*

21. "Ethereum roadmap", *https://steemit.com/cryptocurrency/@ ctyptouniverse/ethereum roadmap*

22. "What is the gas in Ethereum", *https://www.cryptocompare.com/coins/ guides/what is-the-gas-in-ethereum/*

23. *https://www.coindesk.com/markets/2016/05/12/the-dao-or-how-a-leaderless-ethereum-project-raised-50-million/*

24. *https://www.stateoftheDapps.com/*

25. *https://neo.org/*

26. *https://acchain.network*

27. *https://bitcointalk.org/index.php?topic=1908143.0*

28. *https://www.connectcre.com/stories/blockchain-tokens-backed-by-655m-fort-worth-area-mpc/*

6

MUTUAL DISTRIBUTED LEDGERS AND DIGITAL CURRENCY

Blockchain, an encrypted and distributed database, has many applications beyond cryptocurrency. In fact, any application that needs to record data as a ledger for the purpose of bookkeeping can use blockchain and take advantage of its secure, distributed, and immutable qualities.

6.1   IDENTITY, TRANSACTION, AND CONTENT MDLS

There are three types of permissioned, or private, Mutual Distributed Ledgers (MDLs): Identity MDL, which holds the entity's identity, Transaction MDL, which holds hashes of all transactions, and Content MDL which holds all original documents. The Content MDL holds original documents. For example, a bank account has a customer's identity in the Identity MDL. It has transaction records in the Transaction MDL, and all other accounts related information is in the Content MDL. These three databases are separate but interlinked. One only has complete information about an account after putting all three MDLs together. Only when all three MDLs are put together does one have the complete information about an account. When a customer has several accounts, such as savings, checking, and IRA, each account has its own Transaction MDL and Content MDL. As another example, your social security number can be in the Identity MDL. Your bank accounts, credit card accounts, DMV records, medical records, and any other record can be in separate Transaction MDLs, with detailed information in the Content MDL.

The Content MDL can be very large, like a database in a data center; nevertheless, it is still distributed. Since all documents in the Content MDL are hashed and stored in the Transaction MDL, any alternation in the original document in the Content MDL will have a discrepancy with its hash in the Transaction MDL. Therefore, the Content MDL is safe from unauthorized alteration.

One can combine these three types of MDLs into a single MDL. The three-in-one MDL has the advantages of a simple data structure, including ease of implementation and searching easy to implement and to search, reduced risk of data loss, the simple link between data and content, and more options for storing sensitive content. The disadvantages are that the MDL will be bigger and there is a potential lack of oversight over sensitive personal information. Sharing with other MDLs can be more difficult. It makes sense to have three separate MDLs linked together. The transaction and content MDLs are unique to a particular application or organization, but the Identity MDL can be shared among many different entities or organizations.

The only structural difference between the Identity, Transaction, and Content MDLs is that the first two MDLs have a fixed-length hash field while the Content MDL has a variable length field to hold documents, pictures, videos, spreadsheets, and other types of documents. These three types of MDLs are separate and stored in separate locations, but since they are linked, their functionality is integrated.

Separate MDLs make data sharing flexible. One MDL can interface with many different MDLs. For example, the MDLs of different organizations may want to share the same Identity MDL. The police department may use the same Identity MDL as the department of motor vehicles, but each department holds a different Transaction and Content MDL. The police department and DMV each hold different Transaction MDL and Content MDL. When the police issue a traffic ticket, a transaction is created in the police Transaction MDL, and is shared with DMV Transaction MDL through the shared Identity MDL. The same is true that an insurance company may use the same Identity MDL as a hospital.

The economics of multiple users drives the modularization of MDLs, which leads to cross-organizational systems. This flexibility makes it possible to share part of the MDL (but not all of the MDL) using Quorum-like public/private states, or even multiple private states in the database. For example, a hospital may share part of its private Identity MDL with one insurance company and a different part with another insurance company. Likewise, because each insurance company has its own provider network, an insurance company may share part of its Identity MDL with one provider and a different part with another provider. A credit card company may share part of its Identity MDLs with a bank.

With all these MDLs established in a cloud, the transactions between different organizations can be fast, secure, and only involve relevant parties. Eventually, the cross-organizational MDLs can be so extensive that they link most of the organizations together.

Standard and data sharing protocols need to be developed to integrate several blockchains into one. To integrate several blockchains into one, standard and data sharing protocols need to be developed. The data sharing protocols validate the data links for different chains networks, which opens completely new possibilities for different MDLs to work together when necessary. A standard protocol involves the registration, inspection, certification, and checking of the underlying MDLs.

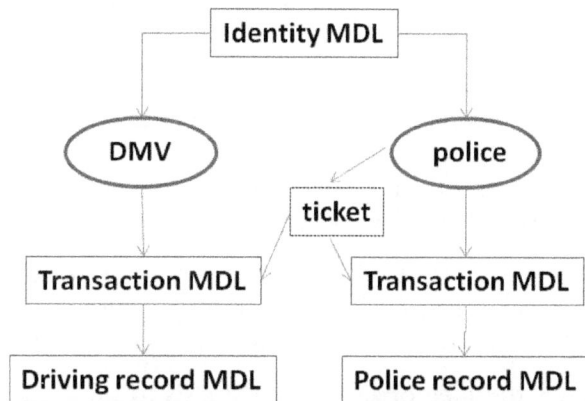

FIGURE 6.1 An example of a shared MDL.

It is essential to develop the ability of these three functionally different MDLs to exchange information, even though they do not belong to the same entity or must be modular. Figure 6.1 shows two organizations: the DMV and Police Department, which share the same Identity MDL. However, each has different Transaction MDLs and Content MDLs.

When a police officer writes a traffic ticket, he is creating a transaction in the transaction MDLs of the DMV and the Police department at the same time. These two MDLs are not necessarily in the same cloud. The P2P network serves as a bridge between clouds. The DMV has its own transaction MDL and content MDL. They integrate with the Identity MDL to form an archiving system in the DMV. Such an archive contains the drivers' identities, their driving records, and all their identity data, such as their address, photo, birthday, and eye color. Likewise, the police department also has its own archiving database, containing Transaction and Content MDLs. It contains all a person's police-related data. These triple MDLs can support and interact with other MDL ledgers.

Today, the DMV and police department have their own database, containing the same data. However, they lack the ability to interact with other databases and they are less secure than MDLs using blockchain.

Multiple databases, such as healthcare data, insurance certificates, credit history, contracts, and real estate deeds, can be classified, encrypted, and tracked. This MDL can be distributed across several platforms, over the Internet, or in the cloud, and provides the same level of security and the convenience of an asset transfer.

The interactive nature of an MDL is realized by a technique called side-chaining.[1] A *sidechain* is a separate blockchain from the main blockchain, which has tokens. *Sidechaining* is the mechanism that allows the system to use tokens from the main blockchain securely. The tokens can always move back to the original chain if necessary.

For example, a private Ethereum-based network that had a linkage allowing Ether to move securely from the public Ethereum main chain onto it and back would be considered a sidechain of the public network.

However, the idea of sidechain extends to more than just tokens; it can exchange anything of value across MDLs, as well. In doing so, the MDL is no longer isolated and valuable assets can move across different MDLs. Once the modularity of the MDL is developed, a true Internet of Value becomes a reality.

The concept of immutable data could materially alter the way society views identity, privacy, and security. But before MDL technology solutions are more widely adopted, several conditions need to be met, including developing standards for interoperability, and creating a cohesive regulatory position on MDL technology applications.

6.2 IDENTITY MDLS

In the sharing economy, identity becomes the most important trust element. For example, in a bike-sharing platform, without identity, anyone can just take the bike and never return it or get a free ride without paying for it. Therefore, identity is necessary to do transactions and hold assets.

Identity MDLs could make possible a wide array of asset-related tasks. Efficient identity systems are fundamental to efficient financial and trading systems. The persistence and pervasiveness of MDLs make them ideal for providing a lifetime record.

Theoretically, a single Identity MDL can serve any number of transactions that require an identity. Thus, the idea is born to develop the Identity MDL as a stand-alone MDL that can serve many different clients.

In June 2017, the Decentralized Identity Foundation (DIF) was launched at the Consensus blockchain tech conference in New York.[2] The founding members included Microsoft, Accenture, IBM and many others. The goal of the DIF is to develop the foundational elements for an open ecosystem for decentralized identity and to ensure interoperability between all parties.

Blockstack[3], one of the foundation's founding members, has released a set of programming tools to create a decentralized Internet and to construct Identity MDLs.[3] The Blockstack toolset decentralizes the application layer of the Internet by enabling decentralized storage and authentication, and users can run Dapps (discussed in Chapter 5) through the Blockstack browser. Information is encrypted and stored on users' personal devices.

Microsoft has collaborated with Blockstack Labs and ConsenSys to build an open-source identity platform for integrating the Bitcoin and Ethereum blockchains. This joint effort aims to create a global standard for blockchain identity applications.

Microsoft launched an open-source framework[4] with the cross-chain applicability on Azure, where developers can build their own identity applications. Microsoft's Identity MDL connects with the Ethereum blockchain via ConsenSys's uPort[5] solution and with the Bitcoin blockchain via Blockstack's OneName.[6]

The project has found growing interest among global organizations because of its use of a blockchain technology that can address long-standing identity issues. A readily available Identity MDL, such as the one built by Microsoft, can facilitate the creation of new Identity MDLs by eliminating the need to build new Identity MDLs from scratch.

Okta is another leading independent provider of Identity MDL for the enterprise, offering the Identity Cloud service. Its Identity Cloud helps people securely connect to the technologies and services that allow them to work efficiently. It helps Human Resources, workplace, and IT organizations provide security and protection to their employees regardless of location. Okta offers products and services to facilitate remote work and keep people employed and productive, even when they cannot be in an office. It also provides the solutions and tools to build secure, seamless customer experiences, empowering them to still generate revenue and drive growth.

The Decentralized Identity Foundation is not alone in developing Identity MDL; the open-source Hyperledger Project is also working on a decentralized identity project called Indy.[7]

Identity MDL could empower people with personal data storage and management, or permission frameworks for access by third parties such as banks or insurance companies, and even distributed reputation ratings. Such applications could reduce identity theft and fraud, increase confidence in products, and lower costs.[8]

There is an infinite number of potential applications, including the ability to link to education, driving, tax, medical, marriage, and employment records. For example, an Identity MDL can link to an education record, driving record, tax record, medical record, marriage record, employment record and many more. MDL technology and related applications could transform the way we manage digital identity and personal information.

In addition to individuals, juridical entities, such as companies, also have their own identities. DueDil offers a platform that provides authoritative data on over 40 million private companies in Europe so that the same information that is available about public companies will be now also available about private companies.[9] This helps businesses to evaluate risks in dealing with these private companies.

An ID scheme relying on decentralized MDLs combining a public ledger of records with an adequate level of privacy could rival state-backed identity systems. One day it may replace driver's licenses, social security cards, and passports. Eventually, one's fingerprints, face, and any other biometrics, even DNA, will be in a person's Identity MDL.

To establish an Identity MDL, the first step is to input identity data into the ledger. These data include the data in driver's licenses, passports and any form of ID cards, birth or death certificates, signature records, criminal records, educational degrees, professional qualifications, certifi-cations, human resources records, medical records, bank records, business transaction records, location data, and DNA and genealogy records.

The data entry can be from any system using identity validators. Data from different sources are cross-referenced. Data can be collected from birth and can continue to be collected throughout one's lifetime. Combining authen-tication and personal data management functionalities with secure MDLs could lead to new frameworks for identity management. Any activity of an individual becomes a transaction record in the MDL. Each of these transac-tions is a permanent record to an identity in the Identity MDL.

MDL technology and related applications could transform the way we manage digital identity and personal information. An Identity MDL could replace many of today's state-owned identity systems, due to the superiority of the available information, speed of verification, fraud prevention, and all-in-one features. Several digital ID schemes are emerging, including OpenID Connect, which allows clients to request and receive information about the authenticated session.[10]

India is embarking on a comprehensive national ID system, and it is not alone. Governments around the world are trying to set up digital ID systems and authentication processes. Countries like the U.K. and Estonia all have similar projects in progress. The U.K., for example, unveiled Gov.UK Verify in September 2014, a proposed public service identity assurance program that would use a network of trusted and vetted third-party providers instead of relying on a centralized database.[11] Estonia has been operating a national dig-ital ID scheme for a decade and is now updating to MDL structures.

When an entity such as a government owns an Identity MDL, it is a per-missioned Identity MDL. By possessing such a large amount of personal data, the government holds tremendous power over its people. This has raised fear of governments creating such Identity MDLs. Therefore, creating a trusted and widespread digital ID system is a social as well as a technical task. The nationwide implementation of such a system may meet much resis-tance and mistrust if it is understood as a tool of absolute totalitarian control. Establishing an efficient identity system is the core global development chal-lenge for MDLs.

Like any system, there are pros and cons of a nationwide Identity MDL. On the positive side, an efficient identity system is fundamental to efficient financial and trading systems. With the explosive growth of MDL into the

Internet of Value and the storage and transfer of assets, it is unimaginable that the storage and transfer of assets – such as land and property, business ownership, regulatory records, court records, smart contracts, vital documents, medical and health records, or eventually genome and DNA records – can function securely without a proper MDL.

In contrast to the permissioned Identity MDL created, which is owned by the government, a permissionless Identity MDL belongs to the public. It retains all the advantages of the permissioned Identity MDL but without a controlling authority.

In the permissionless Identity MDL, you have access to, and control over, your own data. This scheme will empower individuals to store, update, and manage access to their identity data, much like today's social media. However, social media networks fail to meet the basic trust requirements, as most data in social media has no verification and is not secure.

Permissionless Identity MDLs require the data to be authenticated and notarized by identity validators, which serve as a "notary public" of data. An identity validator might be a government agency, an accounting firm, or a credit-referencing agency. People will need to go to an identity validator to encode biometrics, such as DNA, retinal scans, photos, facial scans, and fingerprint identifications, thus time-stamping their physical identity. Validators notarize the data as a trusted third party. In InterChainZ, the identity validator is a notary of data onto a personal or corporate MDL. Once validated, the data in the permissionless Identity MDL can be trusted, and is secure, private, and safe from any misuse.

Co-stamping and validation themselves are important aspects of development for a permissionless MDL, since identity data varies greatly (such as health records, driving records, financial records, biometric data, and academic records). The validation or co-stamping of these data can be complex.

Developing an efficient and functional permissionless MDL free from government or any other authority control is the key to maximizing the benefits and minimizing the downsides. Combining authentication and personal data management functionalities with secure MDLs could lead to new frameworks for identity management. If successful, such identity schemes could remove government monopolies in managing their citizens' identities and data. At a time where access and control over one's own data are becoming increasingly sensitive, empowering individuals to store, update, and manage access to their data seems rather appealing.

6.3   TOKENLESS MDLS

We have discussed that a token is not necessary for a permissioned block-chain. Tokes are an incentive for people to do the validation work, or a means to exchange value. When the tokenless blockchain was first proposed, there were some doubts as to whether there were benefits to MDLs without Proof-of-Work/Proof-of-Stake validation mechanisms, which are the core of MDL.

In a permissioned blockchain, all the network nodes belong to the owner. Permissioned ledgers are normally either within a single organization or have strong structures for multiple parties, such as regulators, or the ledger is within a single organization. In this type of environment, the institution of the blockchain provides the trust.

In fact, securely processing transactions to make the transaction securely processed is incentive enough and tokens are not necessary to provide incentives for the nodes to do the validation work. At the same time, the smart contract governs the terms and conditions of the exchange of value.

InterChainZ Consortium, launched by Z/Yen, a commercial think tank based in London, proposed MDL applications without using currencies or tokens.[12] By getting rid of the token, the transaction speed is improved. InterChainZ permissioned ledgers can achieve 5,000 transactions per second, which is several hundred times faster than the transaction times of token-based MDLs.

The project developed several MDLs that directly stored documents, as well as MDLs that only recorded the "hash" of documents. InterChainZ demonstrated how MDL technology might provide such capabilities for current financial services. It builds software providing an interface to MDLs for tasks performing a sharing economy. It has demonstrated MDLs' functionality in an identity validation service, and the functionality to use them to validate company's identity and report on their finances.

6.4   BUILDING MDLS FOR FINANCIAL SERVICES

There are several types of financial services, all which serve different purposes and have different complexities. Possible applications of blockchain in financial services not discussed previously include private banking, capital market service, certificates of deposit, bonds, derivatives, voting rights associated with financial instruments, commodities, stocks, credit data, mortgages, or loans, P2P lending, donations, airline miles, business license, business ownership/incorporation/dissolution, and chain of custody.

In general, the trusted third parties in financial services provide three functions: validation, safeguarding, and preservation. In principle, any financial services that perform these three functions can deploy a blockchain.

In developing a blockchain application, the important questions to ask are as follows:

- How can we construct a blockchain that will best meet the application requirements?
- What kind of consensus mechanism is the best (Is it Proof-of-Stake, Proof-of-Work, Proof-of-Concept, dBFT, or hybrid)?
- What elements of the trusted third party are to be replaced by the blockchain?
- How are transactions authorized, as true peer-to-peer or merely decentralized?
- Are all nodes equal and performing the same tasks, or do some nodes have more power and additional tasks?
- Are tokens needed?
- Is the blockchain application in question going to interface with other blockchains?
- Does it need a sidechain?
- Is there a need to separate the Identity MDL, Transaction MDL, and Content MDL?
- What technical choices are there for cryptography standards, peer-to-peer arrangements, guaranteed distribution approaches, partial cryptography, programming languages, and communication protocols?
- Is it a private or public?
- Is it permissioned or permissionless?
- Is it P2P based or cloud based?
- How scalable does it need to be?

For example, if the application already has trusted third parties – such as banks, regulators, or the government – PoW will not be required. If scalability is needed, PoW cannot be used. Furthermore, if the trusted third party is still present, does the blockchain still offer any advantages? Only when these questions have definite answers can the framework design of the blockchain be defined.

After defining the scope of the MDL in question, the next task is to build the blockchain itself as well as a small suite of software providing an interface to MDLs for tasks such as selection and storage of documents, document encryption, sharing keys, viewing the MDL transactions, and viewing the MDL contents subject to encrypted limits. A suite of software is needed to test various configurations and simulated situations for MDLs, the outputs of which are to be shared and revised with participants.

The InterChainZ project was a consortium research project, pioneered by London-based Z/Yen to provide a real learning experience on blockchain. The project intended to demonstrate how the blockchain could work for financial services. The tool used is the online demonstrator of InterChainZ, an online MDL, which can be configured and explored for how they might work in different environments. The outputs are interlinked MDLs along with software, explanatory materials, and website information.

Blockchain has significant potential in financial services, such as know-your-customer (KYC), anti-money-laundering (AML), insurance, credit, and wholesale financial services. In addition, the encryption of MDLs produces immutable records.

InterChainZ demonstrated many potential applications for its project, for example, as a data ledger, identity application, insurance policy database, large-scale archive, and voting validation service. It also worked with partners on specific case uses:

Validation: Used blockchain to validate identity. A third-party bank confirmed the validation of the identity and financial information. Such a validation service is useful to individuals who need to comply with AML or KYC requirements.

Audit: Used blockchain for credit audit. In this demonstration, MDL functionality allows companies to validate their identity and finance report. A trusted third party reviews the information, confirms it, and adds it to the MDL. The potential creditors or business partners are provided with a public key so that they can confirm the validation and view the information.

Insurance policy databases: Uses blockchain to validate insurance history and relevant data of an individual or business. When the user applies a new insurance policy, they share the key with the insurance company. It saves the insurance company significant time and effort in verifying historical data relevant to the applicant. New policy details are added to the MDL as an update. In the same way, one's credit history can also be validated easily.

Z/Yen also explored InterChainZ storage options and network architectures using both Content MDL and Identity MDL and tested the scalability of InterChainZ. The InterChainZ MDL has the advantages of a centrally controlled ledger, simple approval rules, fast entry to the ledger, simple implementation, and maintenance; it is reliant on a single trusted third party, and not dependent on specific nodes to be available. Without the burden of PoW, InterChainZ can validate 3,000 to 5,000 transactions per second, almost as fast as credit cards.

6.5   DIGITAL CURRENCIES

A *digital currency* is a currency created and stored electronically. It provides an alternative to traditional fiat currency as store and transfer of value. Bitcoin is the most popular digital currency today, but as we have discussed in Chapter 3, Bitcoin has its limitations, and is not equipped currently for large-scale use.

A national digital currency is also a form of cryptocurrency. However, it is unique in the sense that it is sovereign and has a centralized authority. Due to its relationship to the circulation of national currency, it is considered a different kind of blockchain application.

Because currency is the blood of an economy, governments unequivocally want to maintain absolute control of issuance, circulation, and supply of their currency. A national digital currency is a fiat currency in digital form. However, it adapts many technologies of the cryptocurrency to make it difficult to counterfeit and easy to use. It has all the characteristics of a paper currency. It must be anonymous to all except the issuing government and allows currency to change hands without the need for an account or an Internet connection.

According to the Atlantic Council, a think tank in Washington, D.C., there are 87 countries exploring CBDC as of March 2022.[13] G7 authorities are looking into the risks and opportunities associated with central bank digital currencies. The European Central Bank expressed the desire to issue digital Euro. The Bank of England is also considering a digital pound sterling to settle interbank transactions directly between parties without an intermediary. G7 countries have been planning a collective move on CBDC. In October,

2021, G7 has published public policy principles for CBDC.[14] In April, 2022, the Bank of Japan launched the first phase CBDC experiment to match the rapid pace of private innovation.[15] Initially, The United States resisted the idea of a digital U.S. dollar. But its attitude toward the digital dollar is warming up. While Federal Reserve has not made any decision on digital dollar yet, it admits that it is studying its possibility.[16]

Beyond developed countries, many developing countries have CBDC plans. The LBCoin digital currency issued by Lithuania in July 2020 claimed the title of the world's first digital currency issued by the central bank of a sovereign state. Brazil plans to launch digital Real by 2024.[17] In Africa, Senegal announced a blockchain-based national digital currency. In 2016, the Bank of Russia announced the development of an Ethereum-based interbank blockchain prototype called Masterchain.[18] Some of the largest commercial banks in Russia participated in the pilot test. Russia officially launched the digital ruble in early 2022.[19] Such a trend is universal, and more countries regard CBDC as the competitive edge that they cannot do without.

Many critics said that CBDC is not truly anonymous. The issuing central bank knows exactly the identity of transaction parties. The identity data will be used to authenticate the person when he or she makes a purchase, receives a payment, or makes a smart contract transaction in the same platform. This is the downside of CBDC.

The next sections discuss Indian and Chinese digital currencies in more detail.

6.6 THE INDIAN DIGITAL CURRENCY PROJECT

In November 2016, the Indian government announced the demonetization of all 500 Rupees ($8) and 1,000 ($16) banknotes.[20] The government claimed that the action would curtail the shadow economy and crack down on the use of illicit and counterfeit cash to fund illegal activity and terrorism. The sudden nature of the announcement—and the prolonged cash shortages in the weeks that followed—created a significant disruption in the economy, threatening economic output. At the same time, India introduced India Stack as a part of Digital India program.

The Digital India program is more than just a digital currency program; a program called Aadhaar digitizes the identification of all its citizens, which would be analogous to digitizing the social security number, driver's license, and passport for all the citizens in the U.S. Once this system is fully implemented, every Indian citizen will be immediately identifiable through his or her records in the national database.

The government has launched an open Application Programming Interface platform, which includes the Aadhaar for authentication, e-KYC for customer interface, and e-Sign. India Stack's API allows governments, businesses, startups, and developers to utilize a unique digital infrastructure to facilitate India's paperless and cashless service delivery.

E-KYC is a paperless Know Your Customer (KYC) process, where a person's identity and address are verified electronically through Aadhaar Authentication. It replaces the current processes using physical photocopies of the original documents for ID proof and Address proof.

The e-Sign service allows an Aadhaar ID holder (and in theory, eventually every Indian citizen) to electronically sign a document anytime, anywhere, and on any device legally in India. It facilitates a significant reduction in paper handling costs, improves efficiency, and offers convenience to customers. The e-Sign service is carried out on a backend server of the e-Sign providers, which are trusted third party service providers called Certifying Authorities (CA).

A Unified Payments Interface is on top of India's Immediate Payment System. Tech start-ups can use this framework to develop mobile apps and make services available to a large section of the population.

A system called UIDAI (Unique Identification Authority of India),[21] is a Demographic Authentication and Biometric Authentication system in India. It authenticates a person's identity against the data in the demographic database, which contained the data for 99% of all Indian citizens in 2022.[14] During the authentication transaction, the resident's record is selected using the Aadhaar Number (ID number) and then the demographic/biometric inputs are matched against the stored data provided by the resident during enrollment. Aadhaar is a 12-digit random number, issued to the residents of India by the UIDAI.

Every resident receives an assigned Aadhaar number by voluntarily submitting their minimal demographic and biometric information during the enrollment stage or when a baby is born. The biometric data include iris scans and fingerprints. Without Aadhaar or the UIDAI-issued ID number, people will not be able to use digital cash, which will eventually be the only form of cash in India. The Aadhaar program is already at an advanced stage and serves as a model for such large-scale blockchain projects going forward.

The government now can transfer welfare payments directly to Aadhaar-linked bank accounts, cutting out India's notoriously corrupt intermediaries. Today, many Indians do not even have birth certificates. Once this system is in place, anyone can be identified through a centralized achieve, which stores birth, education, marriage, and many other pieces of identity-related data in one central database. Aadhaar is an ideal platform for digital currency verification.

The State Bank of India (SBI) launched blockchain-based know-your-customer (KYC) processes in 2017. A consortium of 27 banks developed the KYC system. The platform is called Bankchain, which is a system for sharing information about customers.[22] The consortium is working with Primechain Technologies, a Mumbai-based startup, as well as IBM and Microsoft, with the objective of reducing fraud and creating an alternative system for remittances and SWIFT.

SBI has also planned to explore new technologies such as blockchain, artificial intelligence, and machine learning. In such a system, all the transactions and life events such as births, graduations, marriages, and real estate transactions would be handled by blockchain.

However, instead of using the anonymous cryptocurrency addresses, the system will use the real identity of the person, including all of the biometric data. Once the system is in use, nothing an individual does can be hidden from the government, including transactions as small as a petty cash payment.

This Aadhaar project was developed in parallel with the creation of the India Stack, the Indian digital currency. It is truly revolutionary, and even a petty cash transaction, such as buying a cup of coffee, can be carried out electronically; the identity of both payer and receiver will be authenticated by the UIA. Eventually, billions of people will be instantly identifiable by everything they have done or possessed since birth. The power of Identity MDLs will transform the world forever.

6.7   CHINESE DIGITAL CURRENCY – DCEP

China is already at the vanguard of mobile payment and digital currency would be a natural step forward. China's digital currency aims to integrate into the existing banking system, with commercial banks operating the digital wallets for the central bank's currency. The Chinese digital currency uses a distributed ledger in a limited way, different from well-known cryptocurrencies, such as Bitcoin. The issuing bank can verify the ownership of the digital currency to realize peer-to-peer cash transactions. The goal is not to replace the paper currency, but to allow digital and paper currencies to circulate side by side.

China conducted a limited test of its national digital currency in June 2017.[23] The earliest tests involved prototype transactions between the digital currency and some of China's commercial banks. Because there was no guarantee that the digital currency would be able to meet its intended purposes without negative consequences, the test provided a valuable experience.

Since the test was successful, China officially announced a digital currency, called Digital Currency Electronic Payment, or DCEP, issued by the Central Bank of China in 2020. It is also known as eCNY. It is freely exchangeable with the RMB, the paper currency. People can obtain DCEP by linking their DCEP wallet to their bank account, or by exchanging between cash and DCEP in an authorized money exchange, such as a bank. In this manner, cash and DCEP can be exchanged freely.

If people have the DCEP digital wallets on their mobile phones, transferring funds can be as simple as tapping two phones (even without Internet access) because it uses near-field communication (NFC) to complete the payment.

DCEP may pave the way for the internationalization of the renminbi. With digital currency ledgers, it is possible to analyze data and draw economic insights in real time. This would certainly help the government in the development of its broad plans and strategies. It can also facilitate cross-border transactions, as well as the use of the renminbi outside of China. It could lower the cost of financial transactions and make financial services more efficient.

In August 2020, large scale testing began. The four largest commercial banks, Bank of China, China Construction Bank, Industrial and Commercial Bank of China, and Agricultural Bank of China, began testing DCEP.

By testing a digital currency, China was seriously exploring the technical, logistical, economic, and operational challenges involved in deploying digital money, something that could ultimately have broad implications for its economy and for the financial system.

During the test, people used DCEP to pay for purchases, and withdrew and transferred money after pairing the digital currency with their phone number.

6.8 FACEBOOK LIBRA/DIEM

In 2019, Facebook announced its digital currency called Libra, which would be backed up by real currencies. The company partnered with payment companies such as Visa, Stripe, PayPal, and Mercado Pago; tech companies such as eBay, Lyft, Uber, Spotify, and Mercado Pago; telecom companies such as Vodafone and Iliad; venture capital companies such as Breakthrough Initiatives, Andreessen Horowitz, and Ribit Capital; and blockchain companies, such as Anchorage, Bison Trails, and Coinbase. These companies were the founding members of Libra and formed an association to manage nodes in the Libra network. Like the nodes in the Bitcoin network, they validated Libra transactions.

Libra scaled back and changed its name to Diem in December 2020. Although it is not a national currency, considering Facebook's billions of active worldwide users, Diem may assert significant influence in the financial world. It could become more powerful than any single national digital currency, including the U.S. dollar: there are 1.7 billion people in the world without access to a bank and other financial services.

Diem uses a token, like other cryptocurrencies like Bitcoin, and uses a blockchain network as the technical foundation of the token and the tool for verifying transactions and token ownership. To make Diem less volatile and speculative, it has to be supported by the existing currencies from around the world.

Facebook created a new subsidiary, Calibra, to support Diem and build a digital wallet for the storage and exchange of Libra using Facebook apps. It also formed Libra Association, based in Geneva, Switzerland, for the governance of the Libra network and the development of the Diem project.

Diem's blockchain is open-source. Anyone can build an app or develop a service using Diem and people can obtain Diem either by linking their bank account, using a credit card, or exchanging Diem with cash at any authorized dealer, which means that Diem is freely exchangeable with many real currencies.

However, not long after Facebook announced the creation of Libra, the project was met with a strong backlash from across the political spectrum. Regulators were concerned about Facebook's potential outsize influence on the project, and the unforeseen consequences of allowing for-profit companies to begin issuing currencies and injecting themselves into global economics and geopolitics.

Most governments in the world are against such a digital currency. In October 2019, the financial leaders of the world's seven biggest economies, G7, openly opposed Libra, citing the lack of regulation. Since the Libra platform was permissioned and centralized, the organization which runs Libra – The Libra Association, may wield unruly power in the future.

There were also concerns over how to classify the Libra token, and how the entire platform would be properly regulated and by whom, especially as it moved toward offering banking services like lending. Chief among the concerns was the ability of the currency and technology to allow people to move money around undetected and away from the banking system, potentially leading to money laundering and other criminal activities.

On October 23, 2019, Mark Zuckerberg appeared at the House Financial Services Committee hearing to present the case for Libra. It catalyzed a rare alignment of opposition from the party's members of Congress and some Trump administration officials, who were concerned that Libra could unsettle the global financial system in an unexpected way. The Committee strongly disapproved of Libra. Representative Maxine Waters expressed concerns that a large tech company created a privately controlled, alternative global currency.

Under the regulatory pressure, several founding members such as Mastercard, PayPal, Stripe, and Visa all bowed out of the Libra Association.

Facebook scaled down its plans for its Diem project following months of severe regulatory pressure and political pushback. Instead of making the Calibra wallet available all over the world at launch, it restricted the availability to the currencies the Diem project supports to the app. The downsizing of the Diem project is symbolic, but the real essence remains the same. There is nothing to prevent the Diem Association from adding more currencies to its app.

In early 2022, Meta (formerly known as Facebook) decided to sell Diem Association to Diem Association to Silvergate Capital Corporation for $182 million, when it became clear that federal regulators would not allow Diem project to move ahead.[24,25]

6.9   NON-FUNGIBLE TOKENS (NFTS)

NFTs (Non-Fungible Tokens) are Ethereum-blockchain-based tokens, representing ownership of an asset, whether physical or digital, including art, collectibles, IPs such as music or video, and even real estate. Like any article with ownership, it has one unique owner at a time. It can be traded on an Ethereum marketplace.

Like Bitcoin or Ethereum, NFTs are unique digitally, and each NFT has an owner and a public record, which can be verified. Content creators can sell their work.

NFTs are minted through smart contracts that assign ownership and manage their transferability. NFTs cannot be replicated because in order to do so, one must go through the same process of transfer for the replication, i.e., create a new block, validate it, and record the information into the blockchain. Each NFT has a unique identifier that is directly linked to one Ethereum address. NFTs can be bought and sold on any Ethereum-based NFT market. Like Bitcoin, the private key of NFT is proof-of-ownership of the original. The public key serves as a certificate of authenticity for that digital artifact. NFTs are held in an Ethereum wallet.

NFTs have easily verifiable transaction histories and tokens, making them ideal for many applications. It is simple to prove ownership history. Once a transaction is confirmed, it is nearly impossible to manipulate the data. Therefore, ownership is secure from alteration. Trading NFTs can happen peer-to-peer with minimum transaction costs.

Because an NFT is smart-contract-based, it can be programmed to automatically pay out royalties to its creators when it is sold. In this way, it collects royalties for the creative artists. NFTs are popular today in the digital content realm. Many content creators publish their work on social media platforms such as YouTube. In return, they receive very little income from advertisers. By using NFTs, creators do not give ownership of their content over to the platforms. They receive royalties directly from those who use the content.

When the creators sell their content, the funds go directly to them. If the new owner then sells the NFT, the original creator can automatically receive royalties. This is guaranteed every time it is sold because the creator's address is part of the token's metadata – metadata which can't be modified.

Physical assets can also be represented by NFTs, which can be considered as deeds. In doing so, an Ethereum wallet becomes the safe in which to deposit the ownership documents for assets such as a car or home. The property represented on Ethereum by NFTs can be used as collateral in decentralized loans. The decentralized loan is a financial service of DeFi (Decentralized Finance). One can take out a loan in DeFi applications using an NFT as collateral. In the DeFi world, there is potentially an equivalent service for every service provided to users in the existing financial world. NFTs are acting as one of the key elements.

Like Bitcoin, NFTs are created by miners. To create an NFT, one needs to confirm the asset on the blockchain. The confirmation, considered a transaction, needs to be added to a block to be part of the blockchain. The block needs to be confirmed by everyone in the network – a process of consensus. All these tasks are done by Ethereum miners who let the rest of the network know about the newly created NFT and who owns it. The difficulty of mining and making Ethereum tamper-proof ensures the security of the block. Ethereum blocks are created every 12 seconds.

The downside of Ethereum mining, like Bitcoin, is that it is energy intensive; it still uses the PoW consensus mechanism. However, Ethereum is going through upgrades to replace PoW by staking, as discussed in Chapter 5. This will reduce Ethereum's carbon footprint drastically. However, stakers must commit funds to secure the network.

The energy-cost of Ethereum will become the cost of running a home computer multiplied by the number of nodes in the network. If there are 10,000 nodes in the network and the cost of running a home computer is roughly 525 kWh per year. That's 5,250,000 kWh per year for the entire network.

We can use this to compare the future of Ethereum to a global service like Visa, where 100,000 Visa transactions use 149 kWh of energy. In proof-of-stake Ethereum, 100,000 transactions would consume 17.4 kWh of energy. This improves the energy efficiency while preserving Ethereum's decentralization and security. Ethereum does more than just financial transactions; it is also a platform for applications such as smart contracts (which Visa does not offer).

There are other cryptocurrencies using staking, but they are secured by fewer stakers than Ethereum, and the more stakers there are, the more secure the system.

REFERENCES

1. "A simple explanation of Bitcoin sidechain": Richard G. Brown, *https://gendal.me/2014/10/26/a-simple- explanation-of-Bitcoin-sidechains/*

2. *http://identity.foundation/*

3. *https://blockstack.org/*

4. *https://www.microsoft.com/en-us/security/business/identity-access-management/microsoft-identity-management-platform*

5. *https://www.uport.me/*

6. *https://onename.com/*

7. "Hyperledger welcomes Indy", *https://www.hyperledger.org/blog/2017/05/02/hyperledger-welcomes-project-indy*

8. "Next consensus architecture proposal." E. Androulaki, et. al. *https://github.com/hyperledger/fabric/blob/master/proposals/r1/Next-Consensus-Architecture-Proposal.md,2016.*

9. *https://www.duedil.com/*

10. *https://www.pingidentity.com/en*

11. *https://www.gov.uk/government/publications/introducing-govuk-verify/introducing-govuk-verify*

12. *www.zyen.com*

13. *https://www.investopedia.com/countries-developing-central-bank-digital-currency-cbdc-5221005*

14. *https://www.gov.uk/government/publications/g7-public-policy-principles-for-retail-central-bank-digital-currencies-and-g7-finance-ministers-and-central-bank-governors-statement-on-central-bank*

15. *https://www.reuters.com/world/asia-pacific/japans-digital-yen-plan-become-clearer-late-2022-says-ruling-party-official-2021-07-05/*

16. *https://www.federalreserve.gov/central-bank-digital-currency.htm*

17. *https://www.bexs.com.br/blog/digital-real-the-brazilian-digital-currency-is-coming/*

18. *https://cointelegraph.com/news/blockchain-revolution-in-russia-bank-of-russia-tests-masterchain*

19. *https://www.financemagnates.com/cryptocurrency/news/russia-to-launch-digital-ruble-prototype-in-early-2022/*

20. "India tried to get the 'black money' out of its banking system — it ended up doing the opposite", CNBC, *https://www.cnbc.com/2017/09/07/ demonetization-reserve-bank-of-india-suggests-that-demonetisation- allowed-black-money-to-enter-banking-system.html*

21. Unique Identification Authority of India website" *https://uidai.gov.in/*

22. "India's 'BankChain' Consortium Launches Blockchain KYC System", Stan Higgins, *https://www.coindesk.com/indias-bankchain-consortium- launches-blockchain-kyc-system/*

23. "China central bank has begun cautiously testing a digital currency", Will Knight, *https://www.technologyreview.com/s/608088/chinas-central- bank-has-begun-cautiously-testing-a-digital-currency/*

24. *https://abcnews.go.com/Business/wireStory/end-facebook-backed-digital- currency-diem-sold-bank-82603571*

25. *https://www.cryptovantage.com/news/facebook-sells-off-doomed-diem- currency-project-what-does-it-mean-for-crypto/*

7

Blockchain Beyond Cryptocurrency

While all cryptocurrencies are built on the blockchain, there are many other non-crypto applications.

7.1   BIGCHAINDB

The BigchainDB platform, developed by a German company called BigchainDB GmbH in 2016, is an open-source system that adds blockchain-like features to a distributed database. Its objective is to build an MDL with the advantages of both Bitcoin-like blockchain and the traditional distributed database. It takes an approach that is opposite than most MDL approaches. Instead of building the database in the form of a distributed ledger, it builds a distributed ledger out of a database.[1]

BigchainDB takes advantage of a distributed database's own built-in consensus algorithm to tolerate benign faults and use the DB's built-in communication to reduce complexity and security risk. Like any MDL, it has decentralized control and immutability and can transfer digital assets.

Compared to the Bitcoin blockchain, it has a much faster transaction speed with sub-second latency and can store much more data. It removes all the elements in the Bitcoin-like blockchain that slow down the operation and limit the scalability. For example, it uses a hash chain instead of the Merkle tree and replaces PoW with consensus. Mechanisms such as shared replication, reversion of disallowed updates or deletions, regular database backups, cryptographic signing of all transactions, and blocks and votes guarantee the immutability/tamper resistance. Each vote on a block also includes the hash of a previous block. Any entity with asset-issuance permissions can issue an asset. A new owner can acquire an asset if they fulfill its cryptographic conditions.

The permissioned blockchain supports custom assets, transactions, permissions, and transparency. BigchainDB uses Tendermint for consensus and transaction replication. Tendermint is a version of the Byzantine Fault Tolerant protocol. Tendermint can replicate an application on many machines securely and consistently.

Tendermint consists of two components: a blockchain consensus engine and a generic application interface. The consensus engine, called Tendermint Core, ensures that the same transactions are recorded on every machine in the same order. The application interface, called the Application BlockChain Interface (ABCI), can process the transactions in any programming language. Tendermint is easy-to-use, simple-to-understand, and useful for a wide variety of distributed applications.

BigchainDB also gets rid of the token. It can be configured as a permissioned or permissionless MDL. Increasing its number of nodes can increase its throughput and capacity.

An existing database can add BigchainDB to gain decentralization benefits. One can also build a BigchainDB database from scratch into a full-blown decentralization ecosystem. Since it is a database, it can store documents, contracts, or any form of data just like traditional databases without encountering a scalability issue.

In a Bitcoin-like blockchain, every node has a replica of the blockchain and so the database can become very large. It is impossible for the participating nodes to have the capacity to store such a large database. Therefore, it is unlikely that the blockchain is replicated at every node. The solution is partial replication. For example, in Netflix's database, each piece of data has only three replications. Partial replication protects the data and yet does not overload the storage capacity. As the database grows, the number of nodes grows proportionally, but the number of replications remains the same. Thus, the total storage capacity increases with the number of nodes. The capacity of most modern distributed DBs increases linearly with the number of nodes. In such a system, the database's latency and network usage remains the same. Therefore, it scales linearly.

BigchainDB takes the same approach of partial replication to limit the blockchain size. In summary, BigchainDB is an MDL built from a traditional database by adding blockchain characteristics including decentralization, immutability, and built-in support for creation and transfer of assets.

7.2 LIGHTNING NETWORK

The Lightning Network[2] is a micropayments-enabling low cost and instantaneous network that operates bi-directional off-blockchain payment channels, sometimes called *microchannels*.[3] Channels can be created by funding transactions. The funding amount is the maximum amount that can be spent on this channel. The payment is sent in the form of redeemable IOUs. It also works like a debit card. It is able to process thousands of transactions per second, rather than every 10 minutes like Bitcoin today; moreover, there is no transaction fee.

Joseph Poon and Thaddeus Dryja first proposed the idea in a white paper. Multiple developers developed the software. The framework of the Lightning Network is set up to encourage multiple developers to contribute to its development. Functionalities can be introduced without affecting all Bitcoin users. According to its developers, the Lightning Network is safer and more reliable than SegWit.[3] Bitfury Group,[4] a full-service blockchain technology company, has tested the Lightning Network algorithm successfully.

The Lightning Network uses the built-in blockchain smart contracts with the same security and immutability of the Bitcoin blockchain itself, but it is able to overcome the delay in Bitcoin micropayment transactions and to avoid the counterparty risk.

In the Lightning Network, parties use multisig addresses between them for a predetermined period, or the nLockTime for the transaction, which creates a ledger entry on the blockchain. Both parties need to fund the ledger to open the channel.

They also create refund transactions in case the transaction fails (say, one party does not honor the contract). However, this will not happen until the nLockTime elapses to allow sufficient time to complete the transaction.

The parties can transact as many times as they want between them as long as the channel is open (without broadcasting the transaction to the blockchain). The ledger updates itself instantly after each new transaction. When they decide to close the channel, either one of the parties can broadcast the transaction to the blockchain. Upon closing the channel, they receive refunds of the initial funding.

This is somewhat like when you pay a cashier with coins; you lay out the coins on the table one by one and audibly count them. The cashier waits to take the coins until both sides confirm that the sum of the total coins is the transaction amount. Only then does the cashier take the coins and ring up the purchase.

Once the transaction is broadcasted to the Bitcoin network and the channel is closed, the transaction proceeds normally like any other Bitcoin transaction. The multi-micropayments will appear as a single transaction to the Bitcoin platform. This reduces the loading of the Bitcoin transaction and effectively increases the block capacity without touching the blockchain functions.

Since there is no limit on how many channels can be opened in the Bitcoin network, Bitcoin scalability can be achieved using a large network of micropayment channels. This implementation does not require a soft fork and may be used on the Bitcoin blockchain with minimal risk.

In addition to the channel being bi-directional, it also involves more than two parties. When there is no direct channel between two parties, they can create a transaction path through the existing open channels involving third parties. Figure 7.1 shows the payment from Alice to Bob through the four existing channels (Alice to A, A to B, B to C, C to Bob) in the Lightning Network.[5]

The ledger entry data are sent over the network in a manner similar to routing packets on the Internet. The nodes along the path need not be trustworthy because the payment is processed by a script in the smart contract, which enforces the pass-and-fail of the entire payment through a time-lock. Anyone who intercepts the micropayment will not be able to use it since they are only pockets of information which will not turn into a Bitcoin transaction until the transaction is processed by the Bitcoin network. In this way, the transaction is secure without a third party. Thus, transactions can be done off-blockchain and with the confidence of the blockchain enforceability.

A Hashed Time Lock Contract (HTLC) is used to enhance trust when a third party is involved. Since many transactions are off-blockchain, malleability poses a bigger problem. Therefore, the implementation of the Lightning Network solution is possible only after SegWit is activated in the blockchain.

Although miners do not receive fees for off-blockchain transactions, they receive the benefit of dramatically increased transaction volume. The increased transaction volume results in greater income — in the form of fees — for the miners.

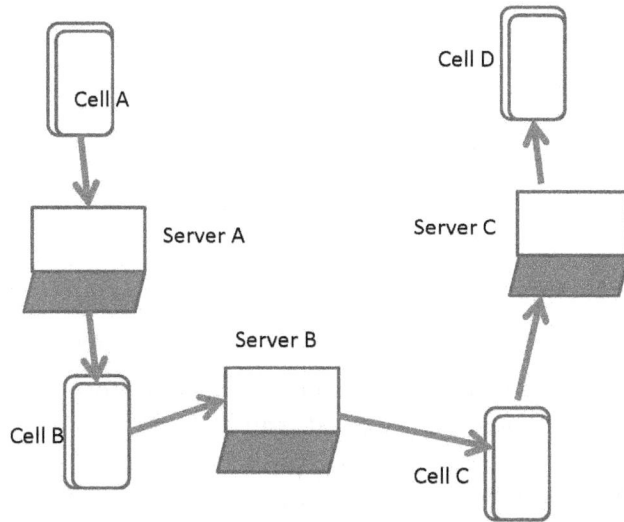

FIGURE 7.1 Payment from Cell A to Cell D through third parties.

The Lightning Lab released a new version called Lightning Network Daemon (LND) in the same month. The new version added a Litecoin operating mode for the cross chain atomic swap, which meets the requirements of all the swapping parties. LDN can manage channels on both Bitcoin and Litecoin blockchain and allow transfer between these two chains.[6]

The Lightning solution has the potential to stream money or allow instant Payment for Value. The idea of Payment for Value or Value-Based Payment (VBP) comes from the healthcare industry. Value-Based Payment is a strategy used by purchasers to promote the quality and value of healthcare services. The goal of the VBP program is to shift from a purely volume-based payment, as exemplified by fee-for-service payments, to payments more closely related to outcomes. Such a strategy evolved from the earlier Payment-for-Performance (P4P) strategy.

The Instant Payment for Value can be applied beyond the healthcare industry. For example, it will be an essential development for IoT where machines will generate billions of transactions per second and clear the transactions immediately.

A structural shift in commerce that creates market liquidity can transform the retail industry by leveling the playing field for smaller businesses to get paid online. The Lightning Network can unlock Bitcoin's massive potential. For example, its ability to handle micropayments utilizing all of the eight decimal places available allows people to trade tiny amounts of value, which is currently not economically sound on the Bitcoin payment rails.

However, the Lightning Network is not without criticism.[7] Some think the Lightning Network can lead to centralization. After all, the banks have all the resources to provide thousands of open channels.[8]

7.3   CORDA

Corda is an open-source distributed ledger platform.[9] It is a product of R3, which was founded in 2014 as a distributed database technology company and headquartered in New York. R3 considers Corda a distributed database rather than an MDL technology.

Corda is designed to be used by regulated financial institutions.[10] It leads a consortium of more than 400 of the world's biggest financial institutions, which represents the largest joint effort among banks, insurers, fund managers, and other institutions working on applications using blockchain technology in regulated markets.

In a traditional distributed database system, the multiple nodes that share the distributed database belong to a single entity or owner, such as a company. There is already a trust between the distributed database system as a whole and its users. Each node in the system trusts the data that it receives from its peers and nodes are trusted to look after the data they have received from their peers. Validation is necessary only when this distributed database exchanges information with the outside world.

Corda's distributed database does not reside in a system with a single owner; rather, it can spread to many independent and unrelated nodes on the Internet. To do so, Corda must build trust by independently verifying the data nodes which they receive from each other.

Corda uses cryptographic techniques, the key element in the blockchain technology, for the security of shared records. Even though Corda does not use PoW and mining, it shares many qualities with Bitcoin, including immutable states and transactions with multiple inputs and outputs.

Nevertheless, Corda does not use blockchain or broadcast the transactions to all the nodes in the network. Instead, Corda sends data only to the relevant parties. Corda relies heavily on secure cryptographic hashes to identify parties and data.

In a Corda system, the ledger has a different definition; it is not a list of all transactions but a set of immutable state objects. It defines states and transactions, where every transaction consumes existing states and produces a new state (Figure 7.2). The issuer and affected nodes must endorse transactions to ensure their validity according to the underlying smart-contract logic.

Only nodes affected by the transaction receive the new state. In other words, only the parties with the privilege to see the data can share the data. This improves the privacy, scalability, and legal-system compatibility of a traditional distributed database. It prevents the sharing of transactions with unrelated parties that occurs with other MDLs. This provides a means for partitioning the data among the nodes.

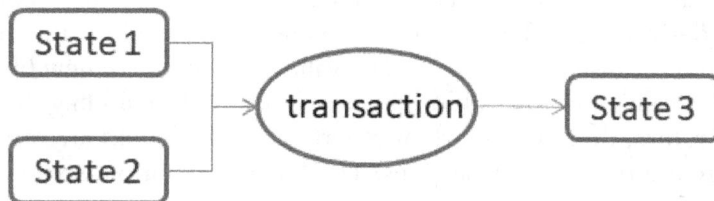

FIGURE 7.2 Corda transaction consumes existing states and produces new state.

Notary, which consists of independent parties running the same contract code and validation logic, verifies the validity and uniqueness of the transaction to all its input states. It must ensure that each state can only be consumed once. The notary also timestamps the transaction and the states pointing to it. The state may also designate an asset, which can be anything controlled by a smart contract or tokens.

An immutable state object in the Corda system is the hash of a legal prose and contract code that governs its transitions. Corda uses smart contract, timestamping, and a framework, which simplifies the process to achieve the immutable state objects. A transaction produces a new state, which represents the change in the input state object.

Corda supports smart contracts with many unique features. For example, it records and manages financial agreements or any other shared data between parties in the legal constructs and regulation by including regulatory and supervisory observer nodes. It organizes workflow, supports consensus, and validates transactions between parties in the transaction.

In summary, the Corda system is a hybrid of a mutual distributed ledger and a distributed database. The Corda application is known as CorDapp (short for Corda Distributed Applications).[11]

7.4 HYDRACHAIN

HydraChain[12] is an open source, permissioned distributed ledger platform based on Ethereum. In essence, it is the permissioned version of permissionless Ethereum. Its protocol is fully compatible with Ethereum's. HydraChain supports the creation of a permissioned distributed ledger using the Ethereum infrastructure.

Like BigchainDB, HydraChain uses a proprietary consensus protocol derived from Tendermint – a consensus based on the Byzantine Fault Tolerant consensus protocol. The validators negotiate new blocks. A quorum of the validators signs off on the new blocks before adding them to the chain. Therefore, there is no fork or revert. The new blocks are created only when there are pending transactions. The block generation is very fast, taking less than a second.

The important feature of HydraChain is that it enables the development of smart contracts in the Python high-level language, which is easy to use and debug. The contract written in Python in HydraChain is compatible with EVM based contracts written in the Solidity or Serpent languages and can co-exist on the same chain. Therefore, it is fully compatible with the Ethereum Protocol. The code runs significantly faster than the codes in Solidity or Serpent.

Users can also customize Hydrachain to their needs. This makes Hydrachain highly useful to many applications.

7.5 MULTICHAIN

The MultiChain blockchain platform,[13] launched by Coin Sciences,[14] allows financial institutions to create a public or private blockchain. MultiChain is a permissioned blockchain and an open source blockchain platform based on Bitcoin's blockchain for multi-asset financial transactions. It uses the Byzantine Fault Tolerant variation of the consensus protocol. Users can tailor these blockchains to their particular needs and deploy either within or between organizations. It allows institutional financial entities to deploy blockchain technology. It also provides the privacy and control they require.[15]

The name MultiChain comes from users' ability to connect to multiple blockchains they created using MultiChain. The owner can also issue assets on the blockchain it created to track and verify assets at the network level and perform multi-asset and multi-party atomic exchange transactions, which simultaneously meet the requirements for multiple assets and multiple parties. It can also create multiple key value, time series, or identity databases on a blockchain for data sharing, time stamping, and encrypted archiving.

MultiChain has the flexibility to allow customers to control many aspects of the blockchain. The chain can be private or public. The user can control the target time for blocks, limit the visibility of the ledger to certain participants, and set the controls on the transactions permitted. The user can also decide who can connect to the network, how these entities interact, and the maximum block size and metadata included in transactions, among other features.

Because MultiChain uses Bitcoin's protocol, transaction, and blockchain architecture, an application of MultiChain can move between Bitcoin and MultiChain with minimal changes to its code. Therefore, it provides smooth transitions between private blockchain and the Bitcoin blockchain. Its interface is fully compatible with that of Bitcoin Core. It can also act as a node on the Bitcoin network.

Like other permissioned blockchains, only nodes in the permitted list can validate blocks and participate in the protocol. Their public keys can identify them. The miner of the first "Genesis" block automatically receives all privileges, including administrator rights to manage the privileges of other users. This administrator grants privileges to other users in transactions whose outputs contain those users' addresses together with metadata denoting the privileges conferred. However, to remove the privileges of a user requires voting of the existing administrators. The voting process increases transparency of the network.

Since the MultiChain platform evolves from Bitcoin, it also relies on "mining" for consensus. However, in the permissioned model, the nodes do not solve computational puzzles. The administrators generate blocks under certain constraints. If two different nodes generate a valid block at the same time, any other node will append the one it encounters first to its chain. This creates a fork. Ultimately, the longer branch will win, and all nodes will continue mining on top of it. Transactions in the blocks of the shorter branch re-enter the memory pool of nodes. That means that they will start the confirmation process over again like any other new transactions.

The modifications to privileges propagate quickly to all nodes in the network. To avoid one participant monopolizing the mining process, MultiChain implemented a restriction on the number of blocks that the same miner can create within a given window.

The user can also grant permissions on a limited basis or to a fixed range of blockchain numbers. In MultiChain, its administrators have the authority to set a list of permitted users that can act as nodes. The user can also grant privileges using transactions with special metadata.

MultiChain uses the consensus mechanism of the Practical Byzantine Fault Tolerance with one validator per block. The MultiChain validation process enables miners to approve transactions in a random rotation. A MultiChain user can also set the percentage of the miners' approval needed to record a block.

MultiChain also allows the chain's owner to control the maximum block size, so that scaling is not a problem. MultiChain uses the public key and private key to restrict blockchain access to a list of permitted users.

The scope of the permissions extends to many other operations on the network. For example, the right to send and receive transactions and mine can be restricted to certain privileged addresses.

For a blockchain to be truly private, at least one administrator must know the real-world identity of the person using the address with permissioned privilege. Most participants in the chain need not know each other's identities.

A key feature of blockchain is allowing peer-to-peer exchange transactions with an anonymous address so that each party does not know the identity of its counterparty. In the real world, this would be like a hotel receptionist who does not disclose the room number of guests to others but delivers messages from others to the guests. One could imagine financial institutions transacting under many different addresses, with only regulators knowing which address belongs to which.

As a blockchain, MultiChain has the advantage over centralized databases in that each participant retains full control over its assets via their private key while the database is simultaneously distributed across many entities. It is also more robust since the malfunctioning of one server will not affect the continued processing of transactions by the network as a whole.

Because MultiChain blockchain is privately owned, there is no transaction fee and block reward. However, MultiChain can be configured to use fiat currency for block rewards, minimum transaction fees, and output quantities.

7.6 QUORUM

Similar to HydraChain, Quorum is another private or Permissioned blockchain technology based on the Ethereum platform.[16] By using Ethereum's core, Quorum can incorporate most Ethereum updates quickly and seamlessly. It uses majority voting BTF, a Raft-based consensus model for faster block times, transaction finality, and on-demand block creation. It focuses on enterprise and industrial applications, which require transaction privacy and control. It is ideal for applications requiring high speed and high throughput processing of private transactions. This suits the financial industry particularly well. J.P. Morgan is experimenting with Quorum for its high speed and high throughput processing of private transactions.[17]

Much of the privacy functionality resides in a separate layer on top of the standard Ethereum protocol layer. Quorum treats public transactions and private transactions differently. Public transactions are visible and validated by all nodes. Only the relevant nodes can see the private transactions and execute its contracts. Other nodes that are not part of the parties involved in the private transaction simply skip this transaction execution. In this way, the state database splits into two databases: a private one and a public one. All nodes in the network are in tune with their public state. Nevertheless, their private state databases are selective to their involvement. However, all nodes fully replicate the distributed blockchain and all the encrypted transactions.

Microsoft's Azure Cloud Computing platform, EBaaS, hosts Quorum platform so that Quorum applications can also run on a cloud. J.P. Morgan's Quorum platform also implements a zero-knowledge security layer, which gives Quorum the same privacy features of Zcash and complies with government regulations.

7.7   HYPERLEDGER

The industry leaders in finance, banking, IoT, supply chains, manufacturing, and technology collaborated to develop the Hyperledger blockchain frameworks. Its collaborators include well known blockchain companies (ConsenSys and R3), technology companies (Cisco, Fujitsu, Hitachi, IBM, Intel, NEC, and NTT Data), financial services firms (ABN AMRO, BNY Mellon, CME Group, CLS Group, and Wells Fargo Bank), and many others. The Linus Foundation facilitated the collaboration. It is an open-source collaborative effort created to advance cross-industry blockchain technologies.

Four Hyperledger blockchain platforms were developed for different applications: Hyperledger Fabric (a private and permissioned blockchain platform for enterprise), Hyperledger Iroha (a version of Hyperledger Fabric focused on mobile applications), Hyperledger Burrow (an Ethereum Virtual Machine), and Hyperledger Sawtooth (Intel's blockchain platform).

Hyperledger Fabric, a private and permissioned blockchain platform for the enterprises, is based on the earlier versions of Blockstream's libconsensus and IBM's OpenBlockchain. The production ready Hyperledger Fabric was announced in July 2017. It has blockchain's advantages of consensus and immutability; moreover, it is modular, meaning it is flexible, scalable, and can support plug-ins of different components to accommodate a wide variety of differences across the enterprise ecosystem. Its trust is not built on PoW, but network members are admitted through the enrollment.

To achieve the maximum flexibility, Hyperledger Fabric stores ledger data in multiple formats. It can customize consensus mechanisms and support different Membership Service Providers (MSP).[18] Members can create their own separate Mutual Distributed Ledgers (MDL) for privacy. Only members can access their MDLs.

As discussed in Chapter 6, like any multi-MDL platform, Hyperledger Fabric has a Transaction MDL and Content MDL. Together they form the Hyperledger Fabric's MDL. The Content MDL in Hyperledger is the current state, or the "world state," and the Transaction MDL contains the transaction log.

Members run applications external to the blockchain to interact with the MDLs. The apps invoke the Hyperledger Fabric smart contracts written in a language called chaincode. The ledger writes the consensus transactions in the order they occur. Each MDL can choose a consensus mechanism that best represents the relationships that exist between its members. The architecture of Hyperledger Fabric is highly elastic and extensible, making it different from other blockchain solutions. Hyperledger Fabric also supports multiple networks to manage different assets, agreements, and transactions.

Hyperledger Fabric has normal database functions such as query and update. Peer nodes validate the submitted transactions against endorsement policies described in a channel's ledger. The endorsement policies also have built-in consensus mechanisms, such as Sumeragi, a Byzantine Fault Tolerant consensus algorithm.[19] The nodes validate these transactions if they meet the policy criteria checks.[20]

Hyperledger Sawtooth Lake is another Hyperledger modular blockchain suite that supports both permissioned and permissionless deployments. It can run general-purpose smart contracts on a distributed ledger. Transaction logic in Hyperledger Sawtooth Lake is separate from the consensus layer. The consensus mechanism used is the Proof of Elapsed Time (PoET).[21,22,23,24] PoET, originally developed by Intel, is based on PoW's mandatory but random imposition of waiting time for leader election. Once the timer expires, the leader node can prove to all others that it has executed the "waiting step" correctly for extending the blockchain. This creates a stable consensus protocol. PoET consensus executes the waiting step in Intel's CPU, using the Intel CPU instruction set, called Intel Software Guard Extensions (SGX). This special hardware component creates an attestation or confirmation. Any node can use this confirmation to verify that the leader has correctly waited for the proper random time. This has the same effect as PoW does with mining.

This process is much more energy efficient than PoW. However, the probability of a node becoming the leader is proportional to the number of hardware modules under its control. As long as there are a large number of trusted nodes, PoET is compatible with a Permissionless blockchain.

In a Permissioned environment, the participating nodes are by invitation only, and all of them are trusted nodes. However, with known nodes, traditional PoET consensus does not offer advantages over BFT consensus protocols; BFT is more efficient and does not rely on a single vendor's hardware.

To enhance the collaboration with the Chinese Hyperledger community, the Hyperledger Technical Steering Committee formed a Technical Working Group China (TWG China) in December 2016.[25]

TWG China is a bridge between the global Hyperledger community, emerging technical users, and contributors in China and other regions, including Hong Kong and Taiwan. TWG China is now led by key contributors from China, who actively contribute to the Hyperledger Technical Community and build the consortium ecosystem. The chairpersons of the working group are from IBM, Wanda, and Huawei.

7.8   DECENTRALIZED INTERNET

Today, Internet Service Providers (ISPs) are the operators of the Internet, meaning users pay ISPs to use the Internet. With the blockchain technology, it is possible to bypass ISPs and communicate through a peer-to-peer network.

The team at Open Internet Socialization Project (OISP) is working on a network called Andrena.[26] This network consists of computers in the vicinity of a certain Wi-Fi network acting as nodes in a wireless grid to help deliver data to each other. The envisioned Andrena network connects the Wi-Fi hotspots in the vicinity to form a local network. The public blockchain manages the flow of information. All users seamlessly transact with each other on the blockchain directly.

The typical household Wi-Fi can project the Wi-Fi signal only up to 1.5 miles. To reach the network beyond this Wi-Fi coverage area, it would require a higher power Wi-Fi router. Someone would have to install such a facility for any connectivity beyond the vicinity. Such a facility may charge for the service, but it is much cheaper than the service provided by an ISP. This concept is illustrated in Figure 7.3.

In this way, the infrastructure is decentralized. The ownership does not belong to one company, but rather the users. This is another example of the sharing economy. Instead of paying ISPs for providing the infrastructure, the community pays each other, which is usually much cheaper. The blockchain technology ensures fairness without trust. It allows Andrena networks to form and organize without a central authority.

Of course, some nodes in the network will be gateways to the Internet outside of the Andrena network. Some users maintain connections to the existing ISP providers. The price of the Internet at this level is much cheaper than the price of the Internet via ISPs.

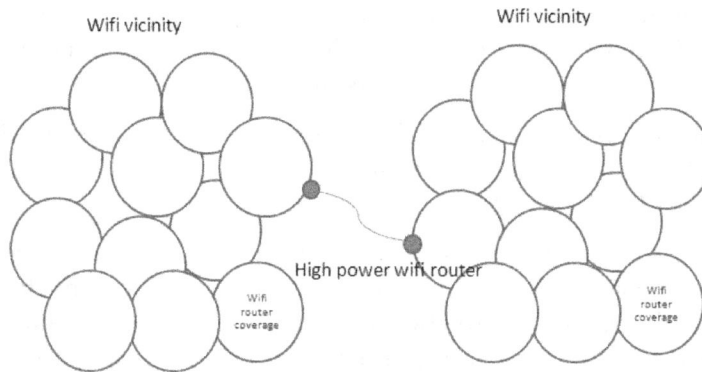

FIGURE 7.3 A P2P Internet.

There are many technical issues to be resolved in this system, such as verifying that nodes are providing their agreed amount of bandwidth. Security is another issue. An encrypted tunnel between users' devices and the gateway nodes needs to be created to ensure that no one in the middle can see the data traffic.

7.9   OTHER BLOCKCHAIN PLATFORMS

There are many other blockchain platforms and their numbers are increasing every day. Openchain[27] is an open-source distributed ledger system for issuing and managing digital assets. Tokens on Openchain can be pegged to Bitcoin, making it a sidechain.[28] The consensus mechanism used by Openchain is the Portioned Consensus. Openchain is a very centralized blockchain. Different authorities validate different transactions depending on the assets exchanged. However, only one authority validates each transaction. Like Hyperledger, each owner controls his or her own Openchain MDL. However, different MDLs can connect to each other. This is similar to the traditional banking system.

Stellar is another open source, distributed payment infrastructure that connects banks and payment systems. Stellar enables the building of mobile wallets, banking tools, and smart devices. An API called Horizon is the user interface, which connects users to the Stellar Core, the backbone of the Stellar network. The consensus mechanism is the Stellar Consensus Protocol.[28]

BitSE's Qtum is a new operating system for blockchain development combined with a modularized basic chain, which combines the advantages of numerous public chains like Bitcoin and Ethereum.

DGX[29] is a new gold-backed Ethereum smart contract coin developed by DigiX. Each GDX is equivalent to 1 gram of gold.[30] One can own, save, and transact Gold in GDX.

Decentralized Capital, a U.K. company, developed DC Assets, which can be exchanged to Dollars, Euros, and six others fiat currencies. DC Assets[30] is a digital currency secured by the Ethereum network and collateralized by customer deposits. Users can transact with DC Assets for products and services on the Ethereum blockchain.

It seems that the potential applications are limited only by imagination. For example, Microsoft is working on a secure ID system to prevent human trafficking. Everledger is developing a system to track of the origin of diamonds.[31] Imogen Heap released a song using a blockchain platform that allows artists to sell their music directly to their fans. Japan and Sweden are experimenting with putting their real estate registration on blockchain to improve efficiency and prevent fraud. The list goes on and on.

Goldman Sachs thinks that blockchain could disrupt everything.[32] The blockchain (MDL) technology, has the potential to transform the way people and businesses handle identity, transactions, and assets, resulting in many disruptive applications similar to those discussed in this chapter.

The most important characteristic of the MDL is that it can replace the trust, which is a necessary element to business transactions in today's world. It does so through three core functions that trusted third parties perform: validation, transaction, and recording. Everyone shares the ledger. The computer systems follow a common protocol to add new transactions.

In addition, MDLs are available instantly anywhere on the globe, and are verifiable, secure, robust, and cheap. Therefore, blockchain technology opens the door to infinite possibilities of business transactions.

Historically, distributed ledgers have suffered from two problems: insecurity and complexity. However, blockchain technology eliminates these problems by employing cryptography, and its integrity to prevent double spending is maintained by the block validation mechanism. The simplicity and robustness of the blockchain ensure that the system is simple to understand and to deploy.

MDLs incorporating trusted third parties had significant potential in financial services, such as know-your-customer (KYC), antimony-laundering

(AML), insurance, credit, and wholesale financial services. Blockchain technology has proven to be robust. It has gained confidence from large companies such as Nasdaq, BNY Mellon, UBS, USAA, IBM, and Samsung, which have used blockchain for various applications. MDLs can provide many competitive advantages.

7.10 BEYOND BLOCKCHAIN

Blockchain is not the only technology that can construct an MDL. Hashgraph is an alternative to the blockchain to build MDLs. Hashgraph can resolve Bitcoin's scaling and security issues, while also pushing the use of distributed consensus applications into new areas. According to Hashgraph, the company that pioneered the technology, Hashgraph is a data structure and consensus algorithm that is faster, fairer, and more secure than blockchain.[33] It uses two special techniques: Gossip about Gossip and Virtual Voting.[34] Gossip about Gossip involves attaching a small additional amount of information to a pair of hashes (Gossip) that contain the last two people talked to. By doing this, a Hashgraph can be built and updated whenever additional information is gossiped on each node.

Hashgraph uses an asynchronous Byzantine process to achieve agreement in the MDL.[35] It makes no assumptions about how fast messages are passed over the Internet, which makes it resilient against DDoS attacks, botnets, and firewalls. The Hashgraph algorithm works without the PoW, and therefore, does not require extensive resources. It can deliver low-cost and high-performance processing. For example, Bitcoin can process at 4.17 transactions per second on average, while Hashgraph can process as many as 250,000 transactions per second.

In addition, Hashgraph allows a fairer system of operations. In the blockchain system, miners can pick and choose any unconfirmed transactions to be included in a block, usually the high fee-paying- transactions, and can delay low-fee-paying transactions indefinitely. Hashgraph utilizes consensus timestamping and prevents any node from changing the consensus order of transactions by denying the ability to manipulate the order of transactions.

Despite its obvious benefits, as a latecomer, Hashgraph has a long way to go before it can boast the popularity enjoyed by blockchain technology. However, in the ever-evolving world of MDL technology, it seems the next paradigm shift is always just around the corner.

REFERENCES

1. "A BigchainDB primer", *https://www.bigchaindb.com/*

2. "The Bitcoin lightning network: scalable off-chain instant payments", Joseph Poon, Thaddeus Dryja, The lightning network white paper.

3. "Understanding the Lightning Network", Aaron van Wirdum, Bitcoin Magazine

4. *http://bitfury.com/*

5. LND overview and development guide, Lightning Network Developers, *http://dev.lightning.community/overview/#payment-channels*

6. "What is the Lightning Network Daemon", JP Buntinx, *http://themerkle.com*

7. "Mathematical proof that Lightning Network cannot be a decentralized Bitcoin solution", Jonald Fyoodball, *http://medium.com*

8. "Simulating a decentralized network with 10 million users", Diane Reynolds, *http://hackernoon.com*

9. *https://www.corda.net/*

10. "Corda: an introduction": Richard G. Brown et. al. *https://docs.corda.net/_static/corda-introductory- whitepaper.pdf*

11. *https://docs.corda.net/cordapp-overview.html*

12. *https://github.com/HydraChain*

13. MultiChain whitepaper: *http://www.MultiChain.com/white- paper/*

14. "An open source project for creating a private blockchain ecosystem preloaded with MultiChain and related tools", YobiChain, https://github.com/Primechain/yobichain

15. MultiChain official site: *http://www.MultiChain.com/developers/*

16. *https://www.jpmorgan.com/country/US/EN/Quorum*

17. *https://github.com/jpmorganchase/quorum*

18. "Membership Service Providers", *http://hyperledger-fabric.readthedocs.io/en/release/msp.html*

19. Hyperledger Iroha's github page: *https://github.com/hyperledger/iroha*

20. Hyperledger Fabric's github page: *https://github.com/hyperledger/fabric 0*T8k7vC_i_Mas85If*

21. Hyperledger Sawtooth's official website: *https://01.org/sawtooth/*

22. Hyperledger Sawtooth's github page: *https://github.com/hyperledger/ sawtooth-core*

23. Hyperledger Sawtooth's demo on "Bringing traceability and accountability to the supply chain": *https://01.org/sawtooth/seafood.html*

24. Hyperledger Sawtooth's demo on "Enabling secure and efficient bond settlement": *https://01.org/sawtooth/bond.html*

25. "Hyperledger Announces Technical Working Group China", *https:// www.hyperledger.org/blog/2017/01/03/hyperledger-announces-technical-working-group-china*

26. "Decentralized internet on blockchain", *https://hackernoon.com/ decentralized-internet-on-blockchain-6b78684358a*

27. *https://www.openchain.org/*

28. "Stellar Consensus Protocol": *https://www.stellar.org*

29. *https://digix.global/*

30. *https://www.decentralizedcapital.com/#!/*

31. *https://www.everledger.io/*

32. "What if I told you", Goldman Sachs, *http://www.goldmansachs.com/our-thinking/pages/macroeconomic-insights-folder/what-if-i-told-you/report.pdf*

33. *https://hashgraph.com/*

34. "Hashgraph vs. Blockchain Is the end of Bitcoin and Ethereum near?", George Kingslay, *https://coincodex.com/article/1151/hashgraph-vs-blockchain-is-the-end-of-Bitcoin-and-ethereum-near/*

35. "Asynchronous Byzantine Agreement Protocols", Gabriel Bracha, *https:// www.sciencedirect.com/science/article/pii/089054018790054X*

8

INDUSTRIAL APPLICATIONS FOR BLOCKCHAIN

Since blockchain is a secured database, any place where data security is required, it will be found useful. This is particularly true when a database is shared by many organizations, and requires end-to-end trust, where a traditional database is vulnerable. In this chapter, we will discuss blockchain applications in some industries. By no means are these all the possible applications.

8.1 INSURANCE

Insurance is a big business. The worldwide insurance market in 2015 was worth around $4.5 trillion.[1] Today, the insurance industry is built on the trust between client and insurer. For example, people who buy long-term care insurance must trust the insurance company to pay the cost of long-term care when needed. An insurance policy is a contract between the insurance company and the insured. The smart contract feature of blockchain is well suited for the insurance application.

Global insurers have been quick to embrace blockchain technology. Insurance companies can benefit from the blockchain technology in many aspects. First, blockchain can simplify the insurance administration and process. However, the most important application of blockchain for insurance is a result of the nature of the insurance contracts, in which certain specific events trigger the obligations. The insurance policy is a contract to transfer risk from the client to the insurer.

The insurance industry has a complex legal and regulatory framework, addressing issues of ownership, responsibility and, potentially, jurisdiction and dispute resolution. Therefore, insurance contracts are usually complex. This is well suited to a smart contract application.

The insurance industry launched the Blockchain Insurance Industry Initiative, or B3i project,[2] in October 2016.[2] B3i is dedicated to developing trading platforms across the insurance value chain using blockchain technologies. It aims to improve efficiency in transacting insurance. Using blockchain to handle insurance contracts eliminates the need for multiple databases and the errors that arise from maintaining and transferring data among them. Most important, it enhances the trust of the insured toward the insurance company.

B3i has 38 members, consisting of insurers, brokers, and reinsurers. Its membership includes big insurance companies, such as Allianz, Swiss Re, Liberty Mutual, Sompo Japan Nipponkoa, Reinsurance Group of America, Hannover, Generali Group, and SCOR. The market share of B3i members is around 43% of the premiums issued and 70% of reinsurers' premiums worldwide. Many applications on the platform have been released for commercial use with still more in the pipeline. For example, the impact of climate change on the insurance industry is significant. Natural disasters occur frequently, resulting in considerable damage. B3i has a catastrophe modeling platform to calculate the physical risks.

Besides B3i, other consortia such as RiskBlock, EY /Microsoft /Maersk, and R3, are working on similar initiatives. The EY /Microsoft /Maersk project's original aim was to facilitate marine insurance but is applicable to other insurance markets, as well. Their blockchain platform resides on Microsoft's Azure. The distributed ledger is used to capture information about shipments, risk, and liability, and to help firms comply with insurance regulations. It will also ensure transparency across an interconnected network of clients, brokers, insurers and other third parties.

Symbiont developed an MDL platform to create smart insurance contracts that can execute payments with little or no human involvement. MDL-based smart insurance contracts can automatically authorize and execute the required payment when the condition meets the contractual parameter. The MDL is also safer than current database technology because of the encrypted MDL data. The MDL platform also allows an individual to establish a global identity protected by encryption but immediately available to individuals and organizations authorized to access the information.

Another growing market is e-insurance. In China, during the first half of 2020, Internet life insurance premium grew by 12.2% year on year, Internet property insurance companies' premium grew by 44.2%.It still has room to grow.[3] An increasingly urbanized and well-educated population, with rising household incomes and personal financial assets drive life insurance in China. China's auto insurance market is already the second largest in the world, but the penetration rate is still behind Western countries. Other types of insurance, such as home insurance and business insurance, are also growing.

Traditional Chinese insurers are scaling up their own digital expertise. More than 100 out of around 130 traditional insurers have introduced online sales platforms, distributing $30 billion more premiums from 2014 to 2015, equivalent to 9% of the aggregated premium value.

As traditional insurance companies have strengthened their online presence, it has become increasingly difficult for fintech firms to penetrate this market without collaborating with more established companies. Therefore, most fintech firms seek to collaborate with the existing insurers. By doing so, fintech firms benefit from traditional insurers' experience in navigating regulatory hurdles, tapping into risk assessment, pricing analytics, and other technical expertise. Traditional insurers benefit from fintech's new channels. Despite its increasing digital capability, the insurance industry remains receptive to fintech collaboration. Fintech companies offer a large database of potential customers, enabling traditional insurers to tailor solutions for customers with different risk profiles at competitive premiums.

China's first online-only insurer, Zhong An, was launched in 2013 as a collaboration between Alibaba, Tencent, and China's second-largest insurance firm, Ping An. Zhong An works with the aim to develop technology based on artificial intelligence and big data to simplify insurance.

In China, e-insurance companies sell insurance policies through e-commerce and online wealth management (WM) platforms. Major players are the People's Insurance Company of China (PICC), Ping An, and Zhong An. Many startups are developing the blockchain solutions for insurance, the most notable of which is Chain B.[4] It aims to develop a decentralized network to provide multiple validation points for claims without the costs associated with traditional insurers.

This development is not limited to startups; China's big banks are also launching blockchain applications aimed at the insurance sector.[5] For example, China Construction Bank (CCB) began using a custom blockchain platform, jointly developed with IBM, in Q3, 2017, to sell third-party insurance products via a distributed ledger.

The Shanghai Insurance Exchange conducted a blockchain trial on insurance businesses with nine large insurance companies, including Cathay Life Insurance, Meiji Yasuda Life Insurance, and AIA Group in China in 2017.[6] The platform, in collaboration with IBM, integrates several new technologies including blockchain, big data, biological recognition, and artificial intelligence.

To develop their fintech products, Baidu formed a joint venture with international insurance giant Allianz and Hillhouse Capital and CPPIC, using big data and machine learning for better risk assessment in e-motor insurance. Some fintech companies engage in acquisitions and mergers. For example, Ant Financial took a 60% stake in Cathay Insurance, the Chinese insurance unit of Taiwanese Cathay Financial Holdings. Alibaba broadened its insurance product offerings and made them available on Leyebao, its online insurance sales platform, while creating insurance products to suit the needs of SMEs operating on Taobao.

8.2   WEALTH MANAGEMENT

Big data and artificial intelligence have already made the transition from concept to application. Artificial-intelligence-related products and applications are gradually replacing the traditional tools to provide personalized service to customers. One example is robot wealth management, or robot investment advisory.

Robot investment advisory provides an online wealth management service. It factors in the assessment of individual investors' risk tolerance, profit goals, and style preferences. It uses machine learning generated by intelligent algorithms and portfolio optimization. Test-proven models offer users investment advice tailored to the dynamics of the market to provide timely recommendations for investment.

Robot investment advisory charges fewer fees than the traditional investment advisory. The robot is obviously devoid of human emotions, and exercises strict implementation of a strategy based on the defined parameters. Robot investment advisory also can absorb, process, and digest a huge quantity of data that humans cannot. More asset management companies now use a "robot" advisor to provide services to their customers.

Many start-up companies, such as Wealthfront,[7] Betterment,[8] Personal Capital,[9] Motif Investing, FutureAdvisor, Hedgeable, and Nutmeg, are providing robot investment advisory services. The demand for such a service is considerable.

Intelligent investment startups often command higher valuations in the market, which is the evidence that the field is gaining popularity. However, the definition of the industry for the intelligent investment is relatively vague. Some intelligent investment businesses are merely P2P platforms. Even some truly intelligent investment startups have not had their investment strategies fully tested by the market. Traditional brokerage houses are also offering intelligent investment services such as Charles Schwab's Intelligent Portfolio service.[10] Based on an investor's answers to a short set of questions, Schwab Intelligent Portfolio selects from among the 53 low-cost professionally selected exchange-traded funds (ETFs) to create a diversified portfolio designed to meet that investor's specific goal. Merrill Edge of the Bank of America also offers a similar service.

In Europe, companies like Wealth Horizon, InvestYourWay, and Swanest in the U.K., MoneyFarm in Italy, Vaamo and Owlhub in Germany, and Moneyvane in Switzerland, all offer intelligent investment services.

China has also quickly developed such a market. In China, intelligent investment products belong to three categories: third-party intelligent investment platform, intelligent products offered by the traditional financial institutions, and Internet wealth management applications. These products include A-share investment advisers and wealth management platforms. Investment vehicles include overseas ETF, A shares, bonds, and funds.

Wealth management (WM) is a rapidly growing market. Although it is unrelated to the blockchain, it is an extension of artificial intelligence into the financial market. It is also considered fintech.

Until now, Chinese investors lacked investment choices. Many of them chose to invest their money in real estate. This has driven up housing prices and created a real estate bubble. Many houses sit unoccupied, while many people cannot afford to buy a house. Wealth management caters to this group of growing middle class consumers with considerable savings looking for better returns. Online fund management offers an outlet for the savers to receive a better return than a bank's low interest rate. The value of wealth management products (WMPs) expanded 56% to $3.5 trillion in 2015. Online fund management apps linked to payment platforms offers ease of access; the investment opportunity is never more than a few clicks away on a smartphone.

The primary participants are Yu'e Bao of Ant Financial, LiCaiTong (Tencent), and Baifu (Baidu). Alibaba's Yu'e Bao is one of the world's top money market funds with over $100 billion of assets in 2021, but it has shrunk significantly since 2017.[11] Licaitong is Tencent's wealth management platform accessible via the WeChat wallet and QQ wallet. It provides Tencent users with quality investment selections in a transparent and user-friendly investment environment. Most of these products offer a yearly return of 4.5% to 5.2%, depending on the investment duration for an amount up to $1.5 million. In 2021, the total transaction amount topped $12 trillion.

Most of the Chinese P2P lenders, such as RenRenDai and CreditEase, are also WM service providers. With their access to massive amounts of social and analytical data about customers' creditworthiness and purchasing trends, these fintech firms can build advanced finance platforms to support elevated expectations from increasingly demanding investors.

In mid-2016, WM firms introduced simplified investment advice services using robo-advisors through sophisticated, automated online platforms incorporating Big Data and artificial intelligence. These robo-advisors use modern portfolio theory, big data algorithms, Xuanji's asset allocation solution, and quantitative modeling and program trading with machine learning. This approach substantially lowers costs to provide universal access to entry-level, affordable, and customized online financial advisory services.

One of the top robo-advisory providers is CreditEase, which launched its robo-advisory product ToumiRA to provide cost-effective access to international WMPs for Chinese retail investors, using trading algorithms to match investor risk preferences and objectives to their optimal portfolio. Another robo-advisory platform, Xuanji, launched by PINTEC, provides intelligent investment advice to retail investors with the ability to customize and automatically rebalance a global portfolio.[12] In addition, PINTEC also offers a B2B version for brokers, independent financial advisors, and financial institutions. Both versions can trade USD ETFs and RMB-denominated Chinese mutual funds.

Other companies offering machine-assisted investment advisory include Baidu Gupiao, PingAn One, MiCai and Clipper Advisor. Robo-advisory could well reshape the future of China's WM business. To survive such competitive market, they will need a breadth and depth of asset offerings, portfolio allocation, and technological superiority in big data analytics and machine learning.

8.3 DEFENSE

Like any other industry, aerospace and defense companies already use a variety of technologies to address operation and product development to improve visibility and efficiency. Yet, due to the nature of their customers and products, which are critical to national security, there are extra burdens and requirements to be met that are not required by other industries, such as agriculture.

Blockchain offers them additional security (or utility) in maintaining classified information along with their supply chains and critical defense-related infrastructures, such as to track and audit transactions across multiple supply chain and operational partners.[13]

Defense industry infrastructure is dispersed across different locations. Some of these locations serve both defense and non-defense markets. Blockchain technology can be used to ensure security against any unauthorized access to these important networks and hardware equipment by consensus-based access.

For example, blockchain can do the certification of people, partners, and parts (e.g., a key component used in the F-35 jet requires certification of the part's origin). The blockchain-based system can manage the supply chain of hundreds of thousands of components going into a highly sophisticated defense product by recording each transaction step of each component from raw material until the finished parts. It can also serve as security clearance to allow certain employees, customers, and partners to have the privilege to use specific facilities and tools or to access data. It eliminates the possibility that a back door or a bug was implanted in a critical electronic component that becomes key in the operation of the final product.

Blockchain technology has applications in both the defense industry and military operations. The blockchain is an ideal platform to deliver hack-proof messages. The blockchain platform-based system can send and receive smart documents and contracts securely.[14] Crypto-Chat,[15] a subsidiary of Indiana Technology and Manufacturing Companies (ITAMCO), developed a secure messaging and transaction platform for the U.S. military.[16]

8.4 HEALTHCARE

One of the most important infrastructures of the healthcare industry is data management. Using digital signatures on blockchain-based data allows access to the health records only by authorized people. A community of people, including hospitals, doctors, patients, and insurance companies, could be part of the overall blockchain, reducing fraud in healthcare payments.

A blockchain-based system could ensure that care allowance is spent exclusively on healthcare activities. The system can save time spent on reconciliation after every transaction, helping with straight-through processing.

IBM has teamed up with the Centers for Disease Control and Prevention (CDC) as well as the U.S. Food and Drug Administration (FDA) to develop blockchain and distributed ledger technology (DLT) applications in the health sector.[17]

The purpose of the project with the FDA is to define a secure, efficient, and scalable exchange of health data using blockchain technology, with an initial focus on oncology-related data. IBM and the FDA are exploring the exchange of owner-mediated data from several sources, such as electronic medical records, clinical trials, genomic data and health data from mobile devices, wearables, and the Internet of Things (IoT).

In 2016, IBM and the New York Genome Center jointly created a comprehensive and open repository of genetic data to accelerate cancer research and scale access to precision medicine using Watson, IBM's artificial intelligence (AI) system.

The CDC is working on several proofs of concept based on blockchain technology. It plans to build real DLT applications for the public health sector.[18] The CDC, state and local health departments, and other organizations routinely share public health data so they can control the spread of a range of infectious diseases. Currently, the task is managed by a traditional database. Such a database is extremely complicated because the vast areas, numerous organizations, and nature of the data involved. Blockchain technology could automate many of the database management processes, and store and share health data faster, more securely, and incorruptibly. Patients' data can have much better privacy and security. Critical data can be trusted. This can be especially important when managing a public health crisis.

In addition, by combining the blockchain and artificial intelligence (AI) technologies, while DLT securely manages and shares data and AI extracts embedded patterns from the data. It opens a vast frontier for exploration.

The amount of research and clinical data in the healthcare sector is exploding. Blockchain technology is coming at the right time to enable the ecosystem of data in healthcare to have more fluidity.

In the healthcare industry, millions of medical records are scattered around in different hospitals, clinics, doctor offices, and insurance companies. Such data form a complete history of a patient and can be vital for diagnosis when needed. Today, these medical data are fragmented and difficult to share. Even the patient does not have access to most of these data. Such low efficiency and transparency are a great waste of social resources. Enhancing sharing is critical to the healthcare industry. However, there is also a privacy concern about these data. Safeguarding these data so that only authorized persons can have access to it is vitally important. Therefore, managing healthcare data makes an ideal case for the blockchain application.

In October 2017, Hangzhou-Yunphant, a blockchain startup based in Hangzhou, entered a strategic partnership with Inspur to integrate the blockchain with healthcare data. Inspur Group[19] is a leading provider of cloud computing and advanced IT products and solutions, one of the largest IT enterprises in China; it serves more than 80 countries and regions around the world.[19]

Once implemented, the blockchain will allow multiple organizations to access peer-to-peer networks without worrying about data security and integrity through encrypted data transmission. The platform synchronizes, consolidates, and shares medical data created by various parties in real-time. The Yunphant Network is an enterprise-class consortium blockchain platform called the YunphantChain. It improves the efficiency and transparency of the medical industry through blockchain technology. It can be quickly deployed for large-scale user application scenarios. The system supports operations such as authority management, monitoring, maintenance, online deployment of Chaincode, and status query.

8.5 FOOD

Food poisoning is a major health issue. Every year, 400,000 people die due to contaminated food worldwide. In the U.S. alone, the CDC estimates 48 million people get sick, 128,000 are hospitalized, and 3,000 die from foodborne diseases each year.[20] In December 2006, an E. coli outbreak affected 71 customers in Taco Bell across five states. Eight people developed kidney failure, and 53 people were hospitalized. From October to November 2015, an E. coli outbreak originating in Chipotle Mexican Grill affected 55 customers.[21] In 2009, the Peanut Corporation of America (PCA) experienced a Salmonella outbreak where 714 people became ill and nine died.

Food contamination can happen due to many reasons: cross-contamination, the spread of food-borne illness, and unsafe practices. The process from outbreak to the identification of the source of contamination can take weeks or longer, causing problems to spread. Blockchain technology can help to trace the contamination quickly, limiting the scope of the damage, both in terms of the people affected and the lost business. IBM entered collaboration with major food suppliers, such as Dole, Walmart, Golden State Foods, and Kroger, to address food safety issues worldwide using blockchain.[22]

Blockchain technology can improve food traceability by providing trusted information on the origin and state of food. All participants in the food supply chain, from growers and distributors to consumers, can gain access to the known and trusted data of the origin and state of food for their transactions. Such chained information greatly shortens the tracing time.

The food supply members of the consortium identify and prioritize deficiencies in the current food tracing system, while IBM provides technical solutions. Once developed, IBM's fully integrated, enterprise-grade production blockchain platform, which runs on IBM Cloud, can be adopted beyond food supply chain applications.[23] The platform includes new features developed in collaboration with the Hyperledger community, including the Hyperledger Fabric and Hyperledger Composer hosted by the Linux Foundation.

Recently, IBM and Walmart conducted platform trials in both China and the U.S. The trial was a success: the platform can track a product throughout the supply chain's every stage in seconds instead of the days or weeks needed in the traditional system. Blockchain technology has enabled a new era of end-to-end transparency in the global food system.

8.6   CREDIT RATING

Most people do not appreciate the importance of the credit rating system to the overall economy. At a personal level, if one does not have a good credit rating, he may have a difficult time obtaining a loan or even a credit card. Rating downgrades can negatively impact company finance. A bad credit rating means there is a higher financial cost. On a larger scale, a bad credit rating can have a detrimental impact on a country's economy. During the East Asia economic crisis of 1997, many countries' economies suffered exacerbated blows due to the downgrade of their credit by rating agencies.[24] These are some examples. However, a credit rating system is impactful in more cases than just when there is a financial problem.

A good credit rating system works to accelerate the economy, similar to how enzymes in a body to act as catalysts to accelerate chemical reactions. Likewise, a bad credit rating system can do harm to the economy. The credit rating to an economy is like temperature checking to the body: You cannot pass the airport temperature checking station if you have a fever.

The flow of capital in an economy is like the flow of blood in a body. Billions of saving deposits in the banks are channeled into entities to produce economic activities. The credit rating can determine where this money goes. Entities with a good credit score obtain capital with a lower borrowing cost. However, this does not mean that these entities will produce more economic activity for the capital they receive than other entities with a lower credit score, especially if the score is not accurate. An inaccurate credit rating system can reduce capital efficiency and increase the overall business cost, just like bad infrastructure. A sound credit rating system can enhance the efficiency of resource allocation and promote economic growth.

Most consumer financing, such as credit cards, is unsecured. Although the individual amount is small, the aggregated amount is large. For example, in 2022, Americans' credit card debt was $800 billion,[25] while the total consumer debt was $15.6 trillion, and it is heading higher.[26] The growth of the debt means the expansion of bad debts. How to establish and strengthen the control capacity and collection capacity is very important.

To finance such a large consumer debt, but not to drive up the cost of financing, is a major challenge. When the consumer debt demand increases, but the financing channels cannot meet the demand, financing costs go up. It may not be as easy to open financing channels – such as the issuance of bonds, asset securitization, and other financing means – because each channel has a different tolerance to risk and requirements to accurately gauge that risk. This is where the credit rating comes in.

The construction of a sound credit system is far from easy. The current consumer finance company data and data integration are insufficient to build a sound credit rating system because of the lack of data coverage, data quality, missing standards, missing data, and rapidly changing personal credit. Data collection and integration deviation can occur during the process of data separation and other issues.

In addition, an entity's creditability is more than just its credit history and related data. It is essential to establish an effective credit score model by associating the credit history to the risk. The credit risk also needs to be quantified to remove the bias associated with subjectivity.

Traditionally, banks have their own credit score model. Banks need to build up their historical data and find suitable forecasting models. However, due to the immense scope of the credit rating, banks are not able to do it effectively and accurately. A complete and effective credit-scoring model requires the overall composition of the targeted entity as well as the circumstances when the data is collected. If the development of the credit system is not comprehensive enough, the risks and costs for banks are high.

An ideal credit agency acquires data from multiple sources; it builds a system that can manage massive amounts of data handling, mining, and processing capability, determines the reliability of each data source with an anti-fraud and filtering model, and does data cross-validation. After acquiring enough data, the building of the credit score model is no less challenging, because the credit data are not always coherent and consistent. Until recently, the tools available to do data collection, mining, and processing have been limited.

Fintech can help the credit rating in two aspects: the acquisition and processing of data, and the creation of a comprehensive model by deploying big data technology and artificial intelligence. Fintech will play an important role in this arena in the future.

Compared to traditional credit companies such as FICO, fintech companies with big data technology have the advantage in the breadth and depth of the data, can gather more dimensions of behavioral information, and can discern a previously undetected pattern, which will, in turn, give a more comprehensive rating. With the big data mining and analysis techniques, the data collected have less asymmetry. Through big data collection and data mining, consumer finance companies can identify their customers' needs and customer portraits. Thus, they can more accurately target marketing and form consumer credit judgments. They can also correlate borrowers to different consumer finance platforms and determine a customer's repayment intention and ability under different economic environments. A stress test will reveal customers' financial capability under different circumstances, such as unemployment or having a health problem.

Applying artificial intelligence and machine learning tools, such as the random forest algorithm, neural networks, and gradient boosted decision trees (GBDTs), can improve the modeling accuracy. Credit scores based on the artificial intelligence can make credit management work more efficient, objective, and focused. Such a score can determine the entity's creditworthiness under certain circumstances.

The current state of credit rating system in China is still immature and this immaturity has caused high social financing costs, lending inefficiency, and the industry's inability to assess risks, which has inhibited economic vitality. Both the government and industry recognized its importance. They are devoting great efforts to develop the credit rating industry by using new technologies, such as big data and artificial intelligence.

In 2009, the China Banking Regulatory Commission (CBRC) issued guidelines for the supervision of an internal credit rating system for the credit risk of commercial banks. In 2013, the Chinese State Council issued the Regulations on the Administration of Credit Industry. By the end of 2014, the central bank credit center had already accessed 1811 data institutions and covered 350 million people and business entities. With the gradual establishment of the modern credit system helped by fintech, a credit rating industry is emerging.

In September 2015, the State Council issued the plan for big data development. In a series of policies, regulations, and guidelines, the PBOC and CBRC encouraged financial institutions to develop innovative consumer credit products.

In 2016, the Chinese government took a consolidated approach to develop an extensive nation-wide Social Credit System (SCS). The SCS is akin to a combination of credit rating systems in the U.S. (such as the FICO, Vantage score, CE score, Moody rating for bonds, S&P credit rating, and Better Business Bureau rating), but even more comprehensive. One difference is that in the U.S., private companies provide scores, but in China, it is the government that provides the SCS.

SCS focuses on honesty in government affairs, commercial integrity, societal integrity, and judicial credibility. The scope embraces both personal and business credit and trustworthiness ratings. Such a rating can easily translate into "trust" for the blockchain validation. In an era when daily business dealings involve totally unknown parties, such a trust system becomes essential. SCS is intending to remove the trust barrier. However, there are critics who condemn such a system, saying it is like "Big Brother."[27] SCS came online in 2020,[28] and still has many supporters and detractors.

The Chinese credit rating industry is by no means limited to the government. The government also has granted licenses to eight private enterprises to develop their credit scoring systems. Among the licensees are e-commerce companies Alibaba, Tencent, Ping An Insurance, and five credit rating companies: Pengyuan Credit Services, China Chengxin Credit Information, IntelliCredit, Credit Arm, and Yin Zhi Jie.

Independently, in September 2016, China's National Internet Finance Association (NIFA) also launched its Internet Financial Industry Information Sharing Platform (IFIISP). NIFA is run by the central bank and 400 traditional financial and Internet finance companies, including heavyweight companies such as Ant Finance, JD Finance, Lufax, and Yirendai. It was established to regulate Chinese fintech firms and control risks in the sector. The IFIISP provides credit data on customers by sending requests to all other member companies and collating the results without divulging the source data to protect competitive insights. NIFA took a giant step forward in developing a proper credit score system with IFIISP.

China's P2P regulations remain less burdensome than those in developed markets, whether by design or by omission. However, as the system evolves, the government sees greater need to tighten the regulations. In 2001, President Bush signed the Patriot Act, which required ID verification for customers to open a bank account. In 2016, China followed suit, with concerns over money laundering and fraud, to set up new regulations that required in-person verification to open a bank account. Since the online-only banks do not have a physical branch, they needed to collaborate with traditional banks. Thus, traditional banks have gained an additional source of business from the online banks.

The Chinese legislature aims to include a more substantive data protection framework. The new framework includes PBOC's additional requirements for non-bank payment institutions around effective protective measures, risk control systems and KYC measures, and storage of sensitive information. The Chinese government will likely continue to take a leadership role in setting the agenda on data privacy and protection, as this will increasingly become a central pillar of the financial services marketplace – critical in enabling the fintech sector to operate and prosper.

In addition, some private enterprises already moved ahead with their own versions of the credit rating. As e-commerce companies already generated a large amount of data from their own platforms about the customers and suppliers, they set up their own credit rating system. For example, the scoring platform Sesame Credit Management was developed by Alibaba's Ant Financial analyses data generated on Alibaba's shopping platforms from 300 million customers and 37 million small businesses. Customers with higher credit scores enjoy special privileges. Other similar systems were built by Tencent using data from its own social media apps, WeChat and WeChat Pay. They also offer the credit rating services to other financial services providers. For example, Jubao uses social media data generated on WeChat and Weibo to assess customers' creditworthiness. JD Finance is collaborating with U.S.-based ZestFinance in a joint venture to develop services of credit risk evaluation and extend consumer access to credit in China.

With such a torrent of activities, China quickly set up a world-class credit rating system. People will feel more confident in transacting with unknown parties, and this pushes China's fintech market even further. People will also be more cautious about doing things that will spoil their credit rating, and the system will support risk-adjusted loan growth to bolster consumer spending, further supporting the growth of fintech.

Currently, China's consumer expenditures are only 39% of the GDP, vs. the U.S. at 68 %, France 55%, and Germany 63%.[29] Stimulating household consumption is one way to boost GDP growth. Fintech will help.

Chinese fintech firms are leveraging big data from e-commerce, messaging, search, social media, and other Internet-based services to personalize the customer experience, provide new services, and leverage operational efficiency. Customer data can be used to support other online revenue streams, such as lending, insurance, investment, and wealth management.

Right now, the development of most of these systems is in progress. As China's mobile financial market matures, the interoperability across mobile wallets and other banking services becomes more efficient, and they will democratize the ecosystem, leveling the playing field between new entrants and incumbents. Such an open-architecture policy would start a race to offer the most innovative solutions as companies attempt to differentiate themselves.

8.7 DATA MANAGEMENT

Blockchain is a database, and its technology can be used to manage data. Blockchain is also known as the Mutual Distributed Ledger or MDL. In the

MDL world, data is classified into three categories: identity, transaction, and content data. The Identity MDL, Transaction MDL, and Content MDL are the three pillars of the data management applications of blockchain technology.

Data contains vital information about persons, organizations, and events. Today, institutions, organizations or companies build their own silos of data and information-management protocols. The protection of these data against unauthorized access or manipulation is important. In 2013, a Target data breach costed the company $18.5 million to settle.[30] In 2015, hackers obtained the personal details, social security numbers, fingerprints, employment history, and financial information of 20 million individuals in a U.S. government database.

Blockchain technology can simplify the management of the trusted information, making it easier for entities/persons to access and use critical public-sector data while maintaining the security of this information.[31] Blockchain technology organizes data into blocks. Once these blocks form a chain, they are secure. Encryption, verification, and distribution protect the data from unauthorized access.

By organizing data with blockchain, companies, government agencies, and any organization can digitize and manage their existing records within a secure infrastructure and make some of these records "smart." Rules and algorithms allow specific data in a blockchain to be shared with the third party once predefined conditions are met and the third-party identity is verified.

Some countries are aggressive in applying such technology. For example, Estonia developed a platform called the Keyless Signature Infrastructure (KSI) to safeguard all public-sector data. KSI creates hashes of the original data. The hashes are stored in a blockchain and distributed across a network of government computers. Whenever the underlying file changes, a new hash value appends to the chain. An unauthorized data change produces a hash not acceptable by the blockchain.

The transparency of the history of each record detects and prevents unauthorized tampering. Government officials can monitor the "who, what, and when" of any data change. The health records of all Estonian citizens are managed using the KSI platform, which is available to all government agencies and private-sector companies in the country.

Besides the protection of data against unauthorized access and change, data sharing is another dilemma in data management. Until now, the data sharing has been a non-reversible process. Once a party shares data, it possesses the data. In the real world, a non-disclosure agreement is a legal instrument to prevent further spread of the data. However, in most circumstances, it is not very practical. For example, if you hand out your credit card information or disclose your social security number, the information is possessed by the party that you disclose to. You must trust the other party not to use your information for any unintended purpose.

To solve this problem, MIT developed a project called Enigma, which is a computation platform that allows datasets to be shared for computational purposes, yet without having the party using the data access the raw data itself.[32] Only the original data owner ever sees the raw data.

The Enigma protocol is a decentralized, open, and secure data marketplace. It opens a new way to share and manage the data and yet keep it private. Using a credit card transaction as an example, the merchant submits the transaction to receive payment but does not have your credit card information for any other unauthorized use.

Besides managing data, blockchain technology decentralizes file storage on the Internet. Today, HTTP downloads a file from a single computer at a time, instead of getting pieces from multiple computers simultaneously. A P2P approach could save 60% in bandwidth costs.

Not only does distributing data throughout the network save bandwidth, but it also protects files from getting hacked or lost. The data stored in the traditional cloud is not as safe as one might think. For example, Dropbox reset passwords for 68 million accounts in response to a 2012 breach.[33]

On August 31, 2014, a collection of almost 500 private pictures of various celebrities was posted on the imageboard 4Chan.[34] The images were hacked due to a security issue in the iCloud API via phishing attacks.

The public cloud is also prone to privacy breaches and potential government surveillance. A proposed solution is to use a private cloud device, yet this does not address the fundamental problem. It could be more vulnerable than the public cloud. The only advantage of a private cloud is its obscurity. With the arrival of blockchain technology, a solution is available to solve such a security issue.

The Inter-Planetary File System (IPFS) conceptualizes how a distributed Web might operate safely.[35] Similar to the way BitTorrent moves data around the Internet, IPFS removes the need for centralized client-server relationships. Each file is broken into many blocks, which possess unique hashes. The hashes are the index to locate where the blocks of files are stored. IPFS tracks the index version history for every file. Each network node stores only one or more blocks of the file. To look up a file, the unique hash index of the file locates the nodes where blocks of the file are stored. The data downloading from the distributed Web is no longer sequential, but parallel. It can speed up file transfer and stream without increasing the bandwidth.

Storj provides blockchain-based end-to-end encrypted distributed object storage. Only the data owner can access the stored data. It is safe, fast, always available, and cheap. It utilizes blockchain to create a decentralized cloud system using spare disk space allocated by a community of "farmers" who receive rent in Storj's native cryptocurrency.

The software fragments the stored files into small packets, much like the packets on the Internet. The blockchain transaction ledger, public/private key encryption, and cryptographic hash functions protect packets and distribute them throughout the network for storage. The blockchain stores information such as the network locations of each packet and its cryptographic hash as proof of storage. Each packet has three copies for redundancy. Even one or more packets are hacked, the hacker has only a small piece of the entire data.

Blockchain storage is a tamper-proof way of storing records such as those for land ownership, business licenses, or birth and death certificates; governments are interested in blockchain-based distributed ledgers.

There is plenty of commercial interest in a file storage solution using blockchain technology as well. A few companies already use specially encoded Satoshis – the smallest denomination of Bitcoin – to store ownership ledgers. For example, Everledger tracks diamonds this way to help fight insurance fraud. Similarly, the companies behind the IBM-led Hyperledger are developing applications using the blockchain-based, permissioned technology to track the ownership and exchange of all sorts of things, from stocks and shares to cars and houses.

One of the largest database and ERP companies, Oracle, considers that blockchain will fundamentally transform how business is done, making business-to-business interactions more secure, transparent, and efficient. Its impact can be bigger than the social Web, big data, the cloud, or even artificial intelligence.

Oracle is offering the service to enable customers to extend their current Oracle ERP and SaaS solutions to the blockchain-based platform.[36] The major advantages include the enabling of the trust in transactions, avoiding the risks of intermediaries, reducing error-prone information exchange processes, avoiding delays of reconciliations, reducing cross-ERP discrepancies, decreasing the cost, and improving visibility within the ecosystem.

The Ethereum network consists of millions of computer nodes. Many of these computer nodes have idle CPU power ready to be harnessed. On November 11, 2016, the Ethereum community funded a project called "Golem," an Ethereum plug-in, which enables users and app providers to rent out their unused CPU power and software. It is like Airbnb of CPU power and apps. Any user, ranging from a single PC owner to a big data center, can contribute resources to Golem network.

Golem is a special type of blockchain platform. Its aim is to harness unused computing power and storage capacity in the network. Golem is a global, open sourced, decentralized supercomputer that anyone can access. It utilizes the combined power of user's machines, from personal laptops to entire datacenters. There is no single point of failure and no trusted authority. The Golem Network is a decentralized sharing economy of computing power, where anyone can make money renting out his or her computing power or developing and selling software.

Computations in Golem nodes take place inside isolated virtual machines for maximum security. Providers decide how many CPU cores, and how much RAM and disk space they wish to rent to the Golem Network. A reputation system enforces the desired behavior of nodes in a decentralized environment, without relying on any supervising institution. This allows nodes to attribute a reputation rank to their peers. A node obtains a lower rank in the case of inappropriate behavior and an increased rank after performing successful computations.

Developers can create and distribute apps on the Golem Network's Application Registry (Golem Store) and choose whether they want to charge for their apps. Thus, the Golem Network has CPU power, storage space, and apps, all the necessary elements of a computer. In fact, it is more powerful than the fastest supercomputer in existence. According to some estimates, Golem can do two trillion operations per second. With such a supercomputer available at one's fingertip, tasks such as scientific research, graphics rendering, artificial intelligence, machine learning, and data analysis all can be done a fraction of the cost and faster than today's supercomputers.

Many advanced technologies have complementary capabilities, such as IPFS/Filecoin[37] (a distributed file sharing and storage service), Whisper[38] (an app to securely broadcast messages between users), DEVp2p[39] (a cross-platform, peer-to-peer client library, for desktops and mobile devices),

Swarm (a BitTorrent-like protocol to enable the transfer of actual files), and Ethereum. By deploying them together, the combined platform can replace the large data centers that currently power the Internet and become the decentralized computing power behind the entire Internet.

There are four types of users on the Golem Network:

Providers supply computing power to the network and get paid for doing so.

Authors build the software on the Application Registry and are paid for their software.

Requestors rent the network's computing power and the software built on it and pay for doing so.

Validators make sure that malicious programs do not damage your computer. They analyze and test the software that Authors put on the Application Registry and create lists for software they trust and for dangerous software.

8.8 INTERNET SECURITY

By nature, the blockchain database or MDL is secure because it is encrypted and distributed. One might ask how can it be used to improve the security of the Internet and telecommunications (such as 5G) in general.

The InterPlanetary File System (IPFS) project was designed exactly for this purpose. The system seeks to replace the existing server-client architecture by the distributed storage of online data. The blockchain manages the storage of Internet data by spreading it to connected participating nodes to make sure that data is not only censor-proof, but also resilient against attack. Nodes get paid with a cryptocurrency called Filecoin as incentive for their contribution to the storage and bandwidth.

The system works like a P2P network, with each new requestor of a file becoming an additional host. That data is represented on a blockchain as a cryptographic hash and linked to a built-in IPNS (InterPlanetary Name System), akin to the Domain Name System. Unlike the conventional DNS, which translates between the numerical IP addresses and more readily memorized domain names, a name in IPNS is the hash of a public key. The hash is created from a dataset signed by the corresponding private key. The identity of the owner of the dataset, such as an email or a financial record, is thus hidden under the hash. This is unlike DNS, in which the domain name and IP can be traced to its owner. This can prevent DDoS attacks and identity tracking.

Orchid is a cryptocurrency-powered VPN, and another project that uses blockchain to enhance Internet securitys. It allows conventional VPN providers to sell their excess bandwidth to users by becoming a part of a decentralized P2P privacy network. The platform allows people to hop between different VNP providers, which contribute bandwidth to the Orchid's VPN platform. This ensures that not even the individual providers have the full picture of users' Web activity.

VPNs route traffic through a separate, encrypted server, so Web activity appears to travel to and from a different IP address than that of the user. From the point of view of an Internet Service Provider (ISP), identifiable traffic is initiated but appears to travel only to the VPN server. On the other end of the journey, the destination website sees visiting traffic as originating from the same encrypted server, rather than the user's actual IP address.

VPNs are not 100% secure. There are several potential weaknesses, also known as leaks. Leaks can be the fault of VPN provider or, the fault of apps, plug-ins, or operating systems routing traffic through default servers. Using social media apps makes it much more difficult to maintain privacy, even with a VPN.

The DNS, which converts Web domain names into numeric IP addresses, can also be a leak. ISPs assign a DNS server to their users to identify and log the Web domains their customers are accessing. When you use a VPN, the privacy solution routes your traffic through a different DNS server, making it harder for the ISP to log you or for destination websites to see who or where you are.

But when DNS requests are sent outside the VPN server, your ISP sees the sites you visit. DNS leaks can occur if an operating system continues to access the default DNS server rather than the one assigned by the VPN.

Blockchain can also offer security solutions to a 5G communication network. Blockchain can provide privacy by distributed trust models, thus making 5G networks capable of protecting themselves from security breaches. Since the bandwidth of 5G is large, the encryption and distribution of blockchain to a 5G network does not present too great of a burden on the 5G network's performance.

5G is a cloud-based communication technology that utilizes a Software Defined Network (SDN), such as NFV (Network Function Virtualization). Its core network resides in the cloud. Many of its functions reside in the Edge Clouds. This makes the integration of blockchain with 5G not only compatible, but also highly desirable. Blockchain opens the opportunity for storing and managing data on 5G networks via a distributed ledger. Blockchain is the key to ensure security and network performance.

A decentralized blockchain makes use of asymmetric cryptography and hash algorithms to help protect the user's identity. Blockchain can register the devices with their blockchain address, further preventing identity loss.

However, to integrate blockchain into the 5G protocol, many structural and technical frameworks need to be developed, including the regulatory frameworks for the implementation of agreements like smart contracts. The scalability of blockchain also needs to be improved to deal with the high number of devices.

8.9   LOGISTICS

In supply chain management, MDLs can offer many breakthrough applications, such as product authentication and innovative supply chain financing.

In product authentication applications, MDLs are the ideal platforms to certify the authenticity, fair trade status, and origin of products, as well as the components or raw materials in a supply chain. Transparency comes with blockchain-based time stamping of a date and location — on ethical diamonds, for instance — that corresponds to a product number. It also reduces the cost, labor, and time in managing the supply chain.

In this arena, U.K.-based Provenance offers supply chain auditions for a range of consumer goods.[40] Making use of the Ethereum blockchain, the Provenance pilot project ensures that the suppliers in Indonesia who harvested the fish sold in sushi restaurants in Japan did so in a sustainable way.

For supply chain financing, companies like Skuchain in Mountain View, California,[41] Hijro, and Fluent in Lexington, Kentucky, are developing financing services for buyers and sellers.

Since the interlocked interests of the parties in a supply chain are across multiple businesses, supply chain financing can be more creative than the regular financing. Supply chain financing provides an invaluable opportunity to strengthen relations with suppliers. The objectives of supply chain financing are more than just to earn interest, but to ensure the deal goes through.

Supply chain financing by blockchain can optimize the utilization of working capital within the supply chain, creating mutually beneficial arrangements between buyers and suppliers. The smart contract can facilitate lending by financiers against purchase orders, invoices, inventory assets, and payment obligations. The automated release of funds triggered by real-world events offers the assurance to the loans. It provides a real-time, reliable view of the transaction state, bringing significant transparency for all participants and helping them build a more trustworthy and stable supply chain ecosystem. It also enhances the liquidity of collateralized assets in a supply chain by improving upon current trade finance instruments such as Factoring, PO Financing, and Vendor Managed Inventory Financing.

Services like IMT offered by Skuchain provide inventory financing. The idea is to assign the original purchase contract between the buyer and the seller on the IMT blockchain. The contract provides the collateral to an investor in the IMT fund. IMT uses its funds to purchase goods from the seller. Each purchase order triggers the shipment of the finished goods according to the order. The buyer then pays IMT for the goods.

The platform developed by Fluent is a Bitcoin-like system for supply chain financing. Buyers approve invoices on the Fluent Network once they receive the goods satisfactorily. The Fluent Network's blockchain operates on top of the existing banking infrastructure. The actual funds always remain in the custody of the banks. On the blockchain, the funds are converted into tokens for the transactions.

Tech startups and many financial institutions and global enterprises that are already part of the existing supply chain network are developing blockchain-based supply chain applications. A single blockchain platform with cryptographically verified invoices, instant settlements, and low operating costs benefits all parties on the system.

Foxconn, the world's largest electronics manufacturing company, which makes all the iPhones in the world, has launched a new blockchain-based supply chain finance platform, called Chained Finance, based in Shanghai, through its financial service arm, FnConn.[42] It collaborates with Dianrong,[43] the first Chinese P2P company to participate in the Hyperledger Blockchain Project. The new platform leverages advanced financial technology to meet the financial needs of the SMEs involved in the supply chain in China.[44] SMEs make up most of the supply chain, but they have limited financing options. Using a dynamic discounting technique can enable buyers and suppliers to negotiate payment terms and discounts when buyers have capital available that can be redeployed to suppliers in exchange for better trading terms. Smart contracts can implement such a dynamic discounting scheme easily. Chained Finance enables the delivery of needed capital to these suppliers and provides large multinational manufacturers with enhanced visibility and transparency.

Chained Finance is initially targeting three major industries: electronics, auto, and garment manufacturing. The blockchain is revolutionizing the finance industry. It can offer solutions to any company operating and financing complicated supply chains. Chained Finance created a unique ecosystem that will provide supply chains with easier access to funding at competitive rates. In return, supply chain operators will gain greater visibility of their suppliers and the many layers of finance embedded in the process.

By using the Chained Finance platform, every payment and supply chain transaction can be more transparent, manageable, and easily authenticated. Chained Finance will help eliminate many of the trust issues faced by counterparties and delivers automated execution. The new platform will be an enabler of supply chains across many major industries and geographies.

Chained Finance has an initial focus on the automotive, electronics, and garment production industries, though it has much wider applications. Chained Finance will provide timely, efficient support to many suppliers of all sizes. It will also help ensure the timely delivery of products to end customers and improve efficiencies across the entire supply chain.

Founded in 2012, Dianrong is now a leader in online marketplace lending in China, dispersing more than $300 million to 3.7 million retail lenders. Its products and services include loan originations, investment products, and marketplace lending solutions in a comprehensive, one-stop financial platform supported by industry-leading technology, compliance, and transparency. The company's sophisticated and flexible infrastructure enables it to design and customize lending and borrowing products and services, based on industry-specific data and insights, all supported by online risk-management and operation tools.

In summary, the blockchain will revolutionize the supply chain system to make it more efficient, less costly and more trustworthy.

8.10 GLOBAL TRADE, SUPPLY CHAINS, AND OTHER AREAS

IBM has developed blockchain applications for global trade, the backbone of the global supply chain, where the data on the movement of goods and currencies are of vital importance. In 2020, the impact of the COVID-19 pandemic caused an economic upheaval. Many supermarket shelves remain half empty.

Blockchain can significantly reduce costs and improve efficiency by eliminating hidden glitches in trade, such as those in paperwork, procedures, and administrative formalities. It can automate many of the processes in global trade. Blockchain has the potential to remove inefficiencies in global business and save time while mitigating risk and creating new business models as it brings a level of trust among participants and in the data shared. Blockchain can also facilitate customs paperwork, cross-border payments, and contracts.

Sharing trusted data on the blockchain across networks help companies build greater flexibility and resilience into operational and supply chain management. A blockchain-enabled marketplace highlights the importance of transparency and insights within the global economy. Trusted marketplaces on blockchain can promote a data-driven, global economy.

In addition, IBM has developed a blockchain application for the automobile industry. Today's car is increasingly a networked computer on wheels, and that was even before the autonomous vehicle became a reality. In the near future, it will be necessary to incorporate an ecosystem of secure, seamless mobility services that handle micropayments and ride-sharing services, a smart transportation infrastructure, 5G connectivity, location services, and electric vehicle charging. IBM developed a blockchain-based eWallet service enabling cashless micropayments for tolls, express lanes, electric charging, and parking payments.

Besides facilitating vehicle operation, IBM's blockchain also streamlines the global supply chain for auto parts. It makes data from across the supply chain accessible to component vendors, owners and maintainers, and regulators. Blockchain's traceability and transparency make it perfect for tracking globally sourced auto parts. When people hear "blockchain," they often think about Bitcoin or cryptocurrency, but there are many more industries that will be revolutionized by the technology, as we scratched the surface within this chapter.

REFERENCES

1. "Global insurance market trend", EY report, *http://www.ey.com/ Publication/vwLUAssets/ey-global-insurance-trends-analysis-2016/$File/ ey-global-insurance-trends-analysis-2016.pdf*

2. *https://b3i.tech/home.html*

3. "China's insurance market", whitepaper, *http://www.aon.com/inpoint/bin/ pdfs/white-papers/ChinaWhitepaper2016.pdf*

4. "Digital insurance in action", The digital insurer, *https://www.the-digital-insurer.com/dia/chain-b-blockchain-enabled-insurance/*

5. "'Big Four' Chinese Bank to Launch Blockchain Bancassurance Product", *https://www.coindesk.com/big-four-chinese-bank-launch-blockchain-bancassurance-product/*

6. "10 insurance firms test blockchain for insurance in China", Wolfie Zhao, *https://www.coindesk.com/insurance-firms-blockchain-test-insurance-china/*

7. *https://www.wealthfront.com/*

8. *https://www.betterment.com/*

9. *https://www.personalcapital.com/*

10. *https://intelligent.schwab.com/*

11. "Alibaba's Yuebao becomes world's largest money market fund", Yang Jing, *https://news.cgtn.com/news/3d41544f79637a4d/share_p.html*

12. "Chinese robo-advisor Xuanji launched by PINTEC group in Beijing", Steven Hatzakis, *https://www.financemagnates.com/fintech/investing/ chinese-robo-advisor-xuanji-launched-by-pintec-group-in-beijing/*

13. "Blockchain in aerospace and defense", Accenture consulting, *https:// www.accenture.com/t20170928T023222Z__w__/us-en/_acnmedia/PDF-61/Accenture-Blockchain-For-Aerospace-Defense-PoV-v2.pdf#zoom=5*

14. "U.S. Defense finding use cases for Blockchain technology?", J R Cornel, *https://steemit.com/blockchain/@jrcornel/u-s-defense-finding-use-cases-for-blockchain-technology*

15. *http://www.crypto-chat.com/* "ITAMCO to Develop Blockchain-Based Secure Messaging App for U.S. Military",

16. *https://www.prnewswire.com/news-releases/itamco-to-develop-blockchain-based-secure-messaging-app-for-us-military-300464063.html*

17. "IBM partners with CDC to bring blockchain to public health" by Giuliu Prisco, http://distributed.com

18. "Why CDC wants in on Blockchain" by Mike Orcutt, MIT Technology Review.

19. *http://en.inspur.com/inspur/2225886/index.html*

20. CDC, *https://www.cdc.gov/foodborneburden/index.html*

21. Worst Food borne Illness Outbreaks in Recent U.S. History", *https://www.healthline.com/health/worst-foodborne-illness-outbreaks*

22. "IBM announces major blockchain collaboration with food suppliers", *http://www-03.ibm.com/press/us/en/pressrelease/53013.wss*

23. "IBM deploys blockchain technology to provide enterprise solutions to food safety", Brigid McDermott

24. "The Procyclical Role of Rating Agencies: Evidence from the East Asian Crisis", G. Ferri, et. al. *http://onlinelibrary.wiley.com/doi/10.1111/1468-0300.00016/full*

25. "US credit card debt skyrockets, approaching $1 trillion", *https://www.rt.com/business/335249-us-credit-card-debt/*

26. *https://www.statista.com/statistics/500814/debt-owned-by-consumers-usa-by-type/#:~:text=Consumers%20in%20the%20United%20States,totaling%201.58%20trillion%20U.S.%20dollars.*

27. "Big Data meets Big Brothers as China moves to rate its citizens", Rachael Botsman, *http://www.wired.co.uk/article/chinese-government-social-credit-score-privacy-invasion*

28. *https://nhglobalpartners.com/china-social-credit-system-explained/*

29. "Household final consumption expenditure (% of GDP)", World Bank, *https://data.worldbank.org/indicator/NE.CON.PETC.ZS*

30. "Target will pay $18.5 million in settlement with states over 2013 data breach", Samantha Masunaga, *http://www.latimes.com/business/la-fi-target-credit-settlement-20170523-story.html*

31. "Using blockchain to improve data management in public sector", Steve Cheng et. al., *https://www.mckinsey.com/business-functions/*

digital-mckinsey/our-insights/using-blockchain-to-improve-data-management-in-the-public-sector

32. *https://www.enigma.co/*

33. "DropBox's 2012 breach was worse than the company first announced", Russell Brandom, *https://www.theverge.com/2016/8/31/12727404/dropbox-breach-passwords-hacked-encrypted*

34. *"4chan Chronicle/The Australian Hack", Wikibooks,*

35. *https://ipfs.io/*

36. "Oracle blockchain cloud service" *https://www.oracle.com/cloud/blockchain/index.html*

37. *https://filecoin.io/*

38. *https://www.ethnews.com/whisper-and-anonymity*

39. *http://devp2p.com/*

40. *https://www.provenance.org/*

41. *http://www.skuchain.com/*

42. "Foxconn reveals plan for blockchain supply chain domination", Michael del Castillo, *https://www.coindesk.com/foxconn-wants-take-global-supply-chain-blockchain/*

43. *http://en.dianrong.com/*

44. "Chained Finance: First Blockchain Platform for Supply Chain Finance", *https://www.prnewswire.com/news-releases/chained-finance-first-blockchain-platform-for-supply-chain-finance-300418265.html*

9

PAYMENT AND LENDING

Besides digital currency, banking, lending, and payments are the most obvious applications of blockchain technology.

9.1   BANKING AND PAYMENT

By 2022, 90% of banks have either employed blockchain or are investigating the best way to implement it. Their goal is to leverage blockchain technology to create a decentralized system that would replace trust. This would significantly decrease all transaction fees and processing times.

However, the term "decentralized" is deceptive, as shown in the discussion of national digital currency. Although blockchain attracts attention as a decentralized system, it can also be a centralized system. In fact, while blockchain applications can be decentralized in their deployment, they can still maintain centralized authorities.

Banks are experimenting with the distributed ledger approach to promote efficiency without giving up control of the financial establishment. Their goals are to automate processes, speed up the transaction, reduce the cost, and enhance data security. To deploy blockchain, banks need to review the existing complex financial structures to determine which processes should move to a blockchain. Blockchain technology itself is constantly evolving, making it difficult for banks to make long-term plans of action. Since it is so new and complex, a transition from a centralized legacy to a fully distributed digital transaction processing may encounter glitches.

In November 2015, the Council of the European Union approved the European Payment Service Directive version 2 (PSD2) legislation created by the European Parliament in response to the upcoming digitalization of the financial services. It provided a basic legislative framework for online payments, the development and use of online and mobile payments, and cross-border European payment services. It was a step towards a digital single market. PSD2 became effective on January 13, 2018. Britain responded with similar plans called Competition and Markets Authority (CMA). With the legislation in place, many European companies rushed to develop online payment platforms.

For example, Moneybookers/Skrill, a company based out of London, specializes in the transfer of foreign exchange into domestic banks in e-banking. Geoswift[1] is involved in the cross-border payment platform. ChinaPnR provides payment services, including online payments, fund management, POS payments, mobile payments, and tailored integrated payment solutions. All in Pay engages in offline payment.

Elsewhere in the world, there are many activities within the same market space. For example, Foxconn, the world leading contract manufacturer, invested in a Californian blockchain start-up called Abra with other investors, including Arbor Ventures, American Express Ventures, Jungle Ventures, Lehrer Hippeau, and RRE. Abra raised a total of $35 million. Abra is in the mobile P2P consumer payment service using Bitcoin. Its app can use blockchain technology to transfer cash between two smartphones. In 2016, the U.K. saw its first online-only bank: the Atom Bank in 2016. Within one year of its opening, it broke the record for most new customer signups in a single day, with 5,000 new customers.[2]

India also developed its own mobile-first financial services company, Paytm.[3] It offers services for payments, banking, lending, and insurance to consumers and merchants. Paytm uses a QR Code for the transaction. Seven million merchants from across India accept payments directly into their bank accounts without a transaction fee. In 2017, the company launched Paytm Payments Bank to bring banking and financial service access to a half billion unserved and underserved Indians. In 2018, it set up Paytm Money to offer investment and Wealth Management products.

Cross-border payment is another market growing with tourist traffic and cross-border retail business across the globe. PayPal is catering to Chinese consumers by collaborating with UnionPay to support outbound cross-border transactions. This enables Chinese consumers to purchase goods from foreign e-retailers directly in countries where UnionPay still has limited acceptance.

Merchants in European countries can also accept payments from UnionPay credit and debit cards through PayPal's Braintree platform for mobile commerce. PayPal and UnionPay also launched PayPal China Connect, allowing Chinese customers to convert renminbi to their payment currency of choice directly.

9.2 THIRD-PARTY PAYMENT MARKET

Mobile payment is a precursor of a digital currency. In China, nonbank third parties handle the payment from the buyer to seller, and thus was born the term "third-party payment." The third-party payment system has its roots in e-commerce, where the platform owner acts as an escrow. When the buyer pays, the e-commerce company tells the seller to ship the product. When the buyer receives the product, the company releases the payment to the seller. The third party transfers the payment from the buyer's bank account to seller's bank account. This method is necessary because very few people in China had a credit card. For example, China had only 0.29 cards per capita at the end of 2015, which is a stark contrast to the average of 2.35 credit cards per capita in the U.S.[4]

Compared with traditional payment methods, including credit card payments, third-party payment has obvious advantages: convenience, cost efficiency, added security features, and accessibility. Certain unique features of China's e-commerce environment have further contributed to its popularity in China. The threshold for applying for credit cards from a bank is high in China. Even for those who have credit cards, many are wary of using them for online purchases for fear of the leakage of personal information. Banks have also imposed stringent maximum transaction limits on online transactions effected through credit cards.

Some people are under the impression that a third-party payment is free from a service fee. It is not exactly true, although its cost is indeed much lower than that of credit cards. When the party works with banks, the banks charge transaction fees. Therefore, even Tencent and Alipay, which used to provide payment transfer for free, now charge customers a small fee. Such a fee is still relatively inexpensive: 0.1% for transaction amounts over $3,000.

The dominant domestic online marketplaces for Chinese consumers are Taobao (Alibaba), Tmall, and JD.com, which handle payment transactions between buyers and sellers as third parties. As e-commerce proliferated, the third-party payment platforms also grew. As mobile phone penetration got deeper, mobile payment apps started to appear to make payments easier. Soon, the convenience of this third-party payment system migrated from e-commerce to physical stores. Today, most of the brick-and-mortar stores, street vendors, mom and pop shops, supermarkets, and restaurants have also joined the mobile payment system.

In a nation where cash historically dominated the consumer market, China is moving from cash to digital payment on smartphones, bypassing credit and debit cards. Fintech and blockchain technology can greatly accelerate the use of a payment platform and enhance its security.

In the U.S. and Europe, fintech evolution has been driven by startups and financial institutions. However, China's Internet giants have largely been the sources of capital for its fintech firms. Ant Financial, which operates the Alipay payment platform, was a spin-off from Alibaba.

In 2019, the Chinese third-party payment market reached $32 trillion dollars and growing at 22% annual rate.[5] It is forecasted that by 2025, the market will reach $109 trillion dollars.[6] The rapid spread of mobile payment platforms in China was led by Alipay, TenPay, JD Pay and UnionPay's Quick, ICBC's e-wallet, and 99bill.

The earliest entry was Alibaba, which launched Alipay in 2004 to serve its Taobao e-commerce platform. Alibaba's Alipay was the most used third-party payment platform. In part, the flourishing Chinese e-commerce market and its adoption of Internet and mobile payments can also be due to the presence of a massive domestic retail market. Alibaba's Alipay is now the largest online payment gateway in China, accounting for half of the Chinese third-party online payments. Apple launched Apple Pay in China.

These e-commerce firms were not content to only providing payment services. The fiercely competitive market serves as a driving force to create new and innovative market applications. E-commerce companies are obligated to act under market forces or foresee big opportunities in using similar technology to create new markets. They used the third-party payment platform as a springboard to enter other fintech businesses, such as online lending, e-insurance, credit rating, wealth management, stock trading, and bike sharing. Once the payment service technology started, it spread like wildfire in all imaginable applications. This is how the Internet and e-commerce giants Tencent, Alibaba, and JD.com entered fintech.

Alibaba spun off its payment service branch as Ant Financial,[7] which manages Alipay. Alipay works with traditional banks and credit card companies, including Visa and MasterCard.

Merchants and customers using Alipay could easily park their excess cash in Yu'e Bao to earn an attractive interest that banks were unable to offer. The natural extension of Alipay's payment service to the money market fund service resulted in exponential growth. In June 2013, Alibaba launched the money market fund Yu'e Bao, run by Tianhong Asset Management, another Alibaba affiliate. By the end of 2021, Yu'e Bao's market fund assets reached $150 billion, and at one time, it was the largest in the world.

In addition to serving its e-commerce platform, Alipay also expanded to more than 460,000 Chinese businesses. It also made inroads into the international markets by signing up overseas merchants and accepting foreign currencies. It has long dominated China's mobile payment market until its competitor Tencent came up with a more innovative mobile payment system, TenPay. By the end of 2016, Alipay saw its share of the market fall from 71% in 2015 to 54%, while the TenPay share rose from 16% to 37% during the same period.

In June 2015, following the success of Yu'e Bao, Ant Financial launched MYbank, a new online-only bank in China. The online-only bank does not have a physical branch office. All the transactions are online.

Chinese mobile device manufacturers, such as Huawei and Xiaomi, also moved into fintech and mobile payment partnerships, e.g., UnionPay. The regulatory environment has been generally receptive to the collaboration on areas as diverse as e-commerce, gaming, chat, and search engines to financial services. The offline-to-online interaction is also popular in China.

Tencent had a meteoric rise in the fintech arena thanks to its social media app called WeChat. WeChat users can transfer money between each other, as well as pay for services such as taxis, digital subscriptions, food deliveries, and restaurant bills using an embedded function called WeChat Pay or TenPay.

TenPay takes advantage of the enormous user base of the WeChat app ecosystem. With over a billion users in the online messaging service, WeChat entered the mobile payment and anyone with an account can send and receive payments to anyone else with a WeChat account. The app allows users to keep funds in their wallets for peer-to-peer payments and in-app purchases. TenPay can also be used in physical stores for off-line merchants, including

Starbucks, which has 2,600 stores in China. By doing so, WeChat transformed itself from a social media platform into a payment platform in 2013. It also launched a personal online investment fund in January 2014. One year later, WeBank, China's first online-only bank, launched the same product.

WeChat Pay's goal was to serve more than 10 million small merchants or stores in China. It has an innovative function called the Digital Red Envelope (or *Hongbao* in Chinese). The traditional Hongbao is a red envelope containing gift money in cash that the elderly give to children during the Chinese New Year or as a wedding gift to newlyweds. The ability to transfer money online via WeChat accounts revolutionized the Hongbao tradition. Using WeChat's Hongbao function, one can send Hongbao electronically instead of face-to-face delivery. It became widely popular. In 2016, 64 billion Digital Red Envelopes were exchanged over the six-day holiday period. An added benefit to the merchants, the mobile payment system collects the data gathered from spending habits and financial information. It allows merchants to target their specific customers.

Facing a threat from Tencent, Alibaba began building its own physical network of stores, both domestically and overseas. It has already signed up more than two million brick-and-mortar shops in China with 10 million merchants on Taobao using Alipay. Ant Financial, a spin-off of Alibaba, provides more financial service offerings than the money market fund giant Yu'e Bao to attract customers.[7]

Apple launched Apple Pay in China in May 2016, and 30 million bank cards were signed up on the first day.[8] However, its market share did not grow as expected due to several reasons. First, Apple Pay was a latecomer. The mobile payment market was already well saturated and dominated by two big players locked in a fierce competition. In addition, Apple Pay uses NFC (Near Field Communication) as opposed to the QR codes used by both Alipay and TenPay, which introduced QR code system in 2011- 2012. Soon afterwards, QR codes spread quickly in major Chinese cities.

There is an underlying reason that NFC cannot duplicate the success of the QR code in China. NFC payment requires dedicated NFC-equipped smartphones and the point-of-sales terminals in the stores. It is unreasonable to expect millions of mom-and-pop shops and street vendors to sign up for the NFC equipment, when one can easily print QR code on a piece of paper. QR codes are inexpensive to create and only need a camera-enabled smartphone to scan. QR codes provide pertinent and relevant information and deliver it quickly and efficiently.

Besides payments, QR codes also serve as a channel of communication from stores to customers. QR codes direct customers instantly to the website link, SMS, or text messages of the physical store. Increasingly, Chinese retailers have started using QR codes on billboards, posters, and flyers to offer discounts and product information. By scanning the codes, smartphone users can use mobile payment options to purchase the product or service immediately – promoting impulsive purchasing.

Once on the website, store owners can deliver any information they want, such as product information, promotions, coupons, discounts, product displays, restaurant menus, price lists, locations of other franchise stores, memberships, or upcoming events. Customers can enter a virtual queue for train tickets or seats in a restaurant, make purchases, or place orders from a QR code. Receipts often contain QR codes, which open the portal to a wealth of information about the store or business, including ads, coupons, and promotions. QR codes can allow easy access to events, and consumers can download various calendars to their phones, ensuring they have the information needed to attend the event. Tipping digital content providers is quite popular in China, and content creators on WeChat's mobile publishing platform use QR codes to collect tips with payment transactions processed by WeChat Payment.

Recognizing this growing trend, PBOC revealed plans to regulate QR based payment technologies and has authorized the China Payment & Clearing Association to draft standards for mobile purchases linked to QR codes.[9] Favorable regulation will support the development of virtual credit cards, providing further stimulus for fintech firms focused on digital payments.

The popularity of the QR code is for both offline and online. Any QR code on the WeChat messaging app can be decoded with the touch of a finger. In the U.S., Amazon experimented with QR code-scanning mobile payments at its Amazon Go locations.

Besides the choice of technology, the failure of Apple Pay to crack the Chinese market has another reason. As a third-party payment service, both Alipay and TenPay are cross-platform services that are open to users on iOS, Android, and any other type of phone. The Android mobile operating system has 75% of the market share in China as compared to 24% of Apple's iOS. This allows the company to reach a much wider market using smartphone apps. Apple Pay only works with iPhone, which automatically excludes most of the Chinese market who use Android phones.

A new segment of digitally perceptive consumers, Millennials and Generation Z, account for 45% of consumption. They drive online retail market and lead the charge in China's mobile payments adoption, with 66% of post-1990 millennials shopping and 54% banking via their mobile devices. A rising number of young Chinese consumers end up accessing financial services for the first time through fintech-developed platforms, rather than traditional banks.

Although third-party payment transaction still involves banks, it cuts traditional banks off from relationships with merchants and retail customers. The banks merely process the transactions for the third party without establishing a relationship with the payment parties. It deprives banks from the potential of other mainstay businesses, such as loans, deposits, and investments. The emergence of such a new payment platform offers significant opportunities for fintech companies to gain substantial scale but can have a potentially devastating effect on the banking status quo in China.

Fintech firms, such as online-only banks like MYbank and WeBank with streamlined lending processes and innovative credit rating assessments, have broadened financial access for a large segment of the population often ignored by traditional banks in China.

Traditional banks are fighting back with their own fintech transformation. For instance, ICBC, the world's largest bank by assets, has been adapting quickly to the fintech revolution. ICBC researched advanced technology and the cultivation of technical talent by establishing seven innovation labs in ICBC's head office for artificial intelligence, cloud computing, blockchain, biometric identification, big data and Internet finance, and blockchain-based financial trading systems. It is ramping up efforts within the payment space to capture customer data. It successfully launched an e-commerce platform, e-Buy mall, which has grown to become one of China's largest e-commerce platforms. ICBC relied on its capabilities as a bank to facilitate e-commerce, payments, and forex. As a quick payment tool, ICBC e-Payment had 60 million customers in September 2015. ICBC also launched an e-based finance product system that offers payments, financing, and wealth management services, with the largest local online revolving loan extending $259 billion to more than 70,000 SMEs.

Other banks have also collaborated with fintech firms to launch digital initiatives. For example, the Postal Savings Bank of China (PSBC), China's largest lender by branch network with 40,000 branches, is working with Ant Financials' MYbank and Tencent in Internet and mobile finance. Through such collaboration, both parties' benefit. Banks will be able to reach a new segment of customers with the online banking capabilities of the large e-commerce players.

More and more e-commerce companies are establishing brick-and-mortar stores, allowing them to lure online customers to physical stores. This is known as Online-to-Offline (O2O) business. Online channels include online store, social media, emails and Internet advertising. This type of strategy incorporates techniques used in online marketing with those used in brick-and-mortar marketing. The most well-known O2O business is when Amazon acquired Whole Food Market in 2017.[8]

The Chinese Government has an open policy promoting the financial inclusion of China's 234 million unbanked people living in rural areas and in the poorest neighborhoods. The collaboration between the online-only bank and traditional bank fulfills the desire of government policymakers.

Before there was an online third-party payment system, there was also an offline third-party payment system. It works like a bank, but has no branch offices. Its physical presence is a kiosk or an ATM-like machine. Lakala, founded in 2005, is China's largest off-line financial service provider.[10] It boasts 60,000 self-service payment stations in China at convenient stores, supermarkets, shopping malls, community centers, and hospitals. People can pay utility bills, buy train or airline tickets, buy movie or show tickets, book hotels, and even buy wealth management products at Lakala kiosks. It also offers mobile payment platform and POS devices like those used in restaurants and cross-border payment services.

In a few short years, China's third-party payment system evolved from an online shopping payment system to an omnipresent payment system replacing cash entirely. The U.S. payment ecosystem is also shifting toward mobile. However, such a shift requires a fundamental overhaul of the current credit/debit card infrastructure and unseats the existing benefactors. This will also depend on the incumbents, e.g., giant credit card companies, to come up with an innovative solution for mobile payments without giving up their exclusive positions in the existing system. The introduction of fintech may have a large impact on the mobile payment system.

On June 21, 2010, the central bank of China issued administrative rules governing payment services by non-financial institutions.[9] These rules were the first set of regulatory measures China has adopted towards nonbank third-party payment processors. They fundamentally affected China's third-party payment service, an important feature and integral link of e-commerce, and e-commerce itself.

9.3 MOBILE WALLETS AND PAYMENT TRANSFERS

The mobile wallet or mobile electronic wallet is a new form of payment using mobile devices, i.e., mobile phones. This payment system is prevalent in China, and it is getting more popular elsewhere. A trend is evident, and sooner or later, it will replace credit cards and cash as it has already happened in China.

The mobile wallet is an app in one's mobile device that stores the payment method, which can be a credit card or link to the bank account. In China, most of the mobile wallets use a third-party payment system. In the U.S., some popular mobile wallets are Apple Pay,[10] Google Pay, and Samsung Pay. Many financial institutions, such as Chase, Capital One, PayPal, and Wells Fargo Bank also have mobile payment apps. Even some retail stores, like Walmart and Starbucks, offer such a service.

Europe has rapidly developed a mobile wallet system. There are many competing wallets operated by various types of domestic and international entities in different countries. An organization called Mobey Forum Digital Wallet Working Group has created profiles of 49 prominent mobile wallets by their strategy, features, functionality, and technology.[11] Banks operate 26 of them. These include iDEAL of Netherlands, MobilePay of Denmark, BKM Express of Turkey, Swish of Sweden, and Vipps of Norway. The other 23 mobile wallets are nonbank operated. While bank operated wallets mostly serve the domestic market, the nonbank wallets are more successful across Europe. They include Neteller, Skrill, PayPal, SEQR, Masterpass, Yoyo, and Amazon Pay. Twenty-seven of these mobile wallets are credit-card based, while the remaining are Automated Clearing House (ACH) network based, which transfers funds between banks.

The advantages of the mobile wallet are ease of use, including eliminating the need to carry multiple credit cards. Many sponsors of mobile wallets provide rewards as incentives to customers. Some mobile wallets also provide a P2P solution. At the merchant Point-of-Sale (POS), some mobile wallets use Near Field Communication (NFC) solutions. Others use QR codes, Bluetooth, or even barcodes.

Square, one of the pioneers in the payment solution technology arena, offers a square-shaped reader that plugs into the audio jack of a smart phone and turns it into a credit card reader to accept contactless payment, including Apple Pay. In doing so, it can turn a smart phone into a POS system. It also offers a virtual gift card in the form of a QR code stored in the customer's smart phone. When the merchant, who accepts such a gift card, scans the QR code, it receives the payment from the gift card.

CashApp is another one of Square's innovative money transfer products. It allows person-to-person money transfer via the app or website. In 2015, this application was expanded into a business that allows individuals and business owners to send and receive money and to buy and sell Bitcoins. By 2019, six years after its launch, with 15 million active digital users, CashApp ranks number six in the U.S. behind JPMorgan Chase, Venmo, Bank of America, Wells Fargo Bank, and Citibank.

One of the major concerns of the mobile wallet is safety. It is inherently less safe than a credit cards because the payments go through mobile devices and mobile networks rather than a dedicated credit card POS device. However, blockchain technology can address such a safety issue.

9.4 CREDIT CARDS AND LOAN APPLICATIONS

Credit card companies do not want to be left behind by the blockchain technology. Blockchain technology may seem like a threat to these companies in that it provides P2P transactions to bypass intermediates. However, they can also benefit from using the new technology to streamline their operations. The credit card system is prone to fraud. Credit card information can be easily stolen and used to create fraudulent transactions. Reported credit fraud losses reached $27.85 billion worldwide in 2018.[12] Credit card companies see blockchain as a remedy to this problem. The payment industry is undergoing a paradigm shift. Moreover, the industry is large: the global consumer payment market reached $47 trillion in 2014, the first year that the share of digital payment volumes exceeded that of paper-based payment methods.

Financial institutions want to attain the Straight-Through- Processing (STP) concept.[13] STP is a scheme to optimize the speed of transactions. It allows for the transferring of electronically entered data from one party to another in the settlement process without manually re-entering the same data repeatedly over the sequence of events. One benefit of STP is a decrease in settlement risk and time.

To do so, it is necessary to streamline the process of transactions across multiple points. Allowing information to be passed along electronically requires the manual entry of data only once at the source. Multiple parties can receive the same information simultaneously, if needed. STP will eliminate human intervention from financial transactions, thus reducing the cost of transaction as well. A true STP will save money in credit card processing.

Blockchain technology, ideal for digital transactions, has the potential to implement STP and transform the global financial network. This technology could accelerate the velocity of money, thus improving the economy's efficiency. It also provides a path for legacy banking systems to interoperate, greatly improving efficiency. The use of distributed ledgers has the potential to disrupt the payment industry in the near future.

Major credit card companies (such as Visa, MasterCard, and American Express), major banks, and financial service firms are all embracing blockchain technology due to a potential reduction in costs and improved product offerings.[14]

Visa operates a proprietary transaction-processing network called VisaNet. VisaNet facilitates the authorization, clearing, and settlement of payment transactions worldwide while offering fraud protection for account holders and rapid payments for merchants. It is capable of handling 24,000 transaction messages per second.

Visa initiated its blockchain development. It considers fintech a unique opportunity at a time when the payments industry is undergoing a digital transformation. Visa partnered with blockchain company BLT Group to streamline cross-border transfers between banks. Visa Europe also partnered with Epiphyte to explore the possibility of using blockchain technology for international remittances.[15] The project created a prototype smartphone wallet app to enable the processing of remittances directly from a Visa card to a destination payment location over the Bitcoin blockchain.

Recently, it issued the popular Bitcoin debit card, the Coinbase Shift Card. Visa has also invested in a blockchain developer platform, Chain.com, which serves an enterprise market. The incorporation of blockchain technology into the VisaNet operation can potentially be very beneficial to Visa. Other credit card companies are not far behind.

Kreditech is a Germany-based fintech company.[16] It uses non-traditional data sources and machine learning to provide financing to people with little to no credit history. It is based on the conviction that not all people without credit history carry high financial risk. Using its proprietary credit decision technology, Kreditech is doing good business to help people with financial needs and reaches the largely untapped market of the financially underserved.

In summary, blockchain-based networks and traditional technology-based alternative payment solutions will continue to merge. The payment service market landscape will be dramatically different in the future.

9.5 PEER-TO-PEER LENDING

ROSCA stands for the Rotating Savings and Credit Association. It is a popular type of P2P lending. Billions of people throughout the world have practiced the traditional form of P2P lending since ancient times.[17] A participant can borrow from the pool of money collectively saved for anything, like buying a car or making a down payment for a house.

A ROSCA is organized by a group of trusted parties, who agree to contribute a fixed amount of money at a fixed interval, called a "round." At the end of each round, the pot contains the sum of everyone's contribution. Users bid on this amount in a reverse auction manner, where the lowest bid wins. The winning bidder then receives his bid. The remaining will be split equally among all the participants as a form of interest payment. If a bidder's desire to get the money is strong, he will have to enter lower bid to ensure that he would win. In effect, he is paying higher interest.

In each round, there is only one winner. Each user is guaranteed to win one round in turn. A winner will have next opportunity to bid only after all the parties receive their winning bid. This ensures a Pareto optimal outcome, where everyone is better off than they would have been had they saved the money alone.

ROSCAs are seeing growing popularity in the U.S., primarily within immigrant populations. They are also becoming popular in places where informal credit is the norm, such as China. Community systems worldwide are another reason why blockchain is great for leveraging reciprocal finance.

The traditional ROSCA requires trust. The scope of ROSCA is limited to a small group of people who know each other and trust each other to be participants. Therefore, its scope is limited. With the rise of blockchain technology, people found that the ROSCA scheme can be extended far beyond the familiar circle because trust is no longer an issue. Blockchain provides the perfect platform for ROSCA applications.

ROSCAs can be a successful supplement to regular financial services — another tool in the toolbox. Reciprocal aid is a perfect fit for blockchain technology, enabling people around the world access to more advanced financial tools. Most of all, ROSCA is a self-financing model. All the profits are distributed to the participants. The idea for ROSCA is to have a community of like-minded people with financial goals.

Anyone can start a ROSCA with the blockchain application, and set rules: the maximum number of participants, the time period of the round, and the amount of the contribution. It can also be dissolved when all the participants receive the bid.

Many kinds of platforms use the ROSCA concept: eMoneyPool, Monk, Puddle, Moneyfellows, ROSCA Finance, Partnerhand, StepLadder, and WeTrust. One of the most successful platforms, WeTrust, raised $6.5 million in market capital in an ICO in April 2017. Its market capitalization tripled within 10 days of coin issuance. As a peer-to-peer financing system, the platform must be permissionless.

The rapidly growing market of P2P lending is loosely regulated and plagued by fraud and defaults. The worst P2P lending fraud happened in China 2014-2015,[15] when 900,000 investors lost over $7.6 billion in a Ponzi P2P lending scheme on Ezubao. As a result, people lost confidence in P2P lending. Half a year after the exposure of the fraud, nearly one-third of all online lending companies in China were in financial trouble, and 40% of the 1,600 P2P lenders exited the market by April 2016. That left the larger, more established online lenders to dominate the largest online lending marketplace in the world.

There are also other types of P2P lending. Using a different business model, China Rapid Finance (CRF) is China's largest consumer lending marketplaces in terms of total number of loans granted. Much like the e-commerce marketplace where the platform operator offers online spaces for buyers, CRF operates the marketplace without taking a credit risk by using machine learning and proprietary technology to select qualified borrowers. For first-time borrowers, the cap loan amount is limited. After customers establish their credentials, the cap loan amount increases. Its board of directors includes reputable global financial executives with extensive experience.[16]

CBRC, China Banking Regulatory Commission, proposed restrictions for banks that would pave the way for P2P lenders to enter the wealth management market and deliver financial advice in an innovative way.

When the Chinese P2P market cooled down, the surviving P2P lenders sought to collaborate with banks to restore their reputation and re-establish their credibility, even though they were not involved in the scam. For example, a collaboration between Dianrong and the regional Bank of Suzhou set up a P2P loan platform targeting SMEs. The Shanghai-based P2P lender China Rapid Finance (CRF) collaborated with China Construction Bank to create a P2P platform providing investors access to CRF's P2P offerings via the bank. Other collaborations are between P2P lenders, such as Jimubox, RenRenDai, Minshengyidai, and China Minsheng Bank, where the bank manages and safeguards investors' funds. Even CreditEase, a Beijing based fintech leading conglomerate with a nationwide network in 255 cities in China, made a similar arrangement with China Citi Bank.[17,20]

Fintech experts believe that artificial intelligence and blockchain technology can prevent fraud. It prompted many P2P lenders to seek blockchain solutions. To prevent the scam from happening again, the Chinese central bank PBOC introduced new regulations to oversee P2P lending and online payments in China, such as imposing credit limits and requiring a principal guaranteed by the platform.

The Ezubao event was a temporary setback for P2P lending. New regulations and platforms with new technologies are gradually restoring the consumer confidence in P2P lending. Once confidence returns, the market is expected to grow at an annual rate of 50% again, because there is an undeniable demand for such a service.

Nonbanks, which appeared on the scene in the last decade due to the flourishing of e-commerce, have an upper hand in China, especially when it comes to competitiveness in offerings, digital functionality and experience, quality, innovation, and trust levels. For these reasons, SMEs and retail consumers are increasingly turning to the non-traditional lenders for financial services.

9.6 ONLINE LENDING

The use of fintech in lending has spread beyond P2P lending, microlending, and SME lending. Now, banks are quickly adapting the same technology for their traditional loan services to decrease costs, reduce risk and improve efficiency. One prime example is the German fintech company Kreditech.[18]

Kreditech uses AI to analyze big data and calculate an individual's credit score. The data it uses to determine a loan applicant's creditworthiness is essentially the digital footprint of the loan applicant. Such data include location information, social networking information, banking data, hardware data, online shopping behavior, and general online behavior. Location information, such as whether one shops at upscale department stores or thrift stores and the types of restaurants one frequents, reveals important information about customers' shopping habits and economic status. The same is true for hardware data, such as whether one uses an iPhone or a generic phone, or the make and model of car one drives.

Another example is CreditEase in China. CreditEase developed a brand-new concept for the P2P lending industry: it matches borrowers and lenders online. The lenders are not banks or financial institutions, but individuals who have money to lend. It is like an auction market for loans. Once the conditions match, the lender grants the loan to the borrower, and the borrower pays back the lender in monthly installments with interest. Most often, the lender's money is dispersed to many borrowers, and the borrower gets a loan from multiple lenders. Such a diversification reduces the risk. If the borrower misses a payment, CreditEase will pay the lender and try to collect from the borrower. Therefore, CreditEase, not the lenders, carries the default risk. CreditEase is acting like matchmaker and guarantor of the loan. In fact, CreditEase operates like a bank, getting money from individual investors and lending it to borrowers.

The lender contributes funds, which can be automatically allocated among approved borrowers or the borrowers of his choice. The lender, also known as an *investor* on the platform, can choose to enroll in the automated investing option, which automatically reinvests their funds when they receive payments from the borrower. Alternatively, the lender can select lending opportunities to the approved borrowers by the lender themselves. Furthermore, the investor's fund is not locked to its maturity. The investor has the option to sell the loan in the company-operated secondary loan market at any time. This liquidity offers investors the opportunity to enter and exit their investments without waiting until maturity.

Chinese fintech firms are increasingly looking for technology solutions to enhance security and reduce risk. In March 2017, CreditEase launched an Ethereum-based blockchain service called Blockworm to enhance its security.[19] The deployment of the Social Credit System (SCS) may boost consumer confidence in P2P lending.[20]

9.7   MICROLENDING AND SME LENDING

Fintech creates opportunities for microlending and lending to SMEs (Small and Medium Enterprises). SME is usually defined as the enterprises with less than 300 employees. Microlending provides the service of lending small amounts of money, not unlike credit cards. SME lending caters to small and medium businesses. Both types of lending are avoided by traditional financial institutions such as banks because the risk to reward ratio is high. Banks demand stringent qualifications and require an extensive and tedious approval process. SMEs, which lack qualified collateral and track records of credit repayment, receive only 20-25% of bank-disbursed loans. However, SMEs make up 97% of all enterprises in China,[21] and are providing 80% of non-governmental employment in 2019[22]. They generated 60% of GDP, 80% of urban employment, and contributed to 50% of fiscal and tax revenues in China. SMEs also suffer from asymmetric information, with limited transparency in their financial positions and credit rating assessments. Even if they do secure bank loans, the interest rates are much higher than that of large corporations, based on the risk concerns. Likewise, retail customers also receive a lower priority at China's banks. This provides a fertile ground for the growth of a nonbank-operated online lending market. About 160 million people in China took out $180 billion in online loans in 2016. There are many companies operating in niche markets. For example, a fintech online financing company, Daikuan, which raised $2 billion in 2017, offers online loans for buyers of second-hand cars.

Fintech fills the void left by banks' lending services. Using fintech, the approval process for such lending is extremely fast, made possible by using personal financial data online or via big data. Unlike the traditional credit data used by banks, such as the credit score, tax documents, bank and/or income statements, and records of asset ownership, the data collected by microlending services is the customers' actual spending data.

Peak Fintech Group (PFG) is a Canadian fintech company with a significant presence in China. It caters to the more than 100 million small businesses in China having a difficult time getting access to credit from banks and traditional lending institutions.

PFG uses AI analytics to help lenders eliminate the risks associated with lending to small and micro businesses. Since AI requires data, PFG's strategy is to offer its solutions to the lending institutions, which have huge amounts of data on their customers. As of 2020, PFG has partnered with 50 lending institutions and 53,000 loan broker reps, whose customers' data become part of PFG's big data.

Lending institutions like the service because PFG's service not only reduces the risk of lending, but also eliminates their labor-intensive work to qualify the potential loan customers, therefore cutting the cost. PFG's AI software platform is an ecosystem that brings together lenders, brokers, SMEs, data providers, and automated risk management capabilities. PFG has demonstrated that its AI analytics generated lending has a default rate around 2%, within the same range as commercial and industrial loans. These services allow banks and lenders to safely tap into a large, previously untapped market that had been deemed "too risky." This also allows small-time borrowers to obtain loans at a reasonable interest rate. There is no need to search for loan customers anymore, as PFG brings clients to them. SMEs obtain loans they would otherwise not have been qualified for. In 2018, PFG generated $15 billion in loan requests.

In December 2020, PFG entered a partnership with e-commerce giant Pinduoduo, the largest interactive e-commerce platform in the world and the second largest online marketplace in China. Such a partnership allowed PFG to bring credit solutions to Pinduoduo's 5.6 million online stores and over 600 million active users.

Other microlenders and SME lenders in China that are market leaders are Lufax of Ping An Insurance, Yirendai of CreditEase, Rendai, Zhai Cai Bao of Alibaba, and Dianrong. The risk for these lenders, without the leverage of an e-commerce platform, is higher, therefore, the interest rates are also higher. However, their service is open to anyone and is not limited to the supply chain participants. Lufax had more than 23.3 million users by June 2016, which had doubled by 2022.

The SME, which takes part in the supply chain of e-commerce, can obtain loans from an e-commerce company, which lends to SMEs by leveraging SMEs' merchandise on its platform. There is no risk to them because once the SME products are sold on their platforms, they receive the customers' payments. Key participants include Ant Financial and Alibaba's MyBank, WeChat's WeBank, JD.com's JD Finance, and Gome Electrical Appliances.

REFERENCES

1. *http://www.geoswift.com/our-company/*

2. *https://en.wikipedia.org/wiki/Atom_Bank*

3. *https://paytm.com/*

4. "Average Number of Credit Cards Per Person: 2017 Card Ownership Statistics", *https://www.valuepenguin.com/average-number-credit-cards-per-person*

5. *http://www.iresearchchina.com/content/details7_58033.html*

6. *https://www.globenewswire.com/news-release/2019/05/30/1859597/0/en/China-Third-Party-Payment-Markets-2019-2025-Market-Size-is-Expected-to-Hit-RMB740-Trillion.html*

7. *https://www.antfin.com/index.htm?locale=en_US*

8. *https://press.aboutamazon.com/news-releases/news-release-details/amazon-acquire-whole-foods-market*

9. *https://www.finextra.com/newsarticle/21525/china-moves-to-regulate-non-bank-online-payment-providers*

10. "Apple pay is coming to China in 2016", Rich McCormick, *https://www.antfin.com/index.htm?locale=en_US*

11. *https://www.mobeyforum.org/european-digital-wallet-landscape/*

12. *https://www.prnewswire.com/news-releases/payment-card-fraud-losses-reach-27-85-billion-300963232.html*

13. Straight Through Processing", *https://www.investopedia.com/terms/s/straightthroughprocessing.asp#ixzz51TkRyllZ*

14. *https://www.nasdaq.com/articles/how-visa-is-embracing-both-the-blockchain-and-cryptocurrency-2020-12-07*

15. "Ezubao", *https://en.wikipedia.org/wiki/Ezubao*

16. China Rapid Finance website, *http://stage.investorroom.com/chinarapidfinance/index.php?s=118*

17. *http://english.creditease.cn/index.html*

18. *https://www.kreditech.com/*

19. "Fintech CreditEase Launches Ethereum-based Blockchain Service", Cindy23, *http://news.8btc.com/fintech-creditease-launches-ethereum-based-blockchain-service*

20. *https://seekingalpha.com/article/4117596-chinas-social-credit-system-and-p2p-lending-opportunity-for-yirendai*

21. *https://www.msadvisory.com/2022-trends-and-growth-of-smes-in-china/*

22. *http://aeconf.com/Articles/May2020/aef210110.pdf*

10

GOVERNANCE AND REGULATION

There are two aspects of the blockchain governance: The first one refers to the governance of the blockchain platform itself. Different public blockchains have different rules and incentives, but fundamentally, they all bring people together to perform its core functionality, ownership, consensus mechanism, potential changes, and future direction. The second aspect refers to the use of blockchain in the governance of the governing body and its members, such as the government and its citizens, legal governance like smart contracts between the signing parties, land title registries, voting, corporate governance, public procurement, and many others. In this chapter, we will discuss a few examples of the applications of blockchain in the governance.

10.1 GOVERNANCE AND VOTING

A public blockchain allows people who do not know each other to agree to a set of rules for governance purposes. For example, blockchain can verify that no one has tampered with the file, which stores digital signatures and provides identity verification. This could allow citizens to self-service many bureaucratic transactions that previously required the attention of civil servants and lawyers.

Blockchain applications for governance can be divided into two categories: permissioned and permissionless. Furthermore, blockchain application for governance must have the rules separate from the governance in order to maintain a high level of transparency. In the permissioned blockchain application, the rules are defined by a central authority, and in the permissionless blockchain application, the rules are defined by public consensus.

By making the results fully transparent and publicly accessible, the blockchain application for governance could bring full transparency to elections or any other kind of poll taking. Ethereum-based smart contracts help to automate the process. As such, there are efforts to develop blockchain technology for the governance purpose that potentially is able to redesign our interactions in business, politics, and society.

A permissionless blockchain application for governance, such as the Decentralized Autonomous Organization (DAO), is a virtual entity comprised of a large number of individuals that respond to a well-defined set of rules. The rules are defined by a social structure that constitutes governance. DAO governance application is most suitable for publicly organized entities with membership participation. Separating corporate governance from the underlying consensus process entirely can improve the integrity of a DAO by providing better transparency. In other words, the public consensus defines the rules, and empower a representative to govern.

In many applications, blockchain platforms can manage social interactions and governing rules. However, there are many cases in which public consensus cannot replace traditional central authorities to define the rules. Thus, those blockchain apps are permissioned blockchains. The ownership must belong to a responsible governing entity rather than an anonymous public.

For example, the app Boardroom enables organizational decision-making to happen on a blockchain.[1] Boardroom is a governance Dapp for individuals and companies to manage their smart contract systems on the permissioned Ethereum blockchain. It can conduct proxy voting for shareholders on a board's proposal. It is an administrative tool for organizations. These are very narrowly defined organizations, simply concerned with the bookkeeping of address balances, but they meet all the requirements of decentralized decision-making.

Another example involves voting, where the government must define the rules. Therefore, a blockchain-based voting application must use permissioned blockchain. Today, the voting systems are either a paper-based system or a digital voting system. The security risk of digital voting is even higher than that of the paper voting system because the digital voting system is more prone to fraud than the paper voting system.

A digital voting system identifies a voter through their ID card. The platform must confirm a voter's identity before they can cast their vote in the polling station. When a voter submits their vote, it goes to a vote storage server. The vote storage server encrypts the vote and strips voter's ID data from the vote before sending it to a vote-counting server. The vote-counting server decrypts and counts the votes and then outputs the results. In today's digital voting platform, there is a risk of an attack before the votes are transferred to the counting server.

Blockchain technology can develop a secure and robust voting system. It offers a decentralized node for online voting or electronic voting with end-to-end verification advantages [2]. The blockchain does not need to replace the current voting system but can improve it. The blockchain voting system first registers the voter into the registration blockchain. The registration creates a transaction unique to the voter. A government miner validates the user. Upon validation, the voter will receive a ballot card with their information on it. This is the same process as the voter registration in the U.S. today, except that the registration is a record in a blockchain.

The voting itself actually takes place in a separate blockchain – the voting blockchain. Each vote is a transaction. The platform validates a voter by three-factor authentication: their identification number, the password supplied on registration, and their ballot card that contains a QR code. The voter can only vote in the constituency where they are registered.

The separation of the registration and voting blockchains ensures voter anonymity. Certified observers and election officials monitor and audit the voting process. Instead of reading the ballots and counting them, they host the nodes in the voting blockchain and verify that the unencrypted results match the encrypted votes. Each transaction is encrypted with public and private keys. The polling station nodes contain the public keys of their voters to allow them to encrypt any vote made to that polling station.

Each constituency counts the votes and builds blocks. They act as miners during the counting process. They build the blocks by including the votes for the same candidate in a block. A block can contain tens of thousands of votes. This is happening in the local constituencies all over the country. The local polling stations then broadcast their voting blocks to all nodes of voting blockchain network of the same constituency to build the blockchain. Once the vote has been confirmed or built into a block, the polling station will then generate a transaction to remove the vote in its pool memory. Such a voting system is tamper-proof.

Besides the voting system, blockchain technology can benefit the government in many other applications. Governments are known for their inefficiency because of their size, inertia, bureaucracy, and lack of incentives. The services are normally slow, negatively impacting citizens. Linking the data between the departments with blockchain ensures the real-time release of critical data. For example, the real-time consumer information can help to make economic and monetary policy. Real-time nationwide clinical data can help to contain the spread of a contagious disease.

Blockchain technology could improve transparency and check corruption in governments worldwide. For example, the U.S. Navy's Innovation department recently announced its interest in using blockchain technology for their manufacturing system.[3] They plan to add blockchain technology to their 3D printing to help securely transfer data through the manufacturing process.[2] The Naval Innovation Advisory Council will test the blockchain technology integration into their system. The initial test is to prove the concepts, share data, and secure digital designs throughout the Navy's network of information.

They also plan to create a data-sharing layer among the 3D printing sites using blockchain technology. Other government departments, such as the Department of Homeland Security Science and Technology Directorate, awarded a total sum of $9.7 million to several small businesses for technology research on blockchain usage, such as contract bidding.[4]

10.2 REGULATORY AND COMPLIANCE APPLICATIONS

Government regulation is possibly one of the most important factors as to whether or how the blockchain technology will eventually develop into a full-fledged fintech industry.

RegTech (Regulatory Technology) is a branch of fintech.[5] It specifically applies to the regulation related challenges of fintech, including fraud detection and prevention. There are challenges to understand, implement, embed, and enforce the new legislation and regulation in the fintech and blockchain systems. RegTech explores how firms can benefit, leverage, better understand, and manage the risks to comply with new legislation and regulations.

Since fintech and blockchain technology are still evolving quickly, so are the related legislation and regulations. This makes RegTech development a moving target. As we have discussed in the previous chapters that the regulation regarding to the cryptocurrency in the U.S. is still not defined. The complexity of U.S. laws lies in several governmental levels — federal and local (state) ones. While federal government recognizes digital currency, many states do not.[6]

Companies engaged in RegTech development must have expert knowledge in both technology and regulation. RegTech provides executives with the tools to introduce new capabilities to leverage systems based on the new legislation and regulations. It also allows them to analyze regulatory data and report in a cost-effective, flexible, and timely manner, and be able to respond and react as new regulations emerge. RegTech can assist industry in complying with regulations and regulators can use RegTech to make better use of the information provided by the industry to update the legislation and regulation.

The scope of RegTech is big: It needs to cover everything from the systems that monitor and control core ledgers to the "purses" on the periphery that store value locally with users. Regulators could insist on people recording transactions externally on MDLs, providing open sources of transaction prices and volumes, or increasing competition through increased data portability.

RegTech solutions are mostly cloud-based with remote mining, maintenance management, and backup of data. RegTech apps provide compliance obligation analysis, risk identification, irregularity detection and prevention and management tools for legislation/regulation gap analysis, compliance, management information, transaction reporting, regulatory reporting, activity monitoring, training, risk data warehouses, and case management. RegTech can help firms to automate the more mundane compliance tasks and reduce operational risks associated with meeting compliance and reporting obligations. It can also empower compliance functions to make informed risk choices and how to mitigate and manage those risks. RegTech is more than the use of technology to meet regulatory requirements. RegTech falls into four major categories: regulatory monitoring, regulatory obligations, compliance management, and execution of compliance.[7] Its regulatory monitoring function provides users to query legislation and regulations in order to identify compliance imperatives.

Companies, such as Hadoop,[8] Tableau, and Pentaho,[9] develop tools to organize data and create a report to meet regulatory requirements.[5,6] In addition, these tools apply analytics to big data. For example, Tableau's namesake product is a visualization tool that makes it easy to look at your data in new ways to help identify trends from a regulatory perspective. Traditional financial institutions are also investing in regulatory fintech: HSBC created a $200 million fund to heighten levels of regulation in the fintech sector, aiming at improving new compliance demands.

Examples of RegTech companies include FundRecs,[10] which developed reconciliation software for the funds industry; Silverfinch,[11] which creates connectivity between asset managers and insurers through a fund data utility in a secure and controlled environment; TransUnion,[12] which prevents online fraud by scanning transactions in real time; and FunDapps,[13] which offers tools for compliance monitoring and reporting.

One of the challenges of RegTech development is that the legislation and regulation vary from country to country. It creates both technical and non-technical difficulties to develop a universal RegTech app. While Europe has a European Banking Authority that guides the region, the U.S. has a different standard. As long as there is no standardized regulatory baseline or data interchange format across the regions, there are certain difficulties to develop a universal app. This is a significant opportunity for RegTech solutions to be at the heart of these standardization data mazes.

10.3 LAND TITLE REGISTRATION AND REAL ESTATE

A number of countries are undertaking blockchain-based land registry projects. Honduras announced such an initiative in 2015. In 2016, the Republic of Georgia contracted the Bitfury Group to develop a blockchain system for property titles. More recently, Sweden also announced it was experimenting with a blockchain application for property titles.

Japan may have put in the largest effort to investigate such blockchain applications. Japanese authorities have a serious problem with real estate, since many ownership cases cannot be properly solved because of insufficient data. The Japanese government wants to upgrade its real-estate registration systems, using blockchain technology to more effectively collect, manage, and update real-estate data, and to make the data tamper-proof. A blockchain-based registry would allow authorities to better manage real-estate property transactions and boost recovery efforts of properties in the event of a natural disaster like the famous tsunami of 2011. The Japanese land ministry launched a trial version of the new system in the summer of 2018. The government selected a few cities for testing. Japanese government is planning to roll out the system nationwide within five years after proving the system's feasibility.

Likewise, the Ukrainian government also plans to implement blockchain solutions to solve problems of a depressed land market due to the lack of suitable financial instruments for leases and land transfers. The lease price is low because of a profound black market. The application of a blockchain system would protect the auctions from black market controls and therefore to stabilize the land price slide and increase income for farmers. Their pilot project is to transfer the State Land Cadastre to blockchain technology.

These are examples of the blockchain applications in the governmental administration of the land ownership. Blockchain technology also finds its use in the private real estate business. Real estate transactions have always been cumbersome and complicated. Property titles are a case in point. They tend to be susceptible to fraud, as well as costly and labor-intensive to administer. Blockchain technology can have a great impact on the financial verification of the sales process itself. As publicly accessible ledgers, blockchain can make many kinds of record-keeping more efficient.

The most costly and complicated process is the use of escrow and title companies for third-party verification, which is, of course, necessary to prevent fraud. With blockchain, there will no need for the escrow company.

By using a blockchain-distributed database to prove authenticity, homeowners could legitimately transfer ownership immediately without the need to pay for third-party verification.

Blockchain technology can be a help in the rental business as well. The blockchain would effectively make forged ownership documents and false listings outdated, making selling or advertising properties you do not own almost impossible.

Blockchain technology also improves the mortgage business, which is always slow and plagued with red tape and administrative issues. Using the blockchain, buyer, seller, as well as the real estate asset, can all have digital IDs. The mortgage process and transfer of ownership would be seamless and much faster. Verifying the credit history and income of the buyer would be instantaneous, avoiding time-consuming trips to banks, lawyers, and estate agents. Homeowners would be able to prove ownership of their property with a record of their purchase transaction. Houses could acquire digital identities as well, including the chain of ownership, a list of repairs and renovations and the history of real estate tax payment. When this is implemented, the real estate transaction can happen not in one or two months, but in one week. This will have a profound impact on the real estate market.

10.4 LAW AND BLOCKCHAIN

Laws are actually contracts between citizens and the government. Blockchain smart contracts can implement many civil laws. For example, the DMV can automatically revoke a driver's license using a smart contract for three consecutive traffic offenses. The fines from traffic tickets can be automatically deducted from offender's bank account. A restaurant's license can be voided if it does not pass the food safety inspection. Smart contracts will have a profound impact on industries. Smart contracts eliminate the intermediary, such as a legal firm, as payment will happen based on meeting certain milestones. By its very nature, the smart contract is easily enforceable electronically, creating a powerful escrow by taking it out of the control of a single party.

Blockchain smart contract will not replace lawyers anytime soon, but they can greatly help lawyers do their jobs more efficiently. In 2017, ten law firms and four legal institutions, including Cooley, Debevoise & Plimpton, and Hogan Lovells, have jointly formed the Ethereum Enterprise Alliance (EEA).[14] Their objective is to create the framework of legally binding smart contracts.

EEA is not the only entity interested in the application of blockchain in the legal field. A large law firm, Frost Brown Todd (FBT), has also taken the initiative to deploy smart contracts in the legal field.[15] FBT developed a prototype smart contract to be used in software escrow agreements.

The smart contract, once written, will execute on its own. As the lawyers are not skillful in programming the smart contract, and the programmers are not well versed in legal terms and conditions, the gap may cause undesirable consequences. However, smart contracts will bring developers and attorneys together to collaborate and provide progressive solutions for the legal industry.

In addition to the blockchain, cloud services can also be used for judicial applications. Ali Cloud is one of China's top providers of cloud computing services, domain services, emails, network security, and big data analysis. With its data and emails preserved for judicial departments as courtroom evidence, this may be the first instance of blockchain being utilized by a state judiciary.

10.5 PROTECTION OF INTELLECTUAL PROPERTY

Computers can easily reproduce digital content, such as movies, music, and books, and widely distribute them, causing rampant pirating of illegal copies of the intellectual property (IP). The unauthorized copies of digital intellectual property deprive the creators of their financial gains. Smart contracts can protect copyrights and automate the sale of creative works online, eliminating the risk of file copying and redistribution. Blockchain protects IP in two ways: registering the content to prove the ownership and collecting the payments when the content is being used.

Blockchain tracks the rights and transactions attached to many types of digital content, such as music, books, and videos. Blockchain technology registers the IP rights, catalogs, stores the original works, and makes the content widely available. By registering the IP rights to a blockchain, authors possess tamper-proof evidence of ownership. This is because a blockchain transaction is immutable, so once a work has been registered to a blockchain, that information can never be lost or changed.

The Ethereum platform uses blockchain to issue smart contracts to verify contractual agreements. There are startups using the Ethereum platform to focus on IP solutions and other alternative blockchain applications. Mycelia uses the blockchain to create a peer-to-peer music distribution system.[16] Founded by the U.K. singer-songwriter Imogen Heap, Mycelia enables musicians to sell songs directly to audiences, as well as license samples to producers and share royalties to songwriters and musicians through automated smart contracts. By doing so, it empowers a fair, sustainable, and vibrant music industry ecosystem involving all online music interaction services.

There are many other startups to do such work. Ascribe, a digital IP platform, offers solutions to solve the issues surrounding IP and digital content on the Internet.[17] InterPlanetary File System (IPFS), another startup company, developed a peer-to-peer protocol to do the same.[18]

The blockchain and timestamping services can be used to create an auditable trail of content ownership from creation through to the transfer of rights and beyond. Platforms such as Blockai[19] and Ascribe allow authors to make a record of copyright ownership, which can then be used to see where and how the work is being used on the Internet and to seek licenses from third parties.

Registering a work in a blockchain gives the author a digital certificate of authenticity, which can help third parties identify the author of a work. The blockchain, being a permanent immutable record, is the perfect solution for providing proof of creation. There is now a universal database for recording the ownership of IP content and paying for its use.

Once a work is registered and verified in the blockchain platform, authors can make the IP content unusable for those who are not paying the right to use it or to be notified to see who is using their work. Blockchain registration reduces the cost of transactions and creates a direct link between authors and users.

No less important is that blockchain can help collect the payments from IP users. Smart contracts assist in the sale and licensing of intellectual property through micropayments. Each time, a potential user using the content makes a small payment to the author. As a result, the author can be remunerated each time when their IP is being used without having to pay broker fees. Such a method is simpler and more transparent than many other existing means of payment for authors.

Ujo Music, an Ethereum-based and ConsenSys-backed music software services company, has used its blockchain application with singer-songwriter Imogen Heap to release her songs on the blockchain.[20] Users are able to purchase licenses to download, stream, remix, and sync the song via smart contracts, with each payment automatically split on the blockchain and sent to Imogen Heap directly.

10.6 CONCLUSION

This chapter only presents a small fraction of what blockchain can do in the governance space. Governance has historically been a polarizing topic. Because the governance has to do with authority and power. And it can affect large number of members in the governance. Therefore, the applications of blockchain in the governance may assert an out-of-proportion influence in the governing body and its population.

Governance deals with the set of rules, processes and practices giving the organization a direction and a framework to ensure its functioning is within the defined parameters Governance is much more than the government related subjects. Today, media, social media and big data companies, such as Amazon, Metaverse, and Google, are exerting large influence to the population in general. What we can expect if these companies develop blockchain based governance platforms?

In general, governance mechanism can be divided into four categories: consensus, incentives, information and governing structure.

Companies like Metaverse operate as centralized hierarchies with top-down power structures. Their governance mechanism will definitely not be by consensus. The fact that U.S. Congress has blocked the Diem project from Metaverse is a good example.

Incentive is the major driver of the structure of the company. Giving free reign to the big company to develop governance apps will definitely be controversial. Information governance, or misinformation governance is a major legitimate issue today. In the past, if you see a picture of a celebrity doing something, you could believe it was true. But, it is no longer the case. How to govern the misinformation and, further more, to let the information to govern is something for debate.

The blockchain based governance app can be off-chain and on-chain, from the point of view of implementation. Off-chain means that the decision making process is not coded into the blockchain, while the on-chain governance means that the decision making process is built into the code. Example in the traditional world of the off-chain governance is the making of traffic laws. Example of the on-chain governance is the voting.

Currently, blockchain governance application is still in the nascent stage, How it will evolve is anyone's guess. However, blockchain governance represents an important new tool for governance since the formation of government in an organized society more than 5,000 years ago.

REFERENCES

1. *http://boardroom.to/*

2. Ometov A., Bardinova Y., Afanasyeva A., Masek P., Zhidanov K., Vanurin S., Sayfullin M., Shubina V., Komarov M., Bezzateev S. An Overview on Blockchain for Smartphones: State-of-the-Art, Consensus, Implementation, Challenges and Future Trends. IEEE Access. 2020;8:103994–104015. doi: 10.1109/ACCESS.2020.2998951

3. "The U.S. Navy wants to connect its 3D printers with a blockchain", Stan Higgins, *https://www.coindesk.com/the-us-navy-wants-to-connect-its-3-d-printers-with-a-blockchain/*

4. "Blockchain applications for Homeland Security analytics", *https://www.sbir.gov/sbirsearch/detail/867813*

5. "Is RegTech the new Fintech?", *https://www2.deloitte.com/ie/en/pages/financial-services/articles/RegTech-is-the-new-FinTech.html*

6. *https://www.executive-magazine.com/cover-story/legal-aspects-of-digital-currencies*

7. *https://www.ascentregtech.com/what-is-regtech/*

8. *http://hadoop.apache.org/*

9. *http://www.pentaho.com/*

10. *https://www.fundrecs.com/*

11. *https://www.silverfinch.com/*

12. *https://www.transunion.com/idvision*

13. *https://www.funDapps.co/*

14. "Legally Binding Smart Contracts? 10 Law Firms Join Enterprise Ethereum Alliance", Michael Del Castillo, *https://www.coindesk.com/legally-binding-smart-contracts-9-law-firms-join-enterprise-ethereum-alliance/*

15. "How the Legal Industry is Adopting Ethereum-based Smart Contracts", *https://cointelegraph.com/news/how-the-legal-industry-is-adopting-ethereum-based-smart-contracts*

16. *http://myceliaformusic.org/*

17. "How Ascribe uses Bitcoin tech to help underserved artists", Stan Higgins, *https://www.coindesk.com/ascribe-Bitcoin-tech-underserved-artists/*

18. "An introduction to IPFS", *https://medium.com/@ConsenSys/an-introduction-to-ipfs-9bba4860abd0*

19. "Blockai taps the Bitcoin blockchain to protect creative content", Martin Hsu, *https://www.ccn.com/blockai-taps-Bitcoin-blockchain-protect-creative-content/*

20. *https://blog.ujomusic.com/*

A GLIMPSE OF THE FUTURE

Meaningful innovations like blockchain can redefine the capabilities of technology and help numerous industries progress.

Since its inception in 1965, Moore's law has driven the development of the electronics industry. The number of transistors on a chip has doubled every two years, which has made it possible for computers, communication equipment, and the Internet to increase their computing power. In 2022, over 50 years later, a transistor is ten times smaller than a virus and the number of transistors on a chip has not been following Moore's law.[1] As a result, many have speculated that the momentum of technological progress will begin to slow down or even stop. Nevertheless, technological progress does not appear to be slowing – it is accelerating.

Instead of trying to make smaller transistors, innovators are taking advantage of the existing technology. Having 60 billion transistors available on a single chip, for example, has allowed for widespread use of Internet and communication tools. This has opened a new frontier of possibilities within big data and AI.

Data-centric applications fit particularly well within one type of computational architecture – the Graphics Processing Unit or GPU. GPUs were originally designed for graphics applications – gaming, in particular – to process a large quantity of data quickly. GPUs demonstrate a faster data processing speed than traditional CPUs. Emerging big data and AI applications benefit from this increased speed, and, as a result, GPUs have been propelled to the forefront of computational applications.

In an increasingly data-centric environment, computing has shifted from instruction-focused to data-focused. One example of this phenomenon is NVIDIA's CUDA parallel computing platform.

TABLE 11.1 Transistor size comparison (1 micron is one millionth of a meter, 1 nm is one billionth of a meter).

Dimension	Object
50 micron	plant or animal cells
8 micron	red blood cells
5 micron	transistors in 1980's
1 micron	bacterias, mitochondria
100 nm	flu virus
60 nm	transistors in 2005
20 nm	transistors in 2015
10 nm	transistors in 2018
8 nm	protein
7 nm	transistors in 2020
5 nm	lipid
5 nm	transistors in 2022
2 nm	transistors in 2025
1 nm	Carbon 60
0.1 nm	atom

Neural processing is a new computer architecture that mimics biological function, which gives the software the ability to adapt to changing situations and to improve its function in response to new information. This ability is the key to AI being able to recognize a human face, predict the weather, analyze speech patterns, and learn new strategies. Intel, the world's largest microprocessor manufacturer, is developing neuromorphic chips that have the capability to self-learning. This technology mimics the brain's neural networks to relay information with pulses, modulate the synaptic strengths, and store these changes locally.

Fintech, including blockchain, is another application of big data and AI. Fintech is primed to radically alter the traditional financial industry in a manner that will deeply affect the established financial services model. The direction and depth of the change may pose major challenges to inflexible financial institutions. Continued, rapid innovation upon baseline technologies is bound to have a drastic impact on the development of fintech. Artificial intelligence, fintech, and other related subjects are discussed in my book *Fintech Fundamentals*.

Regardless of how fintech develops, it cannot violate basic principles concerning the maintenance of financial system stability and market order and the protection of the legitimate rights and interests of consumers. Regulations must keep up with fintech's future development.

11.1 THE FOUNDATION OF FUTURE TECHNOLOGY

Fintech is more than an application of blockchain technology – many other technologies propel fintech development. Graphically, we can see how fintech, blockchain, and other basic technologies relate to each other in Figure 11.1. At the bottom, there is the infrastructure layer. This layer is the foundation upon which all derivative technologies and applications are built. This layer includes the Internet itself, which consists of the P2P network and the cloud. The IoT acts as the interface between the Internet and physical world objects. Communication is indispensable because it allows the transfer and sharing of all digital data. As the speed and bandwidth of communication technology improves, more data can be transferred at a faster rate. This advancement is especially important when applied to big data.

The middle layer is referred to as the *enabling layer* because it contains infrastructure technologies that enable different applications. These

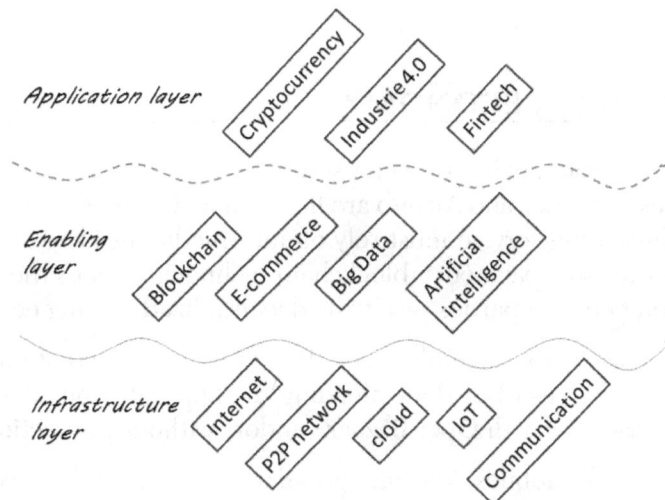

FIGURE 11.1 Elements of future technologies.

infrastructure technologies are the software building blocks from which all the applications are built. This layer includes blockchain, all e-commerce platforms, big data, and AI.

Six major components – AI, blockchain, cloud computing, data, e-commerce, and fintech – are conveniently grouped together as the foundational components of the digital economy. On the very top is the application layer, which contains three major categories: cryptocurrency, Industry 4.0, and fintech.

This graphic is conceptual and illustrative; it is one of the many ways to demonstrate the relationships between different technologies. For example, note that the technologies in the enabling layer are complementary to each other. The combination of these technologies makes it possible to develop the applications within the application layer.

The graphic illustration is not meant to be exclusive or inclusive. For example, Industry 4.0 requires additional infrastructure, such as sensors and robots, that is not shown here. One can argue that e-commerce is an application rather than a component of the baseline technology for applications. In addition, the boundary between AI and fintech is imprecise. The same AI technology, when applied towards financial use, is branded as fintech. For example, when PayPal uses GPU-accelerated deep learning for fraud detection, this is an application of fintech. Nevertheless, the graph can serve as a foundation upon which to build a more nuanced understanding.

11.2 THE SHARING ECONOMY

The sharing economy has proven itself to be a successful business model and companies like Uber and Airbnb are flourishing. Currently, users who want to hail a ride-sharing service must rely on intermediaries like Uber, but by enabling peer-to-peer payments, blockchain technology opens the door to direct interaction between parties — a truly decentralized sharing economy results.

OpenBazaar, for example, uses the blockchain to create a peer-to-peer auction site such as eBay. Downloading the app onto your device allows for direct transactions with OpenBazaar vendors without transaction fees.

Before automobiles became popular in China, bikes were the main method of transportation, a ubiquitous image in the Chinese cities. Now, bikes have made a comeback in a different way. People ride shared bikes. Several Chinese startups have deployed tens of millions of colorful bikes in cities across the country. The rental costs are as little as 15 cents for 30 minutes, and users can pick up and drop off bikes across the city and all you need to rent a bike is a smartphone app. It is convenient, cheap, and ecologically friendly, and the bike sharing business is booming. Ofo and Mobike are the most successful of the bike-sharing companies and are now valued at more than $1 billion.

Peer-to-peer markets, collectively known as the *sharing economy*, have emerged as alternative suppliers of goods and services traditionally provided by long-established industries. Even houses can be shared. The home sharing business Airbnb has over 300,000 shared homes in nearly 200 countries, which has disrupted the hotel business.

11.3 FINTECH AND AI

There are many definitions of AI. One identifies AI as a system that has the capability for self-learning. These machines are based on a neural network and attempt to imitate a living brain. Even the lowest life form can explore, probe, test, and learn in order to complete tasks; systems that can learn from experience will become more intelligent and useful. Thus, in the financial market, the use of neural networks to predict financial indicators has long been a subject of research.

Learning requires experience; this is where big data comes in. The combination of big data and self-learning capability is what produces AI. Financial big data contains people's spending habits, preferences, lifestyle choices, financial capability, and wealth management objectives, alongside information concerning the flow of money, investment trends, and economic activity tendencies.

When it comes to fintech, the goal is to create smarter AI to help with the management and operation of the financial market. Faster decision-making and deeper learning can predict financial behavior. While many of the big data and AI applications in business are not strictly financial services, financial services and other types of business are becoming more interconnected.

AI will help businesses and banks tailor products and services to customers' requirements more effectively. It will also discern economic trends and consumer patterns. Startups have already begun developing AI products and services to improve and expand credit offerings, insurance options, personal finance services, and regulatory software.

Digit uses AI to help people accumulate savings and Kasisto offers an AI chatbot and a mobile app to help companies connect with customers.[2,3,4] Dataminr constantly searches for and identifies high-impact, critical events worldwide to deliver relevant information to personnel, facilities, operations, and interest groups around the world in real time.[5] AlphaSense uses AI to do market research and sentiment analysis.[6] The platform utilizes an AI-powered search engine to provide intelligent search results with critical insights, accuracy, and speed. The search results are significantly more customizable and accurate than a simple Google search, transforming the search function into something more comparable to an expert consulting session.

With increasing frequency, when you dial a service phone number, a chatbot answers the phone. It directs you to a relevant party depending on your input. According to SITA survey, a Geneva-based aviation technology firm, 52% of airlines were planning to use AI programs and 68% of airlines intended to adopt AI-driven chatbots in the next three years.[7] AI-powered chatbots are growing in popularity within numerous service industries.

Another company, Numerai, develops AI algorithms for trading and investment.[8] Numerai is a new type of hedge fund that is built on crowdsourcing knowledge. Through a massive network of hedge funds, the system collects hundreds of thousands of financial models and individual predictions. With this data, Numerai is then able to build their own financial models that incorporate the algorithms submitted through the crowdsourced community.

As AI starts to propagate at asset management and investment banks, AI fintech will replace the role of traditional analysts. This will result in more efficient, accurate, and better investment research at lower costs. Different deep learning AI applications have their own unique performance characteristics, which can be further impacted by their different deployment platforms.

There is a need to benchmark artificial intelligence platforms, since not all AI systems are created equal. Some AI systems are more intelligent than the others. Without benchmarking, there is no way to tell its level of intelligence.

The extent of a machine's capability to learn during deep learning training is referred to as *inference*. Think of the inference as the AI system's IQ. Measuring the AI's inference of neural networks on a given device – which could be a cloud, a network, a computer, or a phone – allows us to know the IQ level of the particular AI device.

Baidu, the dominant search engine company in China, has invested heavily in AI. In 2016, Baidu Research unveiled the next generation of DeepBench, an open-source deep learning benchmark system that operates across multiple hardware platforms.[9] DeepBench benchmarks fundamental operations required for inference, and the inference measurement in DeepBench uses a previously trained model to make predictions on a new dataset, which allows it to measure the deep learning performance after a series of training simulations.

DeepBench is the first open-source tool that has been made available to the deep learning AI community. It has since been used to evaluate how different platforms, or the algorithm/hardware combinations, perform when used to train deep neural networks. Since its release, several companies, including Intel, NVIDIA, and AMD, have used and contributed to the DeepBench platform.[10]

A thorough understanding of inference performance can improve the design of the chips/hardware where the neural networks reside. Among different performance benchmarks, speed is key parameter to consider when training neural networks. With the ability to measure inference, researchers will now have a standard for the performance of their AI hardware.

In addition to measuring inference performance, DeepBench provides new kernels from multiple deep learning models and sets new minimum precision requirements for training.

AI and machine learning can enable banks to become more competitive in other industries like real estate. Fintech sectors, such as the $55 billion property management industry, are using AI and machine learning to increase returns, lower costs, and improve the overall owner and tenant experience for the 50 million rental properties and 100 million tenants in the U.S.

Ecosystem players like mortgage bankers, payment systems, insurers, private bankers, and wealth management companies are now work collaboratively with technology-led property management companies to serve their clients better.

AI can improve the financial market in many ways. One way is by increasing security. Due to its ability to learn and recognize patterns, AI can analyze large volumes of security data and detect abnormal spending patterns, suspicious transactions, and potential future attacks. This helps keep sensitive information secure. AI can also cut processing times by processing data more accurately and quickly; it reduces human error by validating and double-checking the data.

Semiconductor companies are designing chips especially for AI applications that are better equipped to handle the large workloads required to process machine learning and deep learning. These players include Intel, AMD, NVIDIA, IBM, Qualcomm, Infineon, and MediaTek.

NVIDIA's GPU effective use of proprietary NVLink technology has made it one of the more popular AI chips on the market. In combination with IBM's CPU Power9, it can crunch the large amount of data required for AI and machine learning, particularly in cases involving image and voice recognition and credit card fraud prevention.

In addition, Microsoft offers various tools and turnkey solutions to allow developers to create AI apps on its Azure platform. These tools can be used to manage and manipulate virtual machine images, networking, and storage solutions, the blockchain, security and identity, and databases. Many of these tools have direct application in fintech.[11] As a result, companies have formed partnerships to leverage each other's expertise. For example, Microsoft is working with Huawei, and Facebook has partnered with Qualcomm.

AI is by no means limited to big machines. Even mobile devices are going AI. Apple's new iPhone has a neural engine; Huawei's Mate 10 does, as well. Large companies designing mobile chips, such as Qualcomm and ARM, are gearing up to supply AI-capable hardware to power mobile devices. Because AI chips perform more data crunching on the device, less communication with the cloud is required. Thus, AI hardware can offer better performance, longer battery life, improved privacy, and more reliable security. This hardware is also able to work in combination with various apps. Both Android and Apple iOS have APIs that can tap into the power of neural hardware. These APIs leverage the capability of deep learning frameworks such as Google's TensorFlow or Facebook's Caffe2.[12, 13]

The R&D spending on AI-oriented microprocessors has ramped up dramatically because AI chips power AI just like microprocessors power computing. They will be omnipresent in the near future, and the industry will be in the tens of billions of dollars.

In nearly every industry, one of the most common benefits of AI is its automation opportunities. In addition to reducing the manual expense management problem, AI can automatically generate expenditure and expense reports quickly, efficiently, and without errors.

AI can manage approval workflows and allows companies to restructure and automate the expense tracking process. It also helps to prevent reimbursement fraud and guides organizations with their budgeting efforts via automated reports.

One of the most valuable benefits AI provides for organizations is data. The future of fintech is largely reliant on gathering data efficiently enough to stay ahead of the competition, and AI can facilitate that. With AI, one can process a huge volume of data, which allows for game-changing insights. These insights can transform the way one approaches complex decision-making processes.

To keep ahead of competitors, larger enterprises have relied heavily upon algorithms, automation, and analyses achieved with the help of AI. Because this technology is becoming increasingly accessible and affordable, it can begin to help smaller startups and consumers as well, giving them the tools needed to compete with larger players within their industry.

AI is playing an important role in empowering both consumers and fintech companies. AI-powered personal financial applications allow people to balance their budgets based on their specific income and spending patterns. AI acts as a robot advisor to individuals and organizations to cut costs while boosting the bottom line.

AI is not limited to behind-the-scenes roles in the business world. AI-guided chatbots undertake a variety of internal and external communications, such as customer-facing, self-service tools utilized by financial institutions. AI allows fintech companies to eliminate human error while boosting productivity and increasing their bottom line. With the stiff competition in the fintech world today, it's no surprise that companies are adopting new technologies to stay one step ahead of the competition.

11.4 FINTECH REGULATION

One of the biggest obstacles of the fintech industry is the lack of regulation. This is clearly the case for Facebook's Libra project. China has taken a different approach; it will not regulate the industry until it has developed enough to make an impact on the market. This approach allows the nascent industry the room for innovation and growth.

For example, the Chinese government did not regulate Third-Party Payment system (TPP) until 2017, when TPP was several trillion dollars in size. There are roughly 600 companies operating in the TPP space. In August of 2017, the Chinese government established a Network Alliance Platform to regulate third party payments. All third-party payment systems were required to migrate their private platforms to the Network Alliance Platform by within that same year.

From 2018 onward, that new platform has operated as the only clearing house for all third-party payments within China. Third-party payment companies, such as Alipay, no longer need to interface directly with different banks. Their only interface is the Network Alliance Platform, which in turn interfaces with all the banks. This approach is like the Automated Clearing House (ACH) operated by the Federal Reserve Banks and the private Electronic Payment Network in the US.[14]

The Network Alliance Platform is organized in the same way a company is. The two biggest players, Alipay and TenPay, each have 9.6% of shares. The central bank supervises the platform. In this way, the Chinese third-party system is regulated just as the credit card payment system in the US. This relatively new mechanism of third-party payment continues to have a huge impact on the digital payment market.

There are winners and losers. The winners are small third-party payment companies. They no longer need to establish relationships with each individual bank. Through the Network Alliance Platform, they are allowed the same access to all the banks as larger, more established players. These large third-party payment companies are the losers.

In 2017, Chinese third-party mobile payments topped 27 trillion yen, or $4 trillion dollars. When these payment funds stall in the Network Alliance Platform, this does not generate interest for the third party. Any interest earned belongs to the NAP. Even though the holding period is short, the amount of interest can be staggering. For example, if the fund stays in the NAP for three days average, the parked amount at NAP is $45 billion.

In addition, proprietary big data, which used to belong exclusively to third-party payment companies, is now shared with the Network Alliance Platform.

Third-party payment services, acting as escrow, alleviate trust problems and thus have contributed significantly to the growth of e-commerce in China. Still, a serious concern is that the service could become a money-laundering tool or could facilitate other fraudulent behaviors. For example, there was an incident in Suzhou that involved a massive illegal gaming scheme operated by overseas online gaming companies. The perpetrators used third-party payment services to transmit millions of dollars.

There is an urgent need for the legislation to address these problems. Currently, legislation covers online payment services, currency conversion services, issuance and servicing of pre-paid purchase cards, and other payment services conducted by nonfinancial institutions. Providers of these services must now apply for and obtain a Payment Service License. The legislation also established threshold credentials for entities qualified to provide third party payment services and set credentials for entities controlling licensed third-party payment companies. Some estimate that about half of the 300 plus third-party payment companies currently operating in China could not meet these standards.

There are also operational standards for third-party payment companies. These standards address various concerns associated with third-party payment services, including security of customers' funds, prevention of money laundering, and prohibition of potential circumventions of the more stringently regulated banking system.

11.5 DATA-DRIVEN FINTECH

The field of financial technology innovation is very broad. There are plenty of opportunities for asset management, loan businesses, and insurance, payment, and financial market operations. We can look to the experience and establishment of traditional financial institutions for guidance as we implement sound applications, such as risk management, supervision, and operation of the financial industry.

Traditional financial institutions built up a stable and functional financial system over the course of several decades. Fintech will likely require a similar amount of time. The eventual success of fintech depends on its ability to be flexible through several economic cycles. It must be able to safely navigate risks in credit, market, operation, legal, reputation, compliance, and liquidity. As the system evolves over time and accumulates experience and effective control, the market's confidence in the new system will grow.

One of the major driving forces of fintech development is big data. All transactions and financial deals are composed of data. Big data technology includes infrastructure, modeling, data collection, and data mining.

Big data, blockchain, and AI will play an important role in future risk management strategies. In traditional financial systems, as exemplified in the

Chinese and U.S. markets, SMEs and low-income public groups generally have higher financial risk despite possessing high financial demand. Fintech is well suited to tap into this huge potential market through its use of the Internet, big data, AI, and cloud computing.

Fintech can provide solutions to risk, credit intermediaries, and payment settlement issues within the financial industry. This would reduce the cost of financial services with no additional risk. Fintech can also bring under-served and underground financial markets into the mainstream financial market, greatly increasing the market size. For example, illegal gambling in the U.S. alone produces $150 billion dollars annually.[15] The counterfeit product market is similarly massive at $225 billion dollars. Blockchain-based supply chain management can effectively eliminate product counterfeiting. This is one of the many ways that fintech can generate significant economic returns. Customers can benefit from lower interest rates, and financial institutions can generate more returns by reducing costs and serving a larger market. The financial resources that underserved customers obtain can further fuel the economic growth.

Robot investment management is one of the many applications of the AI. A low-cost intelligent investment advisor platform can manage pension savings. AI-based fintech can direct savings into the critical investments needed for economic growth and technological innovation to provide a higher return to investors.

Online, automated consultants can design a personal investment plan for each customer according to their individual circumstances and needs, considering things like risk appetite, duration of investment, and objectives. The service can cover the entire lifecycle of the customer, from infant to old age. The application of data technology makes financial services universal and customized.

Big data management is based on customer behavior and consumption patterns. By capturing and analyzing large amounts of data related to customer service, and mining and sharing this data, new, innovative financial services and cross-industry innovation are able to develop. This results in a more efficient and personalized service.

Consumption habits and consumer demand change over time. The consumption of financial services will have to adapt to the change. In an increasingly competitive financial landscape, companies that integrate fintech adaptors will have an edge on their competition.

All financial transactions, including stocks, private equity, bonds, hedge funds, and derivatives, form immutable chains. Thus, blockchain technology can be applied to effectively register, identify, and transfer all assets and contracts.

Security is a prerequisite for the coming data powered economy. Network security laws and data security supervision will be necessary at a national level. Network security will play a prominent role in the future economic construction, production, and operation. It is safe to say that insufficient data security will compromise economic development in the emerging data-driven economy.

Data and network security involves more than just technological safeguards. Security is affected by management practices, personnel safety awareness, and general business processes. It involves all aspects of an enterprise's operations. This makes it difficult to achieve full-scale security since all the above-mentioned components need to be considered. Security work has brought, and will bring, new challenges as technologies evolve. Mobile Internet, cloud computing, big data, and other new technologies each have their own security challenges.

Most financial services at the global level are exploring the benefits of data analytics and big data. Increasingly, technology will allow financial services to gather large amounts of data to tailor experiences, services, and products to customer needs. Banks will be able to customize products and services based on advanced customer profiling data. Big data and the cloud will lend itself to cross over between industries, leading to a more interconnected world. Multi-organizational MDLs, with smart contracts and IoT sensing, will allow semi-intelligent, autonomous transactions. Ledgers with a smart contract will use cryptographic techniques to provide immutable, long-term records.

Big data and AI are closely linked. In fact, AI is an application of big data. Using AI on big data can provide insights from advanced analytics without requiring professional expertise. In this way, big data and AI coexist in a mutually beneficial relationship. This smart data discovery will accelerate business intelligence capabilities and enable a new generation of data-driven decision-making and innovation.

11.6 COMMUNICATION-DRIVEN FINTECH

Mobile devices account for over 80% of all Internet use globally. Telecommunication technology is in a race to meet the network speed and bandwidth requirements for big data, fintech, IoT, and AI applications.

Fortunately, 5G telecommunication technology deployment is right at the corner.

5G network and devices have improved speed, latency, bandwidth, and power consumption when compared to 4G. Using 5G, a smartphone can perform downloads at over 1 GBps; eventually, phones will be able to download data at 20 GBps. 5G's ultra-low latency is as important as its speed. *Latency* is the time it takes for a device to interact with a remote server. In a 4G network, latency is around 50 milliseconds (ms), but in 5G, latency is only 1 ms. In other words, a 5G device can respond 50 times faster than a 4G device. This will allow 5G providers to meet growing demand for data-intensive services, like streaming video. It is also critically important to the autonomous vehicle.

In 2016, there were 23 billion devices on the 4G network. By 2020, when 5G was starting to be deployed, there were 50 billion devices on the network. 5G will continue to connect more devices with increasing reliability. No matter where you are in a city, you will always be connected. This should lead to a surge in the applications like fintech that require a network connection.

For example, China Merchants Bank (CMBC) is cooperating with Huawei to make use of its agile information and communication technologies to help strengthen its customer-centric experience. Using big data and cloud technologies, CMBC can integrate data in real time, cut the margin of error in financial assets by half, increase conversion rates, and speed up personal credit reporting. As a result, customers can experience on demand, real-time services, no matter what platform they are using or what location they reside in.

With this omnipresent communication link, mobile devices such as phones, smart watches, earphones, activity bands, virtual/augmented reality headsets, flexible sensors on smart clothes, and smart glasses possess a real-time link to the cloud, and can link to devices in their vicinity and swap data. This ability is called Multiple Inputs and Multiple Outputs (MIMO) communication. It is one of the capabilities of 5G set to fully replace Bluetooth, RFID, and other short-range communications.

Critical data, including identity, transaction, and content information, will be stored in MDLs. The sharing of this data will create a powerful feature for fintech. Identity authentication of the wearer will establish all the trust needed for the transaction. 5G will also enable a micro-payment system, in which the unit of payment can be very small.

5G will also revolutionize stock market transactions. Speedy buying and selling are everything in the stock exchange, and a fraction of a second can make a huge difference worth millions of dollars a year. 5G's latency will settle transactions instantly.

Fintech companies can make use of 5G's reliable connectivity and vastly improved download and upload speeds, as well as exponential cloud computing power, to develop new products. For example, banks can develop personal banking assistants using AI, cognitive computing, and machine learning to produce financial and wealth management products tailored to customers' needs. Current robo-advisor services will become more powerful and customizable in the 5G era.

The faster, more responsive, more pervasive wireless coverage of 5G networks will provide the backdrop for breakthrough changes in numerous industries.

The success of the U.K.'s Atom Bank, a bank based on a mobile app, illustrates this trend. Online banking is unstoppable. In response, many assets are moving online. According to some estimates, by the end of the 21st century, the blockchain platforms may contain more than 50% of the assets in the world.

11.7 CONCLUSION

Blockchain technology promises to revolutionize financial technology. This is possible with the advancement of the big data, AI, communication technology, and many other breakthrough technologies. We are at the threshold of a revolution. In the coming decades, there will be an avalanche of innovations that will change our day-to-day life dramatically. These advancements will transform society, business, economy, and even the balance of power.

These new technologies will be also an equalizer. They promise to bring financial services that once catered to the upper class, to the general population. On the other hand, they will make the entry barrier to entering business much higher. Only the biggest and the most well-entrenched entities will be able to carve out a place providing the infrastructure, services, and business. Along the way, profit-oriented businesses may strip most of the benefits from these technologies. The world will be divided between economies with and without access to this technology.

Likewise, privacy and security will be another complex and polarized topic of discussion. Blockchain technology promises anonymous transactions that are private and secure. However, the digitization of identity data, asset data, and other personal information online, such as health data and DNA sequencing, may turn a person into a number.

Like many other technologies before our time, whether the coming disruptive technology revolution will bring greater benefits or disadvantages to humanity is unknown. This trend will continue and accelerate.

Because the pace of this technological revolution is moving extremely fast, the content of this book cannot truly keep pace with the change. Every day, there are new announcements and developments. This book can only serve as an introduction to those who are interested in the subject. Still, with the information provided within this book, you will be able to understand and discuss the coming advancements concerning blockchain, fintech, and many others easily. Congratulations for making it to the end, and good luck!

REFERENCES

1. *https://www.slideteam.net/0614-size-comparison-among-various-atoms-molecules-and-microorganisms-medical-images-for-powerpoint.html*

2. *https://digit.co/*

3. *http://kasisto.com/*

4. *https://www.dataminr.com/*

5. *http://www.alphasense.com/*

6. "How travel companies are using AI to acquire, engage, and retain customers," *http://travelwirenews.com/how-travel-companies-are-using-ai-to-acquire-engage-and-retain-customers-2-580212/*

7. *https://numer.ai/*

8. "DeepBench," Sharan Narang, *https://svail.github.io/DeepBench/*

9. "Intel® Xeon Phi™ Delivers Competitive Performance for Deep Learning—And Getting Better Fast," Andreas R., *https://software.intel.com/en-us/articles/intel-xeon-phi-delivers-competitive-performance-for-deep-learning-and-getting-better-fast*

10. *https://azuremarketplace.microsoft.com/en-us/marketplace/*

11. *https://www.tensorflow.org/*

12. *https://caffe2.ai/docs/getting-started.html?platform=windows&configuration=compile*

13. "Overview of the US payments, clearing and settlement landscape," Federal Reserve of New York, *https://www.newyorkfed.org/medialibrary/media/banking/international/03.Overview-US-PCS-landscape-Merle.pdf*

14. *https://www.statisticbrain.com/black-market-illicit-trade-statistics/*

15. *https://knect365.com/5g-virtualisation/article/a2ba2cab-6977-4858-a500-e4f8392dde51/5g-and-fintech*

INDEX